THE FALKLAND ISLANDS

THE FALKLAND ISLANDS

by IAN J. STRANGE

Third edition, revised
to include the impact
of the Falklands War

DAVID & CHARLES
Newton Abbot London North Pomfret (Vt)

British Library Cataloguing in Publication Data
Strange, Ian J.
    The Falkland Islands—3rd ed.
    1. Falkland Islands—History
    I. Title
    997'.11   F3031
    ISBN 0-7153-8531-3

Printed in Great Britain
by Redwood Burn Limited, Trowbridge, Wiltshire
for David & Charles (Publishers) Limited
Brunel House, Newton Abbot, Devon

Published in the United States of America
by David & Charles Inc
North Pomfret, Vermont 05053, USA

ACKNOWLEDGEMENTS

In this third edition my thanks still go out to all those mentioned in the first work and second edition who, but for reasons of resetting and space, would have been mentioned again. For this new edition I feel tribute should be paid first to every one of those who served with the Task Force, especially our particular friends who arrived early. Without the combined efforts of that Force this edition would perhaps never have appeared. My special thanks also go to many who come within the pages of the chapter on the occupation but whose names do not actually appear there: The Rev Harry Bagnell, Eddie Anderson, Lewis Clifton, Bill Etheridge, the Jaffray family, the Ashworth family, Len and Shirley Middleton, Jeannie and Duffy Sheridan, Mike Harris, Pat Watts, Theo and Kath Fleuret, Kitty and Cecil Bertrand, the late Len Reive, Mike and Alison Bleaney, and all those who lived in East Block! Also one or two individuals to whom I feel we owe a great deal but whose names it is prudent not to mention. Finally the BBC, who became part of every family.

In the revision of the book for this edition thanks go to Wilf Vevers; Maj Timothy Spicer (2 Scots Guards); Maj Dair Farrar Hockley (2 Para); Maj John Charteris, MC (The Royal Scots); EOD Units; Police Provost Unit; R. Barclay (Everards Brewery); A. Mitchell (Standard Chartered Bank); John Reid; John Ferguson; John Brodrick; Michael Gaiger; David McLeod; Brian Summers; Mike Peake; Owen McPhee; Annie Chater; John Smith; Len McGill; Robert Findlayson; Lewis Clifton; Les Halliday; John Fowler; Alison Thom; Linda Lyse; Rosemary

ACKNOWLEDGEMENTS

Allen; Peter King; Marie Baylis; Gerald Cheek; Sandie Clifton; Richard Cockwell; and special thanks to Phyl and Mike Rendell for their help and last but not least to Maria for her great help.

CONTENTS

SOUTH ATLANTIC OCEAN

FALKLAND ISLANDS

SOUTH ATLANTIC OCEAN

Cape Dolphin

Foul
Bay

Middle
Bay

MT
ROSALIE

PORT SAN
CARLOS

DOUGLAS

SALVADOR

RINCON
GRANDE

JOHNSON'S
HARBOUR

PORT
LOUIS

SAN CARLOS

TEAL INLET

GREEN PATCH

Berkeley Sound

SOUND

BIG MT

MT SIMON

Grantham
Sound

NO·MAN'S
LAND

MT KENT

MT CHALLENGER

MT USBORNE

SMOKO MT

BLUFF COVE

MT WICKHAM

STANLEY

FITZROY

DARWIN
GOOSE GREEN

L A F O N I A

WALKER
CREEK

Choiseul Sound

EAST FALKLAND

LIVELY
I.

Lively Is.

Adventure Sound

Low Bay

Lively
Sound

NORTH ARM

Bay of Harbours

BLEAKER
Bleaker I.

Sea Lion Is.

● SETTLEMENTS
ROADS
- - - - TRACKS

0   5   10   15   20   25 miles

ILLUSTRATIONS

LIST OF ILLUSTRATIONS

*All photographs are by the author except no 18, which is reproduced
by kind permission of K. Christ*

MAPS

*(based by kind permission of the Directorate of Overseas Surveys on the
first edition of their 1966 map. Crown Copyright reserved)*

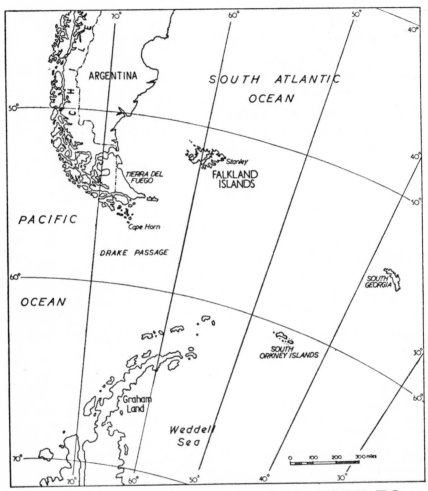

FALKLAND ISLANDS IN RELATION TO
SOUTH AMERICA AND THE
ANTARCTIC

INTRODUCTION

SET deep in the South Atlantic some 300 miles from the tip of South America and Cape Horn lie a mass of islands which, in part, are very similar to the western isles of Scotland.

Their physical appearance, way of life, community spirit, and climate are so similar that a visitor to the islands will find it difficult to appreciate that more than 8,000 miles lie between them and Scotland.

At the present time the Falklands lie on the brink of a new and exciting period of change. Since their first sighting a journey to these Islands has necessitated a sea voyage through some of the most tortuous seas of the southern oceans. Even to the most remote places, however, travel changes and since 1972 the Falklands have had an air link with the outside world. The experience of the sea voyage will be lost by many. By this route the traveller is initiated to the special environment of the Islands. Cool winds carry the smell of the Islands, the scent of kelp, the odour of sea bird rookeries and seal colonies. Entering Port William, the large outer harbour of Port Stanley, it is not difficult to visualise the scene of a 100 years ago, when vessels on the Cape Horn route fought bitter battles with the elements to reach the sanctuary of this harbour.

At the head of Port William, the smell of peat smoke comes as a preliminary to the journey's end. Passing through the 'narrows', a deep but confined sea-way, the vessel enters into the inner, almost land-locked harbour of Port Stanley. The small township of Stanley, capital of the Falklands, lies ahead. Neat, simply-designed houses clutter the low sloping hillside in almost regi-

13

mental order and, as if on parade to approach vessels, all face across the harbour to the north.

Coloured iron roofs give the little town a bright patchwork appearance. On days of intense sunlight such colour adds vivid contrast to the backcloth of the surrounding landscape. When dark clouds predominate, however, the town moulds into the surrounding greys and buffs of the hills putting on a rather sober cloak.

By whatever means one enters the Islands it is at this point that the visitor who is accustomed to the British way of life will find difficulty in appreciating their geographical position. Entrance formalities are no more than one would expect from a local police and customs officer on any Scottish isle. When a plane is due to land, numerous Land-Rovers congregate at the airport to meet friends and relatives coming off the flight. Carrying these new arrivals to their destinations will mean, for those living in Stanley, a drive of only some ten minutes to those houses situated furthest away.

One small hotel copes with visitors and a number of private houses also welcome tourists.

There is a distinctly informal air. Returning residents and visitors share common greetings, and although many Islanders have an insular character on the surface, this is quickly penetrated and one becomes part of the everyday life. It is difficult to remain a stranger.

Entering the homes of these people is like entering a very typical British village home with just a touch of its own special colour. The mid-morning break for coffee makes its appearance as 'smoko time.' Tea making formalities comply as also does the Colonial touch of pre-lunch gins. Breakfasts of bacon and egg remain traditional but through necessity are often supplemented by chops and penguin eggs. The English 'hello' remains but the Islanders' goodbye is 'cheers che'.

Outside this small capital town of Stanley lies the 'camp', a Falkland derivation of the word 'campos' or countryside. Here live the 'campers', the other half of the Falkland population:

14

sheep farmers, shepherds, navvies, roustabouts and their families, who make up the thirty or so settlements where these people have their homes and operate the Islands' only industry of wool production.

In the camp the insular character of the Islands is portrayed even more. Here a natural reserve on the part of the settlement people fights with their overwhelming hospitality. The old tradition of the village manor is replaced in these camp settlements by the 'big house' residence of the farm owner or manager.

At the present time the Falklands and their people are beset with many problems and as in many islands there is a slow and steady migration; the economy balances in the hands of the world's wool markets.

The word evacuation has trembled on the lips of many who have looked at the Falklands from outside and viewed them only as an economic entity. But should economics have the last say in the future of the Islanders and their unique environment? Regrettably words alone cannot convey the powerful attraction these Islands have to those who make their homes here, nor can they describe the finer perfections of island life, the scene, the feel, the sound and even the scent of the environment. All these are dominant factors which can only be appreciated by those who walk these lands.

Such joys are fast becoming rare in the world. They are not only for what society calls the escapist, they will in the future be for the benefit of all and as such deserve their place today. Eventually men will require to sample such unique environments so the Islanders and those who wish to keep such stores of natural richness alive for the future should be encouraged.

PREFACE TO THE THIRD EDITION

For the majority of us on that early morning of 2 April 1982 there was a feeling of utter disbelief as it became increasingly apparent that an Argentine Naval fleet was heading for Port

Stanley. Even in the final hour people attempted to reassure themselves that this could not possibly be an invasion but more of a show of strength, and that the Argentine fleet would return to base. This was however to turn to shocked amazement as troops in heavily armoured amphibious carriers poured ashore to surround the small capital town and its airport.

In my former introduction, written ten years ago, I spoke about the Islands being on the brink of an exciting period of change. Few I believe saw this folly and the changes that we are now experiencing—or those that would now appear to be set for the Falklands.

In an odd twist, the former introduction highlights certain scenes of many years ago which are now being re-staged. The experience of a sea voyage, ironically, has returned; not between the Atlantic and the Pacific, but between the Falklands and Ascension Island. Entering Port William and the smaller inner harbour of Port Stanley—both now full of shipping—it is even easier to visualise the scenes of one-hundred years ago, when vessels on the Cape Horn route sought refuge in these harbours after fighting bitter battles with the elements.

By that action which started on 2 April the Falklands have changed dramatically. They have become a point of focus; they are no longer an obscure group of islands set deep in the South Atlantic. There is even more focus on development, backed by finance such as the islanders have never known before. Changes are inevitable, and many will come hard to those who sought the Falklands as a haven and a refuge from the outside world— perhaps even from the twentieth century. Who knows what the outcome will be. It can only be hoped that at least some of the qualities so many found in these islands will not be lost.

In this new work the decision was taken to leave such chapters as the original Introduction and 'The Future and Development' in the belief that as they stand they are important aspects of the Falklands' immediate past and serve now as a comparison with the present and a new future.

16

1   GEOGRAPHICAL FEATURES

THE Falklands have a cool oceanic climate dominated by westerly winds. Lying on the northern edge of the depression belt which passes through the Drake Passage, the Islands experience continuous variation of weather caused by the air masses and fronts which pass across. Although they lie in the lee of the South American mainland and experience some of the warming and drying influences of the Andes, their separation from the mainland by some 300 miles of relatively cold water modifies these effects. The Falklands' climate has a narrow temperature range. At Stanley the mean monthly temperature during the summer months of January and February is 49° F (9° C) and 36° F (7° C) during the winter months. Strong winds, the annual mean being about 16½ knots, are typical, together with seasonal uniformity and a day to day variability commonly associated with an oceanic situation in temperate latitudes.

Temperatures have never been known to exceed 79° F (26° C) or to fall below 12° F (−11° C). Ground frosts can occur in any month of the year although air frosts are uncommon during the summer. The average values for relative humidity are high and overcast conditions are frequent. Recordings at Stanley show that on only about eighteen days in the year is more than half the sky free of cloud and sunshine levels are low. The indication is, however, that in the west conditions are generally more favourable. The total possible sunshine recorded annually is 35 per cent.

Fog is comparatively rare and normally occurs only on hills and coastal areas. Snowfalls have been recorded in every month

17

but are generally light, rarely lying for more than a few days. An exception was in 1878 when snow fell on fifty-eight days and lay from May until the end of August. Present records indicate snow falls on about fifty-five days of the year.

In Stanley the average rainfall is about twenty-five inches with a trend towards higher rainfall during December and January with a minimum in spring, September and October. Port Stanley is in one of the wettest parts, with the drier stations in the south of the archipelago. Data from West Point Island, in the north-west shows a marked low rainfall. Records indicate that there are a number of local climatic gradients within the Islands.

Comparisons show that the mean winter temperatures are similar to those in Great Britain but the summer mean is more in keeping with that of Scotland. The total possible sunshine recorded is about the same as many parts of England and the mean annual rainfall recorded in Stanley compares with the centre and east of England.

The prevailing winds are from the west and more than two-thirds blow from the quadrant between south-west and north-west. There is little seasonal variation in wind speed although local vessels are wary during the equinoctial periods of September and March. Records show strong winds also during November. Gales are on average recorded about four times a month but storm force winds (forty-eight to fifty-five knots) and gusts above sixty one knots (70 mph) are infrequent. The highest recorded gust in Stanley over the last ten years was 88 knots in June 1976. Statistics show that calm conditions, more prevalent during dawn and dusk, occur more frequently than gales.

History of Observations

The first records of weather in the Falklands were kept by McBride at Port Egmont. These are found in his 'Journal of winds and weather and degrees of heat and cold by the thermometer at the Falkland Islands' dated 1 February 1766 to 19 January 1767.

Records were also kept at Port Louis by the naval officers at intervals between 1832 and 1842. These observations were, however, largely restricted to wind direction and speed and temperature and entered in 'Naval Log Book' fashion. Lt Henry Smith maintained records four times a day at Port Louis between August 1835 and August 1836.

G. T. Whitington appended to his monograph of the Falkland Islands a weather chart kept at Port Louis by Henry Channon a former crew member of the schooner *Unicorn*. Observations were taken over a period of nine months, the weather being noted three times a day, 7–8 am, noon and 4–5 pm. It was kept from 9 November to 26 August 1833 at the settlement and on Turf Island from the 27 August 1833 to 9 January 1834. The change to the latter place was the result of the Port Louis murders (see Chapter 3).

Probably the first detailed and carefully transcribed records were those taken between April and August 1842 by Sir James Ross of HMS *Erebus* and *Terror*. Records were kept at Cape Pembroke Beacon after its establishment in 1850 and continued probably in more detail after 1855 when the lighthouse was built.

In February 1858 Governor Moore reported that he had received observation registers and would employ the lighthouse keeper, Mr Creed, to maintain records. Moore had no meteorological equipment and requested that a barometer and two thermometers be sent from England. These records were then maintained, with some interruptions, until 1947.

In 1875 a station opened in Stanley but operated only spasmodically until 1923. F. E. Cobb of the Falkland Islands Company took records from 1881 to 1883 and from 1885 to 1886 and the Government House gardener, A. Linney made observations from 1905 to 1911.

The Meteorological Station in Stanley first began observations in 1945 under the supervision of the Royal Navy but for most of its life it has been run jointly by the British Meteorological Service, British Antarctic Survey and the Falkland Islands Government. In 1968 it was taken over entirely by the Falkland

Islands Government. Several camp stations send daily weather observations to Stanley and a number have maintained almost continuous records for over twenty years.

The Geological Structure

The oldest rocks in the Falklands belong to the Archaean basement complex, a small exposure appearing at Cape Meredith in the south of West Falkland. Apart from a few Jurassic dolerite dykes these are the only igneous rocks that occur in the archipelago. Most of the islands are composed almost entirely of of Palaeozoic and Mesozoic sedimentary rocks. There is a very strong stratigraphical similarity with those of South Africa and fossil fauna and flora also show a striking similarity between the two regions. Silicified wood found in the south east of East Falkland bears close resemblance to specimens of the Barakar Beds in India and Ecca Series of South Africa. These close relationships add evidence to the suggestion that the group may have moved from the vicinity of south-east Africa and that the rocks now forming these islands represent the missing section of the Karroo basin of Natal and eastern Cape Province.

The Falklands owe their existence to folding movements which probably occurred some time before the laying down of the youngest rocks now to be seen in the archipelago. These folds, which occur in a somewhat winding course on a rough east-west axis on the two main islands of East and West Falkland, give rise to the Wickham Heights range on East Falkland and the mountains on West Falkland, the mountains ranging in a slightly concave form between the extreme north-east and north-west points. A subsidiary folding runs down the east coast of West Falkland forming the Hornby Mountains.

West Falkland and adjacent islands are predominantly composed of Palaeozoic sedimentary rocks, quartzites, sandstones and shales. The northern section of East Falkland is also composed largely of Palaeozoic sedimentary rocks. The Lafonia region of East Falkland and its adjacent islands is composed of the younger Mesozoic rocks, represented by sandstones and mudstones, evi-

20

dence of the extensive Gondwana system of other parts of the southern hemisphere.

Although much of the Falklands may have been ice free during the quaternary era when great parts of the adjacent land mass of South America were glaciated, the mountains of the archipelago which rise over 2,000 feet show evidence of local glaciation.

The broad, dome-shaped Mount Usborne and the Mount Adam and Mount Maria ranges on West Falkland have pronounced corries with small glacial lakes at their bases. Morainic ridges deposited below the corries suggest that the glaciers and ice domes were confined to areas of maximum elevation with other parts of the islands experiencing a periglacial climate.

Stone Runs

During the period of severe cold, large accumulations of boulder formed on the hillsides and valley floors. These are locally called stone runs and undoubtedly present the most controversial feature in the geography of the Falkland Islands.

From the air an obvious contrast is apparent between stone-runs of the block-field type, which may be several square miles in extent, and those which occur in approximately parallel lines in which individual lines may be hundreds of yards long but only a few feet wide. In certain light conditions, stone runs resemble sheets of water. Streaks and patches of white or dark grey cover neighbouring boulders, where lichen varieties differ. Long islands of vegetation fleck the acreage of tumbled, irregular boulders. The rocks may be almost square and flat or cube-shaped, diamond, cigar, or triangular shaped and can be any size from that of a shoe box to boulders of several tons weight. Clusters of rocks of great size occur but other giants are isolated among hundreds of lesser boulders lying at any angle. Water can frequently be heard underneath the stones.

To explain stone runs Sir Wyville Thomson argued that weathering acting differentially on beds of varying hardness in the Quartzitic Sandstones, which form the bulk of the Falkland

Uplands, resulted in the collapse of massively jointed and bedded resistant strata when the supporting softer strata was removed. These blocks were then clothed with vegetation and soil and because of the expansion and contraction of these agents with seasonal variation in water content, the whole mass crept down-hill by settling. Eventually streams washed away the soil exposing the boulders.

J. G. Anderson, who visited the Islands in 1902 believed that the stone runs were formed when solifluction was working on a much larger scale at an earlier period. Freeze-thaw weathering in peri- or sub-glacial conditions, acting on the alternating hard and soft bands of rock typical of the Quartzitic Sandstone uplands reduced the softer material to mud, which acted as the vehicle for the transport of large numbers of hard blocks which collapsed from the ridges as the softer material was removed.

J. R. F. Joyce, writing in 1950, argued that several stone runs have characteristics which are irreconcilable with solifluction. Some, which lie across the tops of dome-like hills, could hardly have flowed into those positions. He remarks on the absence of stone runs on the south slope of the Wickham Heights, where the quartzites reach their highest point and where solifluction would therefore be expected to have produced most spectacular features. Two more objections he raises are the mechanical improbability of such large blocks being moved without jamming, and the doubt of there being a sufficient supply of mud in proportion to rock to create the 'flows' proposed by Anderson.

Joyce accepts that freeze-thaw action and differential disintegration satisfactorily account for loosening the blocks. Solifluction, soil creep and frost-heave he suggests may all have played a minor part in modifying the position of boulders, but the present distribution and location of stone runs is directly dependent on the geological structure of their sites. In 1960, Dr Maling reached the conclusion that Joyce's version may explain hill-side and near-summit stone runs but it cannot account for valley accumulations.

From 1967–70 M. Dodds carried out numerous field observa-

tions of the Falkland stone runs and accepted Anderson's solifluction theory as the most complete explanation of the more
typical stone run forms, whether on hill-sides or in valleys but
also agreed on Joyce's explanation for hill-top and scarp-slope
features. Dodds' investigations found that where beds of quartzite
lie almost horizontally, such as on the summits of Mount Kent
and adjacent peaks, there are extensive areas of loose blocks still
lying in a recognisable relationship to each other. These have
not been transported and so are similar to the stone runs Joyce
observed on other hill tops. On the north-east face of Mount
Usborne, where the crags above Black Tarn form a prominent
three-sided cliffed spur, blocks apparently dislodged from its
exposed faces carpet the steep slope on all sides and the process
of collapse with the retreat of a scarp face as propounded by
Joyce, is clearly illustrated. Both these examples could be explained in terms of frost action and gravitational collapse
alone.

Other examples, however, cannot be explained by Joyce's
theory. The south flank of the Wickham Heights, a dip-slope, is
rich in stone runs, where they ought hardly to occur in terms of
his theory. At the foot of the dip slope of Cantara Mountain,
there is a stone run typically composed of quartzite blocks, on the
Lafonian side of the geological boundary. Nearby a stream bank
exposure reveals a peaty matrix containing quartzite boulders
lying on rocks of Lafonian age. Some form of transport must
explain these features. If transport has occurred in these cases it
seems reasonable to suppose that it has also happened in the case
of other similarly located features which have not crossed the
boundary.

Dodds supports Anderson's theory of solifluction by the evidence of the vegetation 'leads' which lie between the stone lines
referred to earlier. In the Moody Valley quarrying has revealed
sections through such an area. The vegetation is seen to be established on sections of boulder field choked with soil and fine
material. Also, large areas adjacent to stone runs have an uneven
surface suggesting that if soil and vegetation were stripped, further

areas of boulder field would be exposed. These buried stone runs and vegetation leads could represent the original flow-matrix colonised by plants with the amelioration of the climate.

Forest Remains

The only pre-glacial deposit so far discovered in the Falkland Islands is known as the 'forest-bed', on the shore of West Point Island harbour. Mr A. Felton brought it to the notice of the Swedish geologist T. Halle, a member of the Swedish Magellanic Expedition (1907–1909).

Dr Halle made several sections through the bed and discovered, beneath a steep clay bank, a large number of black humified tree remains composed of small branches and tree stumps. Halle identified these as *Podocarpus* and *Libocedrus*, Chilean species of modern ranges of Lat 38–42° and 34–45° S respectively. Halle also discovered in a sample of clay taken from around the deposit, an abundance of pollen grains of two or three conifers, adding evidence to the suggestion that the climate of the Falklands was warmer before the Ice Age than it is now and that they may have been partly forest clad. Halle was satisfied that the fossil trees had grown on the spot immediately before solifluction had taken place and that the resulting flow had buried the trees.

Baker, however, felt that Halle's interpretation might be more convincing if the remains had been found in situ, for no stumps were found in a position of growth. Baker dismissed the find as an accumulation of driftwood from South America. Skottsberg, who accompanied Halle, commented that no other deposits had been found, but also considered it probable that the change in climate at the end of the Tertiary period came slowly. Consequently the forests died and most trunks decayed before solifluction began. Perhaps the West Point deposit remained due to a concatenation of favourable circumstances. It is also worthy of note that no intensive search has yet been made for other deposits of this kind. Mr Felton was keenly interested in such matters and it may yet be proved that other deposits exist.

PHYSICAL FEATURES

Plains

The only large area of land in the Falklands which qualifies as a plain is the undulating land known as Lafonia which seldom rises above 100ft. This plain comprises some 50 per cent of the total land area of East Falkland and forms the entire southern section below Brenton Loch and Choiseul Sound.

Two smaller plains exist. The Bombilla and Chata Flats area, lying central of the northern section of East Falkland and the Warrah river region on West Falkland where a small plain is embraced by the Robinson, Maria and Purvis mountain ranges.

Mountains

The principal mountain ranges follow the folded quartzites on an east-west axis. Mount Usborne 2,312ft is the highest point of the Wickham Heights on East Falkland, while on West Falkland the range continues with Mount Adam, 2,297ft, and Byron Heights, 1,709ft. The Hornby Mountains on West Falkland run parallel to the Falkland Sound with Mount Moody, at 1,816ft while Mount Maria reaches 2,158ft. Although Mount Usborne on the East is the highest point in the archipelago, generally speaking West Falkland is more impressive in its appearance.

Coastlines

The coastlines of the Falklands are deeply indented with many excellent harbours. The underfit rivers and the fact that the river valleys continue below sea level, is an indication that the inlets were caused by river action. This was followed by coastal submergence forming characteristic rias.

Rivers

East and West Falkland abound with streams and small rivers. On East Falkland five rivers are named, the largest and longest of the archipelago being the San Carlos River which, from its upper reaches on the 'Flats' of Mount Usborne to the Cerro Monte area of Port San Carlos is about 24 miles long. The

25

Arroya Malo or Malo River, which runs into Port Salvador waters, has an approximate length of 13 miles. The Murrel, Fitzroy and Swan Inlet Rivers are about 8–9 miles long from their appearance as rejuvenated streams with some degree of maturity to their tidal reaches. These rivers develop from various sources along the slight east to west curve of the Wickham Heights. The San Carlos River flows almost due north with a final swing leading to the west coast. The other rivers flow to the east coast.

On West Falkland, the Warrah and Chartres Rivers have lengths of about 18 and 16 miles respectively. The Warrah is fed from a complex of streams originating on the northern slopes of the Mount Maria and Mount Robinson range. The Chartres River comes from the Hornby Mountain range. Four other rivers exist on West Falkland, the Blackburn River with sources in the Mount Edgworth region, Teal River which flows from the southern slopes of Mount Adam, the River Doyle originating from a complex of streams between Mounts Suliyan and Philomel and Dean's River which flows into Port Stephens. In comparison these latter rivers are very small, being little over four to five miles long.

Lakes

Owing to the generally impervious nature of the soils and peaty areas of the lower regions, large numbers of shallow ponds form. The lowland area of East Falkland which is bordered by the Wickham Heights and the Choiseul Sound is pitted by many ponds some over a mile in length. In the north Loch Head Pond is three miles long in its main section and is the largest on this island. Many ponds are generally under two metres deep being limited by the surrounding peat and base of impervious clay subsoil. In the Falklands there appears to be no qualifying factor as to what is to be classed a pond or lake. On East Falkland no lakes are named. On West Falkland five stretches of water bear the title 'lake'. Lake Sulivan is the largest, being six miles long over its two separate stretches. Lake Hammond is the second largest while Lakes Orrisa, Arthur and Ellen are very small areas of water and Lake Hammond alone drains to the sea.

The Falkland Current

The Southern Ocean Current follows an easterly course southward of the South Atlantic, South Indian and South Pacific oceans. For most of its course this vast current is unrestricted in its movement. Between longitude 60° W and 80° W, however, the land mass of southern South America thrusts its barrier into the current from the north. Similarly, Graham Land Peninsula pushes an almost equal barrier into the current from the south. Until the current reaches this point it flows through ocean for some 1,400 miles but at the point of intersection with these two land masses the current is forced through a comparatively narrow channel of about 450 miles. This channel is the Drake Passage, the most notorious of all sea passages in the southern oceans.

After Drake Passage the current becomes very wide with its northern edge following a north-easterly direction into the South Atlantic. This offshoot splits again to pass the southern and eastern shores of the Falklands. This, the Falkland Current, then continues its cold stream to about Latitude 36° S off the southern part of Rio de la Plata where it ends.

The blunting effect which the Falklands have on the predominantly northern flow of this current is indicated by the large amounts of driftwood which have originated from the densely wooded areas of Tierra del Fuego and which are often stranded on the southern shores of the Islands. Fuegian canoes have been found on the shores of Bleaker Island, and historians wonder if the Fuegians themselves might have arrived in the Falklands with the assistance of this current.

To the north and north-east of the Falklands, the position of the current's flow is often pronounced. Large accumulations of kelp appear, originating from the coastal beds of the islands and the rich, food-bearing waters are followed by sea birds.

27

Around the archipelago the current is largely influenced by a south-easterly tidal wave which causes localised streams among the channels, passages and shores. The general streams running northward and south-westward past the Sea Lion Islands flow between one or two knots but along the southern, western and northern coasts the strength increases. Localised tidal rips develop flowing with tremendous force and in conditions of wind against the flow the seas rise to produce an almost static bore of water above the normal level of the surrounding sea.

Tidal levels are affected greatly by wind conditions and the flow of the main current. Off Bird Island and Beauchene Island, which lie exposed to the stronger sections of the Falkland current, tide levels will remain static for days depending on wind direction.

In the extreme north-west the Falkland current builds up against the underwater mountains which emerge at intervals as the Jason Island group. Here the current develops a force not found in many other parts. The waters are forced over shallow reefs and squeezed between the Jason Islands to develop tidal races of ten knots with an average of six knots. With this general flow to the north and the predominantly north-west winds the seas of the area often produce walls of water unmatched elsewhere in the Islands.

The Falkland current has a cool surface temperature which may vary between a mean of some 48° F (9° C) during the late summer and between 40–42° F (5°C) in the winter months. It is rich in animal and plant life which play an important part in the ecology of bird and marine mammal life of the Falklands. Strong currents and tidal rips cause localised areas of sea to become rich in plankton. *Euphausia* and other crustaceans such as *Munida* tend to form concentrated patches which are valuable feeding areas for birds and seal. (See Chapter 9.)

LAND WEALTH

Mineral wealth of economic value has not been found, although at times speculation has run high regarding such minerals as oil and coal. No extensive exploration has been carried out for these two minerals.

Coal

In a letter to the Earl of Carnarvon, in 1866, Governor Robinson reported on finding coal in the areas of Island Harbour, Bodie Creek and Port Sussex on East Falkland. These specimens were studied by Professor Agassiry in 1865 who said of the Island Harbour coal :

> I can only compare it to the Anthracite of Mausfield in Massachusetts and the adjoining deposits of Rhode Island, though it does not appear quite so pure as the best Anthracite of the United States, but this is an impression derived from surface specimens gathered at random

In 1877 the Port Sussex 'coal' was examined more closely by the *Challenger* Expedition and reported as being bituminous layers which had formed among the clay-slates sometimes becoming a sort of culm. This it was stated might have some value mixed with coal and burnt as fuel in a smithy fire.

In 1920–2, Baker carried out an extensive geological survey for the Falkland Islands Government, a survey which was prompted by interesting discoveries made in 1907–08 by Dr Halle of the Swedish Magellanic Expedition. Halle discovered that formations of Permo-Carboniferous or Gondwana Rocks appeared in the Islands. These rocks in other parts of the world are known to contain valuable deposits of coal.

Some time after Halle's visit the Imperial Institute reported on an interesting specimen of bitumen or cannel with an oil content of some 75 per cent which had been received from the Falklands. The sample was found to be practically identical with the oil-bearing rock of Hartley, New South Wales.

Baker found that the bituminous specimens had come from widely scattered localities, often from areas with no outcrops of Gondwana rocks and all found singly on beaches. He found no exposed seams of bituminous material on the Islands and eventually concluded that the material must have drifted to their

29

shores, possibly from seams which crop out beneath the Falkland Sound or to the north-east of Lafonia. He also commented that cannel or bitumen were once shipped past the Falklands from Australia. It was therefore possible that the few fragments of cannel found in the Islands may have originated in New South Wales.

Oil

Baker considered that the possibility of finding oil in the Falklands was doubtful from the fact that extensive surveys had been carried out in the Cape by South African Geological Surveys, where the rocks have a notable similarity to those of the islands.

No evidence had been found to indicate the existence of oil but the possibility of the occurrence of liquid petroleum in the Falkland Islands could never be definitely settled until exploratory boring was undertaken.

·Recently, interest has been renewed in oil in the Falklands and in 1970 the Falklands Islands Government announced that applications had been received from oil prospecting companies for the right to make offshore drillings.

Search for other minerals

Baker reported that the Islands were discouragingly deficient in minerals of economic importance, although on several occasions hopes of finding valuable metals ran high. In 1873 D'Arcy reported that silver ore had been found in West Falkland but was not economically workable. In 1914 the Government fixed royalties on minerals found in the Colony at one shilling on every ounce of gold and threepence on every ton of coal.

Iron ore as limonite and siderite occurs in the Colony and a sample received at the Imperial Institute in 1907 was found to contain 58·95 per cent of oxide of iron, an amount sufficiently high to make this a valuable ore. Unfortunately, it is not found in commercial quantities.

Kaolin and graphite have also been discovered but again in very small quantities. Gold was thought to have been discovered, particularly at the Archaean exposure of Cape Meredith, but this proved to be iron pyrites.

Sand on the Falkland beaches has attracted attention through the entire period of colonisation of the islands. In 1852 Governor Rennie referred to the large amounts of very fine white sand available over an area of some 400 acres of Cape Pembroke. He sent samples to England to be tested by The Thames Plate Glass Company, of Blackwall. They sent for several tons to prove its value on a larger scale but this project was never developed.

Baker reported that a good glass sand should consist almost entirely of quartz grains with a uniformity of size. In this respect the Falkland sands are quite satisfactory for use in glass manufacture. However, the percentage of iron-oxides in sands to be used for best quality optical glass should not exceed a trace, with up to 1 per cent of iron in sand to be used for the manufacture of plate and window glass. The Falkland sands have an iron content of 0·42 per cent rendering them unsuitable for glass of a quality to make exploitation commercially possible. However, the presence of aluminium in these sands could favour its use in the production of thermometer glass. The only out-crop of limestone is found in the raised beach at Shell Point close to Fitzroy on East Falkland.

Peat

The deposits of peat are relatively recent as indicated by the bird bones in the clay beneath. Hattersley-Smith and Hamilton indicated that these were from the same species which live on the islands today.

From the little evidence available, peat may have accumulated during the post-glacial periods of higher rainfall. Penguin and seal bones left by oil hunters, tools and a layer of charred vegetation probably left by early settlers have also been found beneath the surface of peat, indicating that it is still forming.

Peat develops as a mat layer of vegetation which is often rich in total nitrogen but poor in available nitrogen. Therefore the dead vegetation, often highly acid, remains sour and cannot be broken down by bacterial action, which depends on available nitrogen. Compaction takes place and the older layers become colloidal with a very high water content, eventually being reduced to an amorphous carbonaceous mass with 'mat' continuing to form on the surface.

The deposits of peat vary greatly in both depth and in the origin of 'mat'. On the smaller tussac islands where pure stands of tussac dominate, accumulations of a relatively light peat form. Compaction appears to be less and depths of up to 14 metres have been recorded. On the mainlands depths vary between a few centimetres to 3–4 metres. 'Mat' formation differs greatly, resulting in varying grades of peat.

Professor Sir Wyville Thomson from the *Challenger* Expedition in 1877 reported that the Falkland peat was very different from that of northern Europe. He wrote : 'Cellular plants enter scarcely at all into its composition.' Thomson's investigations showed much of the 'mat' to be formed from roots, stems and foliage of *Empetrum rubrum*, of *Myrtus nummularia*, *Caltha appendiculata* and some sedges and sedge-like plants. Other investigators have found *Gunnera magellanica*, *Chiliotrichum diffusum* and *Pernettya Pumila* forming 'mat' accumulations.

ECOLOGY AND PHYSICAL ENVIRONMENT

The two main islands are deeply cut into intricate patterns but vary greatly in contour. East Falkland is the least severe in its terrain. The plain of Lafonia has coastlines with generally slightly inclined beaches. Long wide stretches of white quartzite sand beaches also feature on this island. In the north, except for the Wickham Heights, much of the land is less than 250ft above sea level, but the shore-line is generally formidable with sharply cut cliffs falling directly to the sea or narrow boulder beaches. The northern shores of East Falkland are unusual in that there is an almost total absence of offshore islands and harbours.

West Falkland is generally more hilly. The east coast has few beaches but several excellent harbours are almost landlocked. To the north the coast is broken into a mass of some fifty islands, islets and reefs. These islands gradually form a gentle curve to the north-west with the Jason group.

The west coast of West Falkland is deeply cut by large bays and intricate inlets. In the north the Byron Heights form almost sheer cliffs broken only by small bays. To the south the maze of inlets, channels and bays have formidable cliffs, stacks and bluffs, and there is a final complex of islands in the Weddell, Beaver and New Island areas.

Offshore Islands

There are some 340 islands or islets other than the two main masses of East and West Falkland. In size these islands vary from some 220km to islets of only a few square metres. Fifteen islands are inhabited permanently. These islands are placed geographically into three regions. In the north-west a chain of these islands, comprising Pebble, Keppel, Saunders, Sedge, Carcass and West Point Islands embraces the northern approaches to West Falkland. At the south-west corner lie New Island, Beaver and the largest of the offshore islands Weddell Island. The third region composing Speedwell, George, and Barren Islands, Sea Lion, Bleaker and Lively Islands which form an arc round the south-east shore of Lafonia, East Falkland. The majority of these islands exhibit characteristics typical of the mainland areas closest to them. Where the islands to the south of West Falkland have been exposed to the continuous action of heavy seas, deep fissures and stacks have been developed.

In sharp contrast the Jason Islands show characteristics of their own. Sharply rising peaks give them a grandeur found in few other areas of the archipelago.

Tussac grass is an important feature of many smaller islands. A coastal fringe is often formed usually 200–300yds in width. On the small islands holding a pure stand of tussac, or on islands narrow enough to allow the fringes to meet, a dome shape develops caused by the build up of tussac peat and wearing of the coastal edge by erosion and passage of animal life.

33

GEOGRAPHICAL FEATURES

Many of the larger islands, which generally have richer pastures, play an important part in the main industry of sheep farming. On the few islands where tussac grass has been carefully preserved, a higher percentage of animals can be held per acre. Offshore islands which are uninhabited and unstocked by domestic animals have unsurpassed value as ecological niches for the populations of bird and animal life.

SETTLEMENTS

The sea remains the Islands' 'main road', and although today the islanders also rely heavily on motor vehicles and the air service, nearly all produce is carried by sea. Sea communications are therefore of major importance. But a settlement could not survive without fuel; coal could be imported but was expensive. A suitable supply of peat had to be easily available and this was the main factor in the placing of a settlement.

The best pastures were found on the coasts and these attracted the wild cattle. When land tenures were first taken out on East Falkland, the best cattle areas were taken up. Corrals were often built close to a peninsula where the cattle could be more easily herded and settlements such as Fitzroy, Salvador, Rincon Grande and San Carlos were thus established. During the early days, the term settlement was not generally used and Lafone's small township at Hope Place was called the 'chief corral'.

With the settlement of West Falkland the interest in cattle was declining. Sheep farming was the main interest with the aim of much larger exports. Sea communications were more important to the settlers on the West who were completely removed from a port such as Stanley, which those on East Falkland could reach overland if the need arose. There is an indication that the first settlements on West Falkland were built on harbours more suitable for larger vessels. A supply of peat still ruled the exact position of settlements and a number of good harbours remain deserted because of the lack of peat.

Houses were often built around a green. Each house was an

individual unit with its own cow sheds, hen runs, meat house and garden, the latter usually situated in some nearby valley. For economic reasons preference was given to level, but usually more exposed sites, resulting in a rather haphazard placing of houses.

Typically, all camp stations have a wool and shearing shed, sheep races, kennels and meat gallows, locally called 'palenkey' from the Spanish 'palenque'. On the larger stations, the 'cook-house' similar in style and use to the 'boffy' of old English estates remains an important building in which the single men are housed.

As the sheep industry grew, the need arose for establishing shepherds in remote areas. This resulted in the building of what are today called 'outside houses', single units housing one family.

Owing to economic re-organisation many of the larger farms discontinued the use of the 'outside house' as a permanent residence in the mid to late 1970s, many such houses being taken down and re-located within the main settlements. Although the original system and use of the outside shepherd's house as was known may not return, the present trend to divide up some of the larger farms into single farming units may see a return to the use of the outside house by these smaller farms.

ADMINISTRATION

The Executive Council consists of the Civil and Military Commissioners (the latter non-voting), the Chief Secretary and Financial Secretary, both ex-officio, one non-official member appointed by the Civil Commissioner and two members elected by the independent members of Legislative Council from that council.

On 4 March 1949, the Colony's new Constitution was inaugurated and universal suffrage was introduced. For the first time four out of six of the non-government-service members of Legislative Council were elected by popular vote, and in 1951 the Islanders obtained an unofficial majority on this Council.

In 1964 the constitutions of both Executive and Legislative Councils were altered to allow for a clear non-official majority. In 1980 the Legislative Council consisted of the Governor as President, the Chief Secretary and the Financial Secretary, and six elected members who represent East and West Falkland, East and West Stanley, 'Camp' Division and Stanley Division respectively. Elections are held every four years. The Constitution is currently under review.

Past Legislature

For many years the Legislature retained an official majority with only one non-official member sitting on council. In July 1882, however, Governor Kerr reported to Earl Kimberly that he had received a petition from eight of the landholders in the Islands for increased representation on Legislative Council. It was suggested that the council might be increased to four members, thus allowing two non-official members to sit. A further suggestion was made that a representative should be appointed from East Falkland and one from West Falkland.

Financially, the Colony was slowly finding its feet and in August 1879, Governor Callaghan reported in the estimates for 1880:

> The estimated revenue, £5,630, for the first time in the Annals of the Colony is I am happy to say in excess of the Expenditure required for the year, which only amounts to £5,511.

The following year, 1881, the Falklands became financially independent, from Britain, and on 29 February 1892, Her Majesty's settlements in the Falklands attained the position of a Colony.

Coinage and Currency

Specie was always in great demand and Governor Moody issued a form of promissory note or paper currency. In 1843 he issued Colonial Notes which were valued for half, one, five, ten, twenty-five and fifty dollars. A dollar at that time was valued at 4s 4d, or about one-fifth of an English pound.

These notes were written out and signed by Moody as required. Half-dollar notes, of which 210 were issued, were used considerably more than the larger values. 170 five-dollar notes were issued and 30 fifty-dollar notes. One note to the value of 1/8th dollar was also issued.

By 1850 the doubloon was becoming less common. It was worth 69s 4d in the Colony and 66s 8d outside. There were divisions of a quarter doubloon, eighth and sixteenth.

In 1845 a variety of English coinage was in circulation, largely sovereigns, crowns, three shilling pieces, shillings, sixpences, fourpenny pieces and half crowns. The last appeared to be one of the most used coins. American coinage was also important and the half and quarter-ounce pieces referred to as 'Eagles of the United States', quarter-dollar, half-dollar and eighth pieces remained in use for many years, largely from the influence of American shipping. About 1855 the Bolivian half-dollar piece of adulterated metal was introduced to the Falklands.

British coinage and currency notes eventually came into general use. In 1898 proposals were made for Islands' currency notes and on 16 October 1899 the first 500 £1 and 100 £5 notes were issued. These were printed with a counterfoil which was detached on issue and each note was signed in person by the Colonial Secretary and Treasurer. A 5s note was issued in 1900 but was replaced a few years later by a 10s note. The £5 and £1 value notes continue to be used, although their design has been changed from time to time. In keeping with Great Britain the Falklands changed over to decimal currency in February 1971 and adopted their own 50 new pence currency note, followed in 1975 by their own coinage. By 1976, £1, £5 and £10 notes were in circulation. In 1980 a 50p coin was released, followed in December 1982 by a 20p piece. Commemorative issues have been minted from time to time, for occasions such as the Silver Jubilee of HM Queen Elizabeth II, the 80th Birthday of HM the Queen Mother, and the Wedding of HRH Prince Charles and Lady Diana Spencer. A 'Liberation Coin' was issued to mark the end of the Falklands Conflict in mid 1982. An attractive set of wild life coins were minted in 1979.

WELFARE SERVICES

Medical Service

The pattern, which was first adopted in the 1880s, of stationing medical officers in Stanley, Darwin and Fox Bay was operated until 1972, when it was discontinued. Now three medical officers live in Stanley and are responsible for patients living in both the town and the Camp. A system of regular Camp visits is in operation, involving both air and sea transport.

All the settlements on East and West Falkland can communicate with a doctor by telephone and those living on outlying islands with no telephone link are connected by radio telephone. All settlements are supplied with a standard medical chest which enables doctors to direct its use and prescribe requirements by radio and telephone. The air service (see Chapter six) is available for the transport of doctors or patients. However, much travelling is done by Land-Rover and occasionally by horseback.

For some years the Government operated a scheme the provisions of which allowed patients to take advantage of extra medical attention in Argentina. No payment was required for this service from those patients who were sent by the medical authorities. In 1979 a compulsory levy was introduced for employers and employees to supplement the service. (See also Chapter 11.)

By 1909 over half the population of the Falklands and the Dependencies was engaged in the whale fishing industry. This hazardous work increased the accident rate greatly. Governor Allardyce suggested building an extra ward in the Cottage Hospital to deal with the situation. At a public meeting in January 1911, it was decided to build a hospital, a memorial to King Edward VII. The King Edward Memorial Hospital was opened in May 1915. In May 1953 the Churchill Wing was opened.

Dentistry

Dentistry had to be carried out by the surgeon and it was not until about 1900 that the services of an occasional visiting dentist could be obtained. In 1913, a Colonial Dentist was appointed at a cost of £300 per annum, free service being given to government employees. For other patients an approved scale of charges was drawn up.

One dentist now provides dental care for patients from both Stanley and the Camp. There is a well-equipped dental block in the Churchill Wing of the King Edward Memorial Hospital, while portable equipment is used for treatment given in the Camp.

Pension Scheme

An old-age contributory pensions scheme was introduced in

1952 and is reviewed annually. It is compulsory for all male and female residents in the Colony. A married contributor, reaching the age of 64, received £22 per week, in 1983. An unmarried man, widow or spinster received £14.50. Employees between the ages of 17–60 years contribute £1.70 and the employers £2.60. Self-employed persons contribute £4.30 per week. To provide for those old persons who are excluded by reason of their age, from the pension scheme of 1952, a non-contributory old age pension scheme was introduced in 1961. Rates paid per week for people under this scheme are £18 for married men, £13.50 for unmarried persons.

Children's allowances are paid at the rate of £7 per month for the first two children and £7 in respect of each child thereafter in any one family.

Labour Organisation

There is no Labour Department in the Colony. In October 1943, the Falkland Islands General Employees Union was formed. This is the only trade union in the Islands, and has about 500 members. There is a full-time Secretary and meetings are held annually with the Sheep-Owners Association and employers in Stanley to review wages and conditions. Labour relations in the Falklands are generally good.

JUSTICE AND POLICE FORCE

The earliest recorded statutes, known as Ordinances, date from 1853 when twelve were enacted. An Ordinance of 1853 applied all Acts and the Common Law and rules of Equity of England to the Colony. The Common Law and Rules of Equity still apply but since 1900 the general laws in force in England in that year and other laws specifically applied by Ordinance apply in the Falklands. In addition to local Ordinances passed by the Legislative Council, subsidiary legislation applies. This is usually made by the Civil Commissioner but occasionally by senior colonial officials.

The law provides for Justices of the Peace and Magistrates who may try minor offences. Most minor cases however are heard by the Senior Magistrate's Court established in 1970. The Supreme Court has unlimited powers to hear civil and criminal cases and appeals from all Justices of the Peace, magistrates and Senior Magistrate's Court. There is a court of Appeal which hears appeals from the Supreme Court. There is a resident Senior Magistrate but no resident Supreme Court or Appeal Court Judge. However the Civil Commissioner may appoint an acting Judge of the Supreme Court. Until late 1982 the Colony had a part-time non-resident legal adviser; since October 1982 a resident Attorney General has been in office.

In 1980 the authorised establishment of the Falkland Islands Police Force consisted of one Chief Police Officer, one inspector, one sergeant and four constables. Temporary constables can be called and there is provision for a cadet. At the present time the department is responsible for all driving tests, registration of vehicles and issuing licences for vehicles, guns, dogs, trout fishing, and penguin egg collection, as well as other normal police duties. The Inspector of Police undertakes, on occasions, the duties of Customs and Immigration Officer and the Police also supervise the quarterly dosing of dogs in Stanley in accordance with the safeguards against hydatid disease. (See also Chapter 11.)

Punishments

Punishment for various offences was generally confined to hard labour, which suited the Administration of a small newly-formed settlement where labour for digging ditches, making roads and peat cutting, was always in great demand. Five murderers have been recorded in the Colony, three of whom paid the supreme penalty, the executions taking place in Stanley. Flogging was introduced as a form of punishment but few people were willing to take part in its administration. It was therefore found necessary to imitate the New Zealand practice, where Licenced Victuallers

41

acted as special constables to assist with this particular form of punishment. Capital punishment was abolished in 1971.

PUBLIC SERVICE

Electrical

Continuous electric .power is supplied to Stanley from a Government Power Station which has three generators manufactured by W. H. Allen of Bedford. One engine has a capacity of 306kW and two 467kW each, generating at 3,300 volts, 50Hertz. Power is distributed by an overhead system of wiring. The switchgear and alternators are made by 'Brush' and the system is manually controlled. The present station was opened in 1973, the installation costing £165,367.

In 1980 there were 395 consumers connected to the supply which produced an annual return in 1979–80 of £152,000 with estimated expenditure for the same period of £111,000. The cost of electricity to the consumer in 1983 was $9\frac{1}{2}$p per unit.

Wind Generators

The 'Shackleton Report' team studied the potential of wind generators especially as a source of power for camp settlements and in 1978 a research team from the Electrical Research Association Ltd visited Stanley to investigate the possibility of installing a fairly large capacity wind generator. The proposal was to supplement the existing Stanley power supply by coupling the wind generator to the grid system. Economics apparently overruled the scheme but undoubtedly the Falklands can look forward to wind powered generators in the near future.

Filtration Plant and Water Supply

Water supplies in the Falklands are generally adequate with all supplies originating from surface sources. A number of bore holes operate from wind-driven pumps but no artesian wells are in use.

The majority of the camp stations have devised various means of obtaining water supplies, usually in the form of enclosed

42

reservoirs fed from springs. They gravity-feed a settlement in the conventional manner. Few systems in the camp have any form of filtration, relying instead on water settlement in the reservoir itself. In isolated shepherds' houses, water is supplied by a catchment system off the roof of the house. In some places, however, the introduction of alkathene piping with its durability and relatively low cost, has opened up the possibilities of tapping new sources of supply which may lie several miles distant.

In Stanley the daily average consumption of water is 76,000 gallons (1971) which is gravity-fed from supply reservoirs above the town. The water originates from Moody Valley Filtration Plant which draws its supply from Moody Brook. The plant cost £36,250 to build and install, of which £32,963 was provided by the Colonial Development and Welfare Fund. The plant was opened in March 1958.

Books and Films

A library with some 23,500 books is administered by the Education Department and provision is made for Camp settlers in the form of a system which enables them to obtain books through the local postal service.

The central film library was established in 1953 having been organised by the Superintendent of Education for the supply of films to the schools and camp stations. Films are obtained from the J. Arthur Rank Overseas Film Distributors Ltd, from the Central Office of Information, London and from other distributors in the United Kingdom.

The Library operates on a non-profit making basis, costs being defrayed by subscriptions. Membership in 1980 was made up of 26 Camp stations and two commercial hirers in Stanley. The cost of membership is £250 per annum. In the case of farm settlements this cost is found by the farm owners. Government contributes £800 towards the cost of films.

Printing

For many years there was no provision for any form of type

43

printing. In 1846, reference is made to Thomas Rolon, a 'Banda Oriental', who was returned in the census as a printer. Rolon appears to have been largely responsible for the writing of public notices in script, these being affixed to the Government Notice Board in the 'Dockyard'.

In 1861 the first lithographic press was indented for and one of the pensioners became established as a printer. In 1883 Government procured a 'Bremner' Plattens supplied by Harrild & Sons of Fleet Works, London. The machine had a printing page size of up to 13 x 8in. Three years later Governor Kerr spoke of the need for a qualified printer, and suggested that the post be combined with that of Police Constable.

In the 1920s the demand for printed material was increasing and a second 'Bremner' Plattens was obtained. These two machines were still in operation in 1971 producing a good standard of work which compliments the engineering of over eighty years ago.

In 1953, the first of two flat-bed stop cylinder machines was erected in the Government Printing Office. This was a SWO size machine by Dawson, Payne and Elliot of Otley, Yorkshire. In 1970 a larger partner to the SWO was acquired second-hand from HM Stationery Office. Of similar design, this is a SW3 with a maximum printing page size of 29 x 30in. In 1964 a Linotype 78 slug casting machine was installed.

Falkland Islands Magazines

The most outstanding magazine to be published in the Islands was the *Falkland Islands Magazine and Church Paper* which first appeared in 1889. Dean Brandon was the founder and was also responsible for editing, printing and distribution. The magazine was printed once a month almost continuously until 1933.

A daily news-sheet, *The Penguin*, followed the *Church Paper*. In June 1938 the Reverend Lowe, in an attempt to revive the original church magazine, published the *Falkland Islands News Weekly and Church Bulletin*. In 1944 this changed to the *Weekly*

News edited by the Rev Forrest McWhan. After a lapse of some years the *Falkland Islands Monthly Review* was established in December 1958 and did not cease publication until 1978. The monthly circulation of the *Review* in the Colony and overseas was about 850. In 1967 a publication named the *Falkland Islands Journal* appeared for the first time. Published once a year, the journal was designed to promote interest in the Falklands and their history.

Penguin News is the only privately printed news sheet currently in circulation. Likewise there is only one official periodical published in the Falklands; the Falkland Islands Government's *Gazette*.

Public Works

In 1947 Stanley Town Council was set up by Sir Miles Clifford to administer municipal affairs. The Council consisted of six publicly elected members and three elected by the government. Elections were held biennially and the Council elected one of their members as Chairman, referred to locally as the 'Mayor'.

The Council was responsible for street lighting, cleaning and ash collection, which was put out for local tender. Bunkering, or supply of water to shipping, represented one of the Council's unusual services, with water being supplied not only to local shipping, but to the increasing number of fishing and research vessels.

The Council was discontinued in the early 1970s, all these services being taken over by the Public Works Department.

The Fire Service

The Public Works Department is also responsible for the operation of the Fire Service which is a voluntary service originally operated by the Police Force in 1875 when a fire engine was purchased through Dean's for £295 16s 8d. In 1898 the Fire Service obtained a new fire engine, the 'Gem of the Tournament', a Merryweather & Sons double-cylinder vertical steam fire engine. The makers stated that it was capable of delivering 360 gallons of water a minute and could generate steam rapidly.

45

ADMINISTRATION

In 1980, the Stanley Fire Service was equipped with four Coventry Climax Godiva fire pumps, two trailer-mounted and two hand-portable, capable of delivering 500 gallons at 100 psi, and three Firefly Land-Rover conversions. Two of the latter being adapted for foam and used at the Stanley Airport.

With the introduction of a Brittain-Norman 'Islander' aircraft for internal use, settlement landing strips are also equipped with Perren AFFF 60 fire fighting foam units.

As a result of the 1982 conflict the Fire Service lost one of the above Firefly engines and this was replaced by a larger, more conventional type Carmichael fire engine. At the time of writing this revision the local fire service no longer has any responsibility for operations at Stanley Airport, which is presently used by the Royal Air Force (1983).

In a town made up mainly of timber-built houses and buildings, one latent fear throughout the occupation and subsequent action in 1982 was that of fires breaking out and spreading out of control. In the event it was only towards the close of the re-occupation campaign that a number of fires broke out in Stanley, and the very limited volunteer force must be commended for their exhaustive efforts to contain and extinguish these; on occasions this meant working through the night.

3   HISTORY

DISCOVERY AND EARLY LANDINGS

IT is generally accepted that the Falkland Islands were first discovered by the Elizabethan navigator, John Davis, whose vessel, *Desire* was driven among the Islands on 14 August 1592.

Bougainville considered that the first sighting was made by the Florentine navigator Amerigo Vespucci, about 1502, but there is also the possibility that one of Magellan's ships could have made the discovery, for certain islands are described as the *Isles de Sanson y de Patos*. Camargo's expedition, which reached the Straits of Magellan in 1540, reported the finding of several islands, the descriptions of conditions, land, birds and seal being similar to the Falklands.

Among other navigators who sighted the islands was Sir Richard Hawkins on his ship the *Dainty*. He sighted the islands in February 1594 but did not land. He named the islands 'Hawkins Maiden-Land'.

In 1598 an expedition left Holland for the South Seas commanded by Jacob Mahu. Misfortune prevailed after the expedition passed through the Straits of Magellan and the *Geloof*, commanded by Sebald de Weert, turned back into the Atlantic. On 24 January 1600, three small islands were sighted and named Sebald de Weert Islands, today identified as the Jason Islands. Le Maire and Schouten, on their way to discover Cape Horn, also sighted Sebald Islands on 16 January 1616.

Two privateers, William Ambrose Cowley and William Dampier, with their 'prize' vessel, made the Sebald Islands on 28 January 1684. Dampier recorded that they anchored and from references to 'dildo bushes growing near the seashore' and that no fresh water was found it appears a landing was made.

The first undisputed landing was made by John Strong, commander of the *Welfare*. Strong sailed from Plymouth on 1 November 1689 bound for the South Seas. Hawkins Land was sighted on 27 January 1690 and a landing made. *Welfare* spent six days sailing about the islands, passing between the two main islands. This stretch of water was named the Falkland Sound and later Viscount Falkland's name was given to the whole group of islands.

In 1701 a landing was recorded by the French navigator Gouin de Beauchene. On that voyage he discovered the island which still bears his name. The French remained in the forefront of Falkland exploration with Captains Fouquet and Poree discovering the Sea Lion group of islands in 1703. They named them Anican Islands after the owner of their vessels. In July 1708 Captain Alain Poree named the northern coast of the Falklands, L'Assomption after his ship.

The French called the archipelago Isles Malouines after St Malo from where many of the South Seas expeditions set forth. The same year that Poree sailed along the north coast, two English privateers, the *Duke* and *Duchess of Bristol*, commanded by Captain Woodes Rogers, were also off the islands. On 23 December 1708 Woodes Rogers made landfall and his log describes it as 'Falkland's Land'. Later, in 1766, Captain McBride changed the name to Falkland Islands and renamed the Sebalds the Jason Islands.

The French Settlement

Lord Anson strongly urged the Admiralty to claim the Falkland Islands and in 1740 wrote of their potential importance to shipping. Others were also interested in the Falklands, or Les Malouines. The young French nobleman Antoine Louis de Bougainville, bitter after the loss of Quebec and the cession of Canada to Britain, viewed the prospects of a new Colony in the Falklands as recompense for the blow struck at France. He pre-

48

Page 49 (above) Offshore island in the extreme NW of the Falkland archipelago: Steeple Jason Island showing mountain formation typical of some other islands in the Jason group; *(below)* typical coastal scene on the northern section of East Falkland: Cape Carysfort region where the beaches are commonly populated with groups of Elephant seal. Piles of rotting kelp litter the beach

Page 50 (above) Extreme east of Stanley looking west. The cathedral tower is the prominent building; *(below)* typical rolling landscape of the northern section of East Falkland: Teal Inlet settlement

pared his expedition secretly. Two ships, *Eagle* and *Sphinx* were built at St Malo and a large variety of stores, seeds and plants made ready for establishing his new colony. In September 1763, the ships left St Malo with 140 crew and settlers from the lost Colony of Acadia, Nova Scotia.

The vessels loaded cattle, pigs, goats, sheep and poultry at Montevideo and sailed on 16 January 1764 for the Falklands. On 31 January 1764 the expedition sighted the Jason Islands and sailing east came across 'la grande baye des Isles Malouines' (Berkeley Sound) on 2 February. The following day a landing party inspected the new land. Dom Pernetty accompanied the expedition as botanist, priest and chronicler and he described in detail their first landing, the vast numbers of birds seen and the vegetation.

On 17 February 1764, a party led by Bougainville and Pernetty set out in search of a site for the new settlement. They chose a small hill at the head of 'Baie Saint-Louis', or Berkeley Sound, where a fort of stone, turf and clay was erected, together with an apartment house and a number of turf huts. The foundations of the fort and some other buildings are still visible. On 5 April 1764, a ceremony of possession took place, the fort having been named Fort Saint Louis and the settlement eventually being called Port Louis.

On 8 April de Bougainville returned to France, leaving behind twenty-eight people including artisans of various trades. The following January he returned with the *Eagle* bringing more settlers. On his return to France in April 1765, eighty persons were left at the settlement.

When Spain heard of the new settlement she protested against the French occupation. In October 1766 de Bougainville agreed to transfer his colony to the Spanish Government on payment of 618,108 livres, 13 sols and 11 deniers, a sum equivalent to £25,000. In November 1766 Bougainville again sailed for the Falkland Islands, being joined at Rio de la Plata by two Spanish frigates, the *Esmeralda* and the *Liebre*. The three vessels reached the islands on 21 March 1767, and on 1 April the colony was formally handed over to Spain, the Governor of the French settlement M de Nerville, being succeeded by the Spaniard, Felipe Ruiz Puente.

A British Settlement

While the French were settling on East Falkland preparations were made in England for a voyage of exploration to the same islands. This expedition, comprising the sloop *Tamar* and frigate *Dolphin*, sailed from England on 21 June 1764, under the command of Captain John Byron. His instructions were to look for Pepys Island and to survey the Falkland Islands. After an unsuccessful search for Pepys Island, Byron concluded that it did not exist and proceeded to the Falklands, reaching them on 12 January 1765. On 15 January Byron entered the harbour which almost a year before Bougainville had named Port de la Croizade. This was at Saunders Island and Byron named it Port Egmont in honour of the First Lord of the Admiralty.

Byron claimed this and adjacent islands for George III in complete ignorance of Bougainville's claim on behalf of France. On 27 January Byron continued from Port Egmont along the northern shores of the archipelago, naming islands and headlands en route such as Cape Tamar, the Eddystone Rock and Cape Dolphin. A day later he came to the entrance of a very wide, deep sound, which he named Berkeley Sound. Had he entered he would no doubt have discovered Fort St Louis. After his departure from England, rumours circulated that the French had already established themselves in the Falkland Islands, and in September 1765 an expeditionary force composed of the frigate *Jason*, the sloop *Carcass* and the store ship *Experiment* sailed for the islands under command of Captain John McBride.

McBride's instructions were to inform any lawless person on the islands that they were on land belonging to Great Britain. Those not wishing to take the oath of allegiance to HM government were to be given six months in which to leave. McBride arrived at Port Egmont on 8 January 1766, and the first few weeks were spent in erecting a shore establishment which included

52

a wooden block house brought from England. During the winter the settlement was extended and with the return of better weather the *Jason* set out to explore.

On 3 December 1766 the French settlement was sighted from a mountain overlooking Berkeley Sound. The following day McBride made contact with the commander, de Nerville. McBride sent him a letter informing him of Britain's claim to the islands, and although it was rejected by de Nerville the meeting was cordial and, in an unofficial sense, a great success. At the time of this meeting both parties were unaware that de Bougainville had agreed to hand over the rights to Spain.

Spanish and British Occupation

Early in 1767 McBride returned to England to report. Port Egmont was then commanded by Captain Rayner. Shortly afterwards Captain Hunt of the *Tamar* took command, while Port Louis, now renamed Port Soledad, was directed by the Spaniard Don Felipe Ruiz Puente.

In September 1769 Hunt, cruising in the *Tamar* saw a Spanish schooner from Port Soledad. Hunt presented the master with formal warning to leave the islands, and a few days later a second meeting occurred. This time Hunt was presented with letters from Puente ordering the British to quit the islands. More letters passed between Ruiz Puente and Hunt, each issuing notice to the other to leave. Spanish frigates were ordered to find the British settlement and force the occupants to leave. Finding this impossible, a group of five frigates were then ordered to sail to the Falkland Islands, or Islas Malvinas, as the Spanish called them.

On 4 June 1770 the *Industria* reached Port Egmont, followed a few days later by four more Spanish frigates. In the port was the sloop *Favourite* commanded by Captain George Farmer. Ashore, the only fortifications were a block-house and a mud-built battery mounting four twelve pound guns.

On 8 June, Farmer having made defence preparations, sent a letter to the commander of the Spanish vessels, Juan Madariaga, requesting him to leave. Madariaga in reply invited Farmer to view the Spanish force. An officer from Port Egmont returned with the news that the Spanish force of soldiers and sailors amounted to some 1,600 men. The following day Madariaga requested the departure of the British force. Farmer refused to yield and on 10 June the Spanish force landed. Defence of the British position was impossible and although shots were fired in retaliation, Farmer ordered a flag of truce to be hoisted. Under articles of capitulation the British surrendered the block-house and settlement to the Spanish, and on 14 July the *Favourite* sailed for England, having been purposely delayed by the Spanish so that news of the surrender could first reach Buenos Aires and Spain.

The two countries almost went to war but negotiations resulted in an order for restitution being signed on 7 February 1771. In September an expedition commanded by Captain Stott, with the frigates *Juno*, the sloop *Hound* and storeship *Florida*, arrived at Port Egmont and the Spanish officer in command formally relinquished the settlement on 15 September. Three years later the British abandoned the settlement, an action which is still raised in disputes as to ownership of the islands. At the time, Lord Rochford wrote : 'It is neither more nor less than a small part of an economical Naval regulation'.

On 20 May 1774, Lt Samuel Wittewrong Clayton, commander of the settlement took formal leave, his final act being to attach to the door of the block-house a sheet of lead engraved with the following inscription :

'Be it known to all nations that Falkland Islands with this Fort, the Stonehouse, Wharfs and Harbours, Bays and Creeks there-unto belonging are of the Sole Right and Property of His Most Sacred Majesty, George the Third, King of Great Britain, France and Ireland, Defender of the Faith etc. In witness whereof this plate is set up and His Brittanic Majesty's colours left flying as a mark of possession.'

By, S. W. Clayton,
Commanding Officer at Falkland Islands
A.D. 1774.

Spanish Occupation

The settlement at Port Egmont soon fell into disrepair and in 1775 when the Spanish from Port Soledad visited the site they found everything in a state of dilapidation and decay.

For the rest of that century and for part of the nineteenth century, Spain maintained her settlement at Port Soledad. The most progressive of the Spanish Governors was probably Ramon Clairac who took up office in 1785. At this time the settlement had 34 buildings and a population of about eighty. Although Clairac made efforts to develop the colony, Puerto de la Soledad was never a success and in 1783 Juan Jose de Vertiz, Viceroy of Buenos Aires, suggested that the settlement be abandoned.

In 1785 administration of the Falkland Islands was amalgamated with Puerto Deseado. (Today Argentina, in her claim to the Islands, places them within the administration of Tierra del Fuego.) In 1806 came the war in Buenos Aires and the Spanish Governor of the Malvinas, Juan Cristomo Martinez, having received news of the British occupation abandoned Port Soledad and fled to Montevideo. Four years later revolution resulted in the final separation between Spain and her South American Colonies. Martinez never returned to Port Soledad and Spain's jurisdiction over the Falklands lapsed. A period of disorder and confusion reigned during the revolution until on 9 July 1816 there emerged the United Provinces of the Rio de la Plata. They claimed to succeed Spain in the sovereignty she had held over her South American territories, including the abandoned Islas Malvinas. However, not until 1820 were representatives of the new government sent to take possession of the islands again.

The Neglected Islands

From 1806-20 the islands were abandoned by authority, and they became a haven for whalers and sealers. New Island, West Point Island, the abandoned Port Egmont and other harbours became temporary homes of ships and men engaged about the islands. Charles Barnard's *A Narrative of the Sufferings and Adventures in a Voyage round the World* (New York 1829) tells

55

of the scene in the Falklands at this time, but authoritative records are few.

On 1 November 1820 the frigate *Heroina*, commanded by Colonel Daniel Jewitt of the United Provinces Marine, arrived at Port Soledad and on 6 November formal rights of possession were declared in the name of the newly created United Provinces.

The year 1823 saw the appointment of the first Argentine Governor of the Malvinas, Don Pablo Areguati. Shortly afterwards attempts were made at colonisation but this failed. Louis Vernet, a merchant of Hamburg, of French birth but South American by naturalisation, was granted thirty leagues of land, together with the fishery and cattle rights of East Falkland. He had great plans for creating 'a great national fishery' (See Chapter Seven). Between 1826 and 1831 Vernet established 90 settlers of various nationalities; Dutch, English, German, Spanish, Portugese, French and Indians from South America. In January 1828 Vernet was granted rights to the entire East Falkland and on 10 June 1828, he was appointed Governor of the Falkland Islands and Tierra del Fuego.

Vernet attempted to prevent sealing operations by foreign vessels but his efforts met with little success so he seized three United States sealing schooners. His action brought reprisals and on 28 December 1831, the United States corvette *Lexington* commanded by Sylas Duncan, took revenge by sacking Port Soledad settlement. The destruction of years of work by Duncan's action at the settlement was a great blow to Vernet. Absent from the colony at the time, Vernet never returned to the Falklands. Later, he attempted to obtain compensation from the British Government for stock and produce he had left behind and which had subsequently come under British care in 1833. Of the £14,295 claimed, he was eventually awarded £2,400, twenty-six years after leaving the Malvinas.

In September 1832 a temporary Spanish Governor, Major Juan Esteban Mestivier, took over Port Soledad. His office came to an abrupt end when he was killed by a gang of mutineers.

There followed a period of disquiet during which there was a rather unexpected arrival.

Return of the British

When Vernet became governor, Woodbine Parish, British Ambassador in Buenos Aires, was instructed to forward British claim to the islands, which he did in a letter to the Minister of Foreign Affairs in Buenos Aires in November 1829. Although the matter was promised special attention, no settlement was forthcoming.

In 1832 the *Clio*, commander Captain J. J. Onslow, and the *Tyne*, Captain C. Hope, were despatched to take possession, the *Clio* arriving at Port Egmont on 20 December 1832. Onslow, finding the settlement in ruins attempted to repair the block-house, Fort George, and then sailed to Berkeley Sound, unexpectedly arriving there on 2 January 1833.

With the murder of Mestivier the commander of the *Sarandi*, Don Jose Maria Pinedo, was in charge of the settlement. Onslow issued Pinedo with a letter of his intention to : 'exercise the right of sovereignty over these islands'. To Pinedo this was an insult but no doubt, after the death of Mestivier, he was not sorry when on 5 January 1833 he was able to sail for Buenos Aires aboard the *Sarandi*.

The Port Louis Murders

A few days later Onslow departed in the *Clio*, leaving William Dickson in charge with instructions to hoist the flag whenever vessels appeared. Dickson had been employed by Louis Vernet as a storekeeper.

In March 1833 the *Beagle* commanded by Captain Fitzroy, called at the port. Charles Darwin was on board and both he and Fitzroy were dismayed at the ruined settlement in which sealers, whalers and gauchos took full advantage of the absence of authority. During Fitzroy's visit, Captain Matthew Brisbane returned and, as senior British resident, took charge of the settlement. He was Vernet's agent and had been taken prisoner by

Sylas Duncan of the *Lexington*. Fitzroy described Brisbane, Dickson and another British settler, William Lowe, as the handful of honest settlers whose conduct shone out in contrast to the others.

Brisbane attempted to salvage Vernet's business and create law and order in the community. Much of Vernet's labour force had been composed of Indian convicts and having tasted freedom they were unwilling to return to the lawful state. Secretly plotting against Brisbane, five of the convicts and three gauchos took their chance and on 26 August 1833 when Lowe left with four of his men to go sealing, they attacked and murdered Brisbane, Juan Simon, *capitaz* of the gauchos, William Dickson, Anton Wagner a German settler and Don Ventura Pasos. All but one of the other settlers (thirteen men, three women and two children) escaped to Turf Island in Berkeley Sound on 29 August, where they remained until help arrived.

On hearing of the murders, HMS *Challenger*, previously given orders to call at the Falklands to land Lt Smith, set off from Rio de Janeiro and on 9 January arrived at Port Louis. On 10 January Smith was installed as Governor. Anxious to put his new establishment to rights, Smith set about the capture of the murderers. Of the original eight murderers, five were captured early in March 1834. Eventually four were taken to England, but their arrest posed a problem, for under which law could they be tried? The murders had been committed on land claimed by Britain but before government of the islands had been formed and to have sent them to Buenos Aires for trial would have been recognition of Argentina's claim to the Falklands. Eventually, after a term of imprisonment in Newgate, they were sent back to Montevideo as free men.

Colonisation by Britain

Probably the first to urge colonisation was G. T. Whitington who enquired about prospects in the islands about 1828. An associate of Whitington's, Lt William Langdon, who was both sailor and sheep farmer, had called at the Falklands when he

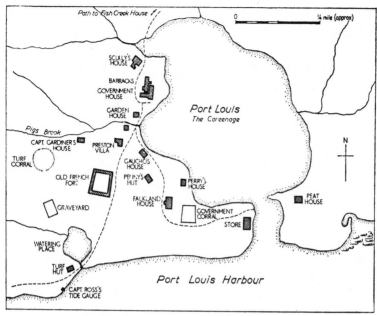

Port Louis settlement area circa 1842

commanded the vessels *Hugh Crawford* and *Thomas Laurie*. From Vernet he obtained for himself and Whitington, grants of land amounting to 6,400 acres in East Falkland.

When Britain took possession, Whitington hoped that with the concessions he had obtained he could continue an establishment similar to Vernet's, namely the salting of fish and beef, sealing and agriculture. In 1834, he formed the Falkland Islands Commercial Fishery and Agricultural Association, forwarding his proposals to the Government. Approval was not given, for to have done so would have been to recognise Vernet's claim on the Islands and, indirectly, that of the Buenos Aires Government. Whitington then applied for new rights, offering to pay not only for his expedition to the Islands, but also the salary of a Governor who might be named by the Crown. The British Government continued to ignore Whitington's applications and his efforts to force their recognition of his requests. Finally in 1840, Whitington's brother, J. B. Whitington, set sail for the Islands prepared to settle there with eighteen other people aboard the two ships *Susan* and *Acton*.

Colonisation was also advocated by Thomas Cochrane who became 10th Earl of Dundonald. He wrote to Whitington in 1834 about the prospects, not only commercially but from the viewpoint of the Islands' value as a Naval station.

Early Administration

Between the years 1834–42 the Islands were supervised by naval superintendents with the assistance of a small naval party to keep law and order and bear some of the administrative duties. Naval influences appeared in the administration. Musters were held every Sunday and the articles of war read, and such formalities were embraced by the civilian settlers. Mutual contracts and letters of agreement were signed by the superintendents and settlers in an attempt to co-ordinate general behaviour.

The superintendent also acted as judge, registrar and shipping master. Marriages were performed, minor offences tried in open court and the first recorded Sailing letter issued at Government House, Port Louis, to the *Alonzo*, owner Richard Penney, on 11 March 1839.

Civil Administration

In 1840 the Colonial Lands and Emigration Commissioners proposed that the Islands be colonised, and on 2 August 1841, Richard C. Moody, aged 28, was appointed in London as Lt Governor and ordered to proceed to the Islands to carry out the proposals.

Moody was left to plan his operations and in a letter to Vernon Smith dated 5 August 1841, he stated that he considered £2,870 necessary to cover the expenses of his plans for a year's operations. By October, Moody had gathered together a small party and supplies. He found the brig *Hebe*, master Captain Anderson, preparing to go to the Falkland Islands and was able to ship his expedition.

On 15 January 1842 at 1.50pm the 190 ton *Hebe* anchored

at Port Louis and on 22 January 1842, after Moody had already visited Port William on horseback, an official landing was made from HMS *Sparrow* at 9.30am. Moody then informed the settlers that Her Majesty's government would look after the Islands.

On 28 November 1843, Moody acknowledged a despatch from Lord Stanley, transmitting the Charter under the Great Seal for the Constitution of the Government of the Falkland Islands. At the same time he received the Commission and Instructions for his appointment as Governor and Commander in Chief of the settlement and Dependencies, both documents dated 23 June 1843.

On 2 April 1845, Moody formed the Executive Council, members being the colonial surgeon, Hamblin, the magistrate, Mr Moore and Moody himself. On 13 November Moody reported the formation of Legislative Council, with Chaplain Moody and Moore sitting as members. The chaplain was the unofficial member and the Governor's brother.

Moody's task of establishing a basis for future colonisation was not easy. Whitehall's view was that he should firmly lead the settlers by example rather than control by the enforcement of laws. Moody was impressed by the Islands. He had great hopes for their future and their capacity to survive on their own natural resources. Many sound practical suggestions were made which, had he been able to implement them, would have benefited the Colony today. Moody was hampered by insufficient financial support from the British Government. Administrative support was also lacking, making it difficult for him to form his Legislative Council. Moody imposed few restrictions although in a great effort to reduce the amount of liquor which 'are fiery spirits which rapidly produce the most maddening effects and disorderly excesses', he imposed an importation tax of 20s per gallon on spirits.

Port Stanley: A New Seat of Government

In 1838 Lt B. J. Sulivan surveyed Port William and the waters of Jackson's Harbour, later named Stanley Harbour. His survey showed much deeper water in these two harbours than at the head of Berkeley Sound. The general lie of Port William, south-west by north-east, presented easier access for sailing vessels against the prevailing westerlies, a point against the use of Port Louis, as Berkeley Sound lay due east and west.

Following instructions from Lord Stanley, Moody continued investigations of Port William in 1842, later reporting that, having viewed the area at the onset of winter, he was concerned about the wet state of the land and considered Port Louis a more favourable site. At this time the Ross Antarctic Expedition was anchored at Port Louis. On 1 June, Moody asked Captain Ross for his advice on the selection of Port William as the new town site. Shortly afterwards, accompanied by Captains Ross, Crozier and Sulivan, the area was again inspected. Four sites were chosen : Sparrow Cove, two positions on the south side of Jackson's Harbour and Weir Creek, which was favoured by Ross and Moody.

Moody was still doubtful and in October 1842 he reported that he had laid out a new town at Port Louis, to be called Anson. Moody's idea was to make Anson a 'temporary' principal town, awaiting the growth of colonisation before embarking on the building of another. His report was not favourably received by the Land and Emigration Commission who wrote to Lord Stanley : 'We have expressed our conviction that the site of the capital should be fixed at whichever port should be decided by competent authority to afford the greatest advantage to shipping. The report from Captain Ross will we should apprehend to be considered as conclusive upon this point'.

Lord Stanley wrote to Moody on 24 March 1843 : 'I confess that I entertain a very strong objection to an arrangement of a temporary nature in a matter of this kind', and concluded : 'You will therefore take the necessary steps for removing to that place (Port William) as early as possible'.

In July 1843 work began on the new town site, Moody having selected the narrow and sharply rising strip of land forming the southern shore of Jackson's Harbour, although the surrounding

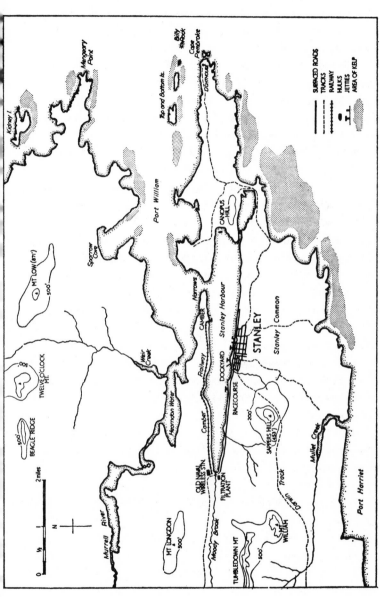

PORT STANLEY AREA

country was some of the wettest and roughest in the islands, with access being restricted by the Wickham Heights to the west. On the credit side it offered vast deposits of peat, which Moody estimated as covering fifty-six square miles.

In August 1843 Moody embarked on moving the seat of Government to Port William and in September reported: 'As winter had not yet ended I could do little more than make arrangements for commencing the change of quarters and return. Since then I have constructed a turf hut and have a small wooden cottage in progress.' By January 1844 HMS *Philomel*, the *Columbian Packet* and the *Hebe*, were still assisting with the removal of stores from Port Louis. The change-over was slow, for Moody's small detachment spent their time constructing buildings by day and were required to guard their stores by night.

The first official letter marked 'Stanley', was dated 16 August 1844, written to Lord Stanley suggesting the name for the new capital. Officially the town came into being on 18 July 1845. Correctly titled 'Stanley' the prefix 'Port' refers to the harbour although the name 'Port Stanley' is commonly used for the town.

Facing north, to the sun, the town was laid out in grid form with a few variations to break the regimental precision of its streets. Between the intersecting roads the land was sub-divided into half-acre plots available at £50 each. Later, finding sales unsatisfactory, they were divided into quarter acre sites. Murrel Robinson had the task of marking out the town and naming the main streets. Ross, Crozier, Moody, Fitzroy, Sulivan's vessel *Philomel* and the brig *Hebe* are all immortalised in street names. Today Stanley remains in its original form and continues to follow Moody's plan, growing slowly and tending to develop towards the west.

The Government buildings were placed on the edge of the harbour west of the main town site. This was known as the 'dockyard' and by July 1844 there was a carpenter's shop, a smithy built of sods, bricks and clay, two wooden cottages, a cottage of sods and stone 'built by one of the married men of the detachment at his own expense and in his own time', and a storehouse which was eventually used as a barracks, a hospital and a gaol. The building still stands today.

The move to the new town had not met with unqualified approval from the settlers. Whitington wrote : 'of all the miserable bog-holes in the Falkland Islands I believe Mr Moody has selected one of the worst for the site of the town'.

By the end of 1844 most of the settlers had moved and it was estimated that property on the new site was worth £5,000 as against £3,000 worth of property remaining at Anson. In February 1846, Moody wrote : 'the entire satisfaction with which the removal of the settlement from Anson to the present site is now regarded, I believe, by every individual in the Colony'.

Work had begun on roads and drains, three jetties were constructed and a sea wall built on the town frontage. The total capital invested in the town was now estimated at about £10,000. The same year 164 persons resided in Stanley, the number of residences the following year being fifteen cottages, twelve houses and three huts.

Little of architectural merit stands in Stanley. High costs of building materials kept design to the basic requirements. Christ Church Cathedral, a building of red brick and local stone, is the most imposing structure. Simplicity in design does, however, have its merits and the town, viewed as a whole, presents a pleasing array of colour against its backcloth of sober moorland and hills.

Lawless Element

Moody's task of founding a new colony was not greatly assisted by the unruly seafaring community around him. Governor Rennie imposed a number of restrictions in attempts to bring some order to the Colony. A Magistrate's Court was formed, and many offences became punishable by law. Rennie also made a bold effort to bring some law to the coasts (see *Hudson* and *Washington*, p 69). He wrote : 'Of good dependable colonists there are few. There are a number of single men, some from the River Plate and others who had been shipwrecked on the Islands. These,' he continued, 'are the only description of emigrants that come here'.

The Chelsea Pensioners

With the formation of Lafone's contract (see Lafone, p 82), the hope had been for a more suitable system of colonisation, Lafone having indicated his desire to import immigrants from Great Britain for his estate. Failure by Lafone to maintain his contract caused Rennie to write to Earl Grey asking if their original plan of bringing out settlers might be embarked upon. In February 1849 Rennie received instructions for the establishment of a group of Pensioners. On 13 October 1849 a detachment of Marines, with thirty army pensioners, their wives and families arrived. The youngest pensioner was 26 years, the oldest 53 years old, the average age being 42 years. However, from a life in the barracks to the life of a pioneer settler was more than some could endure. Cottages and land had been provided but the requirements by government that they should cultivate their land led to difficulties. Eventually the government announced in 1857 that those wishing to return to England could do so, passages being provided. Seven families left, five staying in the islands to become established as excellent gardeners or tradesmen.

MARITIME HISTORY

A New Port

In 1847 Moody spoke rather despondently of the large number of vessels seen passing daily but of the estimated thousand seen in the course of the year, only thirty had called at the port. The following year shipping round Cape Horn increased with the 'gold rush' to California and establishment of the Peruvian guano trade, but the increase was not encouraging. Rennie felt this was due to lack of charts and sailing directions for the port. In 1848 Rennie had Mr Phillips, an experienced and careful pilot, draw up the required sailing directions for Port Stanley. In 1850 there was a sudden increase in the number of visiting passenger vessels

Page 67 (above) A West Falkland settlement: Port Howard with Mount Maria range rising to the back of the settlement; *(below)* New Island, West Falkland, illustrating typical coastline of the SW corner of the archipelago. Part of a large colony of Rockhopper penguins is shown in the foreground

Page 68 Bluff and stack formations typical of the SW regions. Staats Island Bluff

and although the Colony's population did not exceed 500, within six months the number of passengers and crews calling for stores was greater than this figure. Later there was a steady increase in revenue from this source, a rise from £148 10s in 1849 to £442 14s 2d in 1850. Local produce found a ready sale to shipping and a market place was laid out close to the public jetty. Labour was in great demand at this time and high wages were paid, unskilled men earning 2s 6d to 4s 6d a day, mechanics from 5s–8s per day.

Although the colony was well established under British sovereignty by 1850, its status was either unknown or casually ignored by foreign whaling and sealing crews. This led to an incident which had far-reaching effects.

In 1853, concerned about continuing depredations by American vessels, the British government politely notified the United States that it intended sending a naval force to the Falklands to prevent further spoliation. Accepted by the United States, a notice was issued to masters of whaling and sealing vessels bound for the islands, warning them that if they committed depredations 'they will incur the penalties which may be prescribed therefor'.

Depredations continued and shortly afterwards Rennie informed Captain Smyley (see p 75) as United States Commercial Agent, of these acts. In March 1854 Rennie reported on the circumstances leading to the arrest of Captain Hiram Clift, master of the American whaling vessel *Hudson* and Captain Eldridge of the tender vessel *Washington*. Both vessels had been heavily fined in September 1849 for killing cattle.

Rennie wrote :

In the beginning of January last, six deserters belonging to the above vessels arrived in this port in a boat which they had stolen from the *Washington*. They deposed before Mr Montagu (Magistrate) that they left the *Hudson* moored in Ship Harbour New Island, serving as a depot for the *Washington* which was employed to capture whales within the headlands of these Islands, this being the season when whales come near the shore to produce their young. That while so employed Captain Clift and Eldridge

69

had killed a large number of hogs belonging to the Falkland Islands Company on Saunders Island and likewise destroyed a great many seals on the Government rookeries. They also stated that for about eight months the crew amounting to thirty-six men, had lived entirely on pork and geese killed on the Islands.

Rennie requested naval assistance from Admiral Henderson, but before his letter was delivered, HMS *Express*, commanded by Captain Boys, arrived on 18 February. On 20 February, Dale the Colonial Manager of the Falkland Islands Company, took out a warrant for the arrest of the Americans on charges of pig killing and requested Captain Boys to convey the Chief Constable to New Island to arrest the accused. Smyley wrote to the American Consul in Montevideo informing him of the measures to be taken against his countrymen. As a result the American corvette *Germantown* was sent from Montevideo. She was a vessel of 1,000 tons, with an armament of 16 long 32 pound and six long 64 pound cannons. The *Express* was only 360 tons with six 32 pound cannons. The *Germantown* arrived in Stanley Harbour on 2 March. On the following day at about 9am, the schooner *Washington* arrived under her American colours, and the *Germantown*, commanded by Captain Lynch, seeing that the schooner was under arrest, 'beat to quarters and shotted his guns' which, according to Rennie: 'This in sight and hearing of a small settlement totally defenceless naturally created alarm to the inhabitants.' Some hours later the whaler *Hudson*, accompanied by the *Express* arrived in the harbour. Shortly after the arrival of the *Washington* and the action by the *Germantown*, Rennie was visited by Lynch and Smyley who wished to know why and by what authority the whaling captains and their vessels were being brought into the port. Rennie informed Lynch of the charges and produced the notice issued by the United States Secretary of State to all vessels proceeding to the Falklands. Lynch denied that the notice applied to this particular case, also denying that the British sovereign had any rights over the cattle or pigs on the Islands. The warrant was illegal and he could not permit his countrymen to be tried. Rennie replied that in view of the amicable relations between

70

Great Britain and the United States, the decision of the Court of Justice should be awaited. Rennie declared: 'Captain Lynch refused to adopt this course still asserting the illegality of the arrest and that he would not have his countrymen brought to trial. My reply in words to this effect—that whilst I lived, not withstanding the overwhelming force at his immediate disposal, I would never permit him or anyone to dispute the authority with which I was legally invested by Her Majesty to administer the Government of this Colony and to uphold the law'.

On 4 March Captain Clift surrendered to the Police Office. On the following day the *Germantown* moved and re-anchored immediately in front of the Court House. Captain Clift, having accepted responsibility for Eldridge, appeared in court on 7 March and was convicted of unlawfully killing 22 pigs for which he was fined the mitigated penalty of £1 per animal with £5–£16 expenses. The full penalty, according to the ordinance, was £20 per animal. During the day before the hearing and on the day of the trial, Rennie reported that: 'The tompions were out of eight of his guns (The *Germantown*), generally an indication that the piece is loaded, and from the situation of his vessel they pointed direct to the Court House'—an act he considered intimidating to the administration of justice.

On 13 March Rennie received a protest sworn by Captain Clift before Captain Smyley in which Clift wrote an erroneous account of his arrest and informed Rennie that he intended to end his whaling voyage to return to the United States and seek redress. Of this Rennie wrote:

> an extraordinary plea certainly that because in consequence of a few days detention and his not being permitted to provision his crews on the produce of his depredations on the Falkland Islands, the open seas of the whole world being accessible to him, he should have no alternative but to break up his voyage and return to America.

That day the *Hudson* and *Washington* sailed for Mystic, New Jersey, the *Germantown* sailing a week later. On arrival in the United States the sworn information of Clift and Eldridge led to

71

a document being drawn up claiming damages for the owners of the vessels. They claimed 39,000 dollars, 22,000 dollars for the owners and 17,000 dollars for the officers and men. This bill was not presented to the British Government until 1866.

In July 1854 the United States Secretary of State wrote to the British Minister at Washington complaining of Rennie's action and asking for compensation. Some doubt as to British Sovereignty over the Islands was expressed and Britain's regulations of fishing about the Falklands were questioned. The British Government agreed in principle to compensation, although the amount had not been mentioned, but in return for their recognition that Rennie and Boys had acted somewhat undiplomatically, the United States government should indicate that they disapproved of Lynch's behaviour. Not until 1871 were the documents relating to the case printed and then they were overlaid in the large amount of material concerning the Alabama Claims, which arose during the American Civil War.

Ship Repair Trade

This new trade quickly developed in the Colony and in 1854 wages were as much as 25s per day. Of general progress Rennie said :

> When it is considered up to the year 1850, the few inhabitants subsisted on man of war rations sent annually from England, that there was neither cultivation nor trade, that the climate and soil were sufficiently bad to deter the usual class of emigrants from resorting to them, their only resource consisting of a few wild cattle (for the fisheries had nearly been destroyed) the progress which has been made during the last four years proves that the Falkland Islands have great advantages from their geographical position which are susceptible of developments and the energy of the settlers gives me favourable anticipation of continued improvement.

Governor Moore painted a different picture in 1856. Among the Pensioners, he said, he found 'a general tone of despondency', and in the business of the Colony a 'languor' brought about, he considered, by a decline in the ship repair trade. This was undoubtedly caused in part by the reduction of ships on the Peruvian Guano run, but Moore felt that the loss of business had been caused by 'the evil character which the Islands have acquired in the minds of the owners and masters of ships belonging to the United States of North America, at one time our best customer'.

By 1867, the ship repair trade was at its height. Wages soared with the merchants' prices. Unskilled men would not take less than 5s per day and therefore vegetables, although needed, were not produced. In a port where business depended on such a casual trade, the tendency was to take full advantage of opportunity and charge the maximum rates. The cost of materials in a port where every item had to be imported was also high. Stanley could offer few facilities, there being no slip or dock and labour in short supply. Damaged ships usually arrived in considerable numbers after a spell of bad weather. Consequently some ships were kept waiting weeks or even months for repairs.

From about 1870, the ship repair trade was in its final decline. Steam was replacing sail and coal could be bought for £2 per ton at Punta Arenas whereas in the Falklands it was £3 per ton. Mr Plimsoll's efforts had compelled the Board of Trade to impose more stringent regulations on vessels, considerably reducing the number of ships requiring repairs.

D'Arcy wrote : 'The port has seriously felt the movement made by Mr Plimsol in aid of the British Mariner. Many vessels were yearly condemned in the port as unseaworthy and their hulks will never leave the harbour, but during 1873 and 1874 the sale of hulks has quite collapsed and the trade is confined to the repair of sound vessels which have suffered from the violence of the ocean in attempting to round the Horn.'

The Wrecking Trade

Exactly when the 'seed' of this business was sown is difficult to ascertain, but in the 1830s Mackinnon spoke of the unaccountable manner in which vessels were cast away on the shores of the islands. In 1841 the brig *Susan* owned by Whitington and previously condemned as a prize in Sierra Leone for being engaged in the illicit traffic of slaves, was again the subject of some controversy when Whitington was accused of keeping two logbooks for the vessel and, according to her master, of attempting to wreck the vessel.

The sale and purchase of wrecks and their cargoes developed into an important business. To the settler with limited means, a wrecked cargo often supplied the necessities of life. Flour and grain were purchased cheaply and luxuries, otherwise unobtainable, were often suddenly available.

To the larger business houses a wreck was of prime importance and Rennie described how, in 1851, an important commercial gentleman of Stanley approached him 'in an unmistakeably sinister manner' regarding the wreck of a French vessel with valuable cargo of silks and wines. This gentleman requested the loan of a few pounds out the public chest, so that he could make more purchases than his ready cash would allow.

In 1853 Rennie introduced the Auctioneers Ordinance requiring wrecks and cargo to be sold by a licensed auctioneer. A tax was imposed on sales from wrecked cargo, 5 per cent on spirits and wines and two and a half per cent on other goods. Agricultural produce and implements were free of tax. Dean, as agent for Lloyds, and the Falkland Islands Company, took out licences as auctioneers. Rennie's attempt to make wreck sales more respectable was abortive. There was much wrangling between government and the auctioneers and Dean and the Company fought bitter struggles for the right to wrecks. All too often cargoes were reduced in the meantime by other operators working in league with the crews of wrecked vessels. Cargoes of liquor were prized and stories are told of the unusual manner in which such cargoes vanished. Although these stories are no doubt highly coloured, they probably bear much truth.

Often co-operation between masters of ships and people in the Islands brought about the wrecking of ships and the subsequent sale of cargoes to the benefit of all. But among the large number of ships which foundered, there were many whose masters, fighting for the rights of the ship's owners, found it a battle indeed. They encountered what Governor Moore described as an unfairness and unscrupulousness which made the port notorious. Captains began to avoid the colony if at all possible.

In 1871 Governor D'Arcy almost brought to a halt the 'equivocal system of wrecking' by the introduction of the Wreck and Salvage Ordinance. This allowed the government to take charge of wrecks and wrecked cargo and hold them in bond for a year, thereby allowing time for the owners to make claim.

William Horton Smyley

The maritime history of the Falklands would be incomplete without an account of the life and activities of Captain Smyley.

William Horton Smyley was born at Rhode Island, United States in 1792, and when sixteen or seventeen years old made his first appearance in the South American regions. During his early life he had a distinctive career under Admiral Browne of the Argentine Navy when he probably first experienced the seas about Tierra del Fuego and the Falklands. In the 1820s Smyley was sealing on the South Shetlands and according to Christie (*The Antarctic Problem*) was probably the first to prove that the Palmer Peninsula was composed of an archipelago. He was also the first to navigate the Gerlache Strait before 1842.

It is believed that Smyley established himself in business in the islands about 1830. With a group of runaway seamen and equipped with a small chaloupe built from an old wreck, Smyley operated from a small creek in Port San Carlos. Sealing and cattle hunting were his main objectives, selling his spoils to other sealing and whaling vessels. So notorious did Smyley become for killing beef, that he was known as 'Fat Jack of the Bone House'. By 1832 Smyley owned a fine American schooner, the *Saucy Jack*, with which he continued the illicit business of sealing.

By 1839 his reputation as a rogue and even as a pirate was growing, but so was his daring, courage and humanity to other men. About this time he became the owner of a schooner *Benja-*

75

min de Wolf, or *Dandy Wolf*. In 1839, Lt Robinson reported that Smyley represented himself as an officer in the US Services and an employee of that government. This position (probably self-styled), did not deter him from his illegal operations.

In December 1839 Smyley was warned that Great Britain held exclusive rights to all fisheries around the islands and he was forbidden to return another season. Shortly afterwards the crew of HMS *Sparrow* discovered one of his shore depots at Robinson's Bay on West Falkland and recovered a quantity of seal skins and bullock hides. Then Smyley arrived and, dressed in an American Lieutenant's uniform, with cocked hat etc., he boarded HMS *Sparrow*. Brandishing the warning notice before Lt Robinson, he said he would continue to seal and fish anywhere about the islands as he wished and demanded the return of the seal skins removed from his depot.

Smyley continued his sealing activities about the Falklands, Tierra del Fuego, South Shetlands and the South American coast, but his less legal activities were undoubtedly outweighed by the large number of lives he saved.

For some years Smyley assumed his own authority of the seas about the Falklands and even his own countrymen were subjected to his unorthodox methods. In 1846 Magistrate Moore recorded how Smyley discovered an American sealing schooner lying off a seal rookery with the members of its crew engaged in sealing ashore. Donning the uniform of a Lieutenant in the British Navy, Smyley hoisted the blue ensign and pennant on his vessel and threatened the master of the American vessel that if he did not leave forthwith he would sink him as the British Government did not allow foreigners to seal about the Falklands. Upon this the sealing schooner left, leaving Smyley with a rich booty of sealskins.

In 1845 Smyley lost the *Benjamin de Wolf* which was large, well-manned and armed, and replaced it with the schooner *Catherine*. This vessel was also armed with two cannons on carriages which he fired when leaving Stanley Harbour, causing some consternation to the inhabitants. Moody wrote : 'I looked at his Register and Papers and found he was privileged to carry two guns and I was given to understand he fired them by way of a salute to me for whom he professes to entertain a high respect.'

Moody was concerned about Smyley's political activities and when, in 1845, there was the possibility of war between the English and French Governments and the Argentine Republic, Moody reported Smyley's friendship with General Rosas, President of the Republic:

> There is a native of the United States named Smyley possessing lands and other property at Carmon on the Rio Negro. I believe, he was formerly in the service of the Republic; he has the character of being an active, bold, adventurous man with very few scruples in his various pursuits. This individual is on terms of peculiar intimacy with the Commandant at Rio Negro, and I am inclined to think that if the slightest encouragement was given by the Argentine Government he would not hesitate to undertake any daring exploit for the sake of the credit it would give him on the continent independently of the pecuniary advantage he might derive if he could possess himself of the Military Chest and I do him the justice to believe that he would plan the enterprise with skill and attempt it with courage.

Smyley's reputation as a benefactor as well as a rogue was almost a legend in the South Atlantic by 1846. By 1847 he was the owner of the schooners *Alonzo* and *America*, his commercial interests in Stanley increased and on 12 September 1850 his self-imposed position as United States Commercial Agent for the Falkland Islands was approved by the United States President. In 1856, after a few years absence, Smyley returned with a new vessel, the brigantine *Nancy*, which, like his other vessels became instrumental in the rescue of many shipwrecked men. In the winter of 1858, while coasting off the Jason Islands, Smyley spotted a survivor of the Belgian vessel *Leopold* on the Grand Jason Island and although subjecting his own vessel and crew to considerable danger, lay off the island for three days in order to rescue the stranded man.

With his intimate knowledge of Tierra del Fuego and ability

77

to speak Fuegian, he searched for the Keppel Mission schooner *Allen Gardiner* in 1860 and discovered the massacre. Later, on his own initiative, he brought the schooner back to the Islands for the Mission.

In 1861 Smyley was appointed as United States Consul in the Falklands, an appointment recognised by the British Government and the Government of the Islands in February 1863.

The 178-ton schooner *Kate Sergeant* was Smyley's last vessel and made its first appearance in Port Stanley about 1867. This vessel also had its own cannons and was probably the finest of his schooners. In 1868, aged 76, Smyley was still commanding his own vessel but three years later, while on a visit to Montevideo, he contracted cholera and died.

<h2 style="text-align:center">LAND TENURE</h2>

Lt Tyssen, in 1840, first recommended to the British Government that settlers at Port Louis be allowed some land for their own personal property, and in 1842 he sold a number of half-acre town plots at £50 each and one country allotment at Port Salvador. These 389ac were purchased by John Bull Whitington for 12s an acre and were the first farming land taken. Although Whitington retained this land, the sale had been premature, for not until April 1843, was Moody given full legal power to sell Crown Land.

The first large grant of 'country' land was made to Lafone. His agreement was signed in London on 16 March 1846 and he received 200 leagues in the south of East Falkland. The following year regulations were published under which settlers were permitted, by licence, to occupy the unappropriated country lands, on the condition that the purchasers of every allotment of not less than 160ac, should have the right to pasture cattle and sheep within a distance of two miles from each allotment. The first such licence was issued to the Reverend James Leith Moody, brother of Governor Moody. He took a section of land at Fitzroy, the date of the licence being 3 July 1847. These conditions were then modified by Proclamations in 1849 and 1861, the latter providing that each 'grazing station' should comprise an area of 6,000 ac, defined with reference to the nautical chart of the Colony. The first licence under this regulation was for land at Port Harriet, taken by R. C. Packe in July 1849.

Government made gross errors in the land surveys which had repercussions for many years. Governor Kerr reported in August 1882 on how inaccurate had been the survey of land by the use of nautical charts. Bailey, the surveyor, mentioned that capricious allowances were made for mountains and ponds but the measurements were made in nautical miles while the reduction to acres was at the rate of 640 to the mile as if they had been statute miles. In one case a section nominally 6,000ac is described in the lease as bounded on the north and south by lines running five miles and on the west by lines running $2\frac{1}{2}$ miles. This, if measured in statute miles, would contain 8,000ac. If measured in nautical miles it would be 9,200ac.

The government's intention was to encourage immigration and the Emigration Commissioners in England were directed to receive deposits for the purchase of land and to issue in return Land Orders available as Scripat Land Sales in the Falklands on account of which the deposit was made. The deposits were to be expended in sending out emigrants. Although the system was established in 1840 the Falkland Islands Company took advantage of it as a means of sending out emigrants to their farms. Governor Callaghan stated 'the Company have acquired the right of purchasing the large quantity of land without any expenditure towards emigration beyond the interests of their undertaking would have required them to incur' and the Land Order system was ended in 1879.

As another encouragement to immigration provision was made that no person should hold a lease for more than a single section of 6,000ac. However, the leases were transferable and Governor Kerr in 1881 reported that they were taken out in the names of managers or agents and afterwards transferred to the present occupiers, who for the most part leased large districts.

By a Proclamation dated 24 June 1867, the conditions relating to land taken in East Falkland were extended, with modifications to West Falkland to encourage settlement there. By 1869 the entire land area of West Falkland had been leased to eight settlers.

Attempting to assist settlers on West Falkland, who were close to bankruptcy, Governor D'Arcy brought in Ordinance No 6 of 1870 which allowed settlers on East and West Falkland extended leases from ten to twenty-one years. The rental was reduced from £10 to £6 for the first ten years and purchase price per acre of land was reduced from 8s to 2s. D'Arcy had disposed of over 800,000ac when he was informed by the Secretary of State that the ordinance had not been sanctioned and under no circumstances was he to sell land at less than 4s an acre. A new ordinance came into force (No 4 of 1871) placing the price of land at 4s per acre but sanctioning the allotments of land already made.

In 1872 a further ordinance allowed lessees to purchase blocks of land above that of their compulsory purchases. In 1881 Governor Kerr reported that the sheep farmers in the Colony were now quite prosperous and could well afford to pay twice as much as the maximum rent. In 1882 rent was raised from £10 to £20.

The problem of land surveys, knowingly or otherwise, appears to have lain dormant for many years. Governor Kerr tried to correct the situation when he published an enlarged version of a nautical chart showing the various freeholds and leaseholds in the Islands. Kerr suggested that another survey be made. The Colonial Office replied that he should engage the services of a navigating officer from one of HM ships to carry out any necessary surveying. In January 1885 Governor Kerr was prompted by a request from the Board of Trade for details of the Colony's area to remark:

> The whole area of the Colony is occupied either on lease or as freehold, and as stated in the leases or grants would appear as follows: East Island and adjacent islands, 1,082,964ac. West Island and adjacent islands, 999,390ac. Total area, 2,082,354ac.

The figures only represent half the presumed area of the Colony which is returned as 4,159,969ac, and it can only be determined by actual survey.

When Sir Roger Goldsworthy became Governor he continued the investigations and discovered that no less than three different copies of the nautical chart had been used for the surveys. The entire land issue was chaotic and boundaries were marked without any signed approval. Many leases were not registered, others badly drawn up, but the biggest discrepancy was in the acreages.

Goldsworthy refused to issue continuance of leases until a proper survey was made. Disquiet prevailed for the next few years and the matter reached the London press. There was sufficient land to meet the requirements of all who had been attempting to obtain it but until a survey was made, nothing could be done. Leaseholders who held land under the Land Ordinance of 1882 argued that they had been given fixity of tenure when they had submitted to a rent of £20 per section.

Goldsworthy was forced to give way, the Law Officers of the Crown deciding that the existing leases had to be renewed. The only power remaining to the government came under the 1882 ordinance, whereby part of a leasehold could be reserved for a public purpose, or if there was a real demand for land, portions could be put up for sale. On this latter point Goldsworthy said the leaseholders were only prepared to surrender land of a worthless nature, often with no sea frontage.

In 1893 a surveyor arrived in the Colony to see the land to be surrendered. There were further delays and most of the original applicants for land now tired of waiting departed for Patagonia where land could be obtained. For those remaining, the terms of land sales were far more difficult than those imposed on the existing lessees. Goldsworthy attempted to have these conditions altered but with no success. Eventually land reserved for sale was re-let to the original lessees.

In 1903 under the Consolidating Land Ordinance, the right

was extended to all lessees to take their land according to the acreage laid down in their lease at 3s per acre, payment being extended over a period of thirty years. In 1906 purchasers were allowed to anticipate payment and by 1909 the majority of large farms on East and West Falkland had applied to purchase their leaseholds.

Samuel Fisher Lafone

In a report dated 10 October 1842, Governor Moody wrote of the large numbers of cattle and horses to be found on East Falkland, and of the need to exploit these animals by a soundly financed company. His hopes began to materialise in January 1844 when a Mr Martinez, agent for Samuel Fisher Lafone, a merchant of Montevideo, arrived to view the possibilities of such a scheme. In May Martinez returned with proposals from Lafone. In a letter dated 16 March 1844 Lafone made his proposals mentioning that the Falkland Islands first came to his notice in December 1843. He intended to send out a clergyman and an iron church and also to ensure some form of education for the families of his settlers. His first settlers would be sent out in an old ship of about 500 or 700 tons, which was to be broken up for use as housing and shelter. Five-ninths of the settlers were to be from the Shetland Islands, one-ninth to be picked men from the River Plate for the management of cattle, two-ninths from southern Chile 'because they are more docile than those from the Plate' and the rest were to be intelligent Basques from the Saladero to erect buildings etc. Lafone wished to purchase all the land to the south of the Wickham Heights, estimated to be three hundred leagues. Moody refused to allow this and the eventual proposal was for two hundred leagues of land lying south of the isthmus at Darwin Harbour, now known as Lafonia.

Lafone also proposed importing 20,000 ewes in four years and 3,000 tame cows in three years for the use of intending settlers. In payment for the land, he proposed £60,000, £10,000 down and yearly instalments of £5,000. The contract was signed in London on 16 March 1846 and provided not only for the proposals arranged with Moody but also for the complete charge of all wild stock on East Falkland (cattle, horses, goats and swine) for six years, with the proviso that Lafone should have established at the end of his contract a grand total of 20,000 head of horned cattle, horses, mares and geldings on the entire East Falkland.

Lafone experienced difficulties almost immediately. The siege of Montevideo where he lived prevented him from starting operations and it was not until 10 May 1847 that his manager, Williams, arrived at Port Louis aboard the Norwegian vessel *Napoleon*, with horses, stores and 102 men. More problems arose when it was discovered that the territory was smaller than had been estimated. When Lafone's contract was written up, the land had been only half mapped and it was not until the Admiralty had completed the survey that the mistakes came to light. Lafone suggested that he be given more land or that a considerable amount be taken from the original purchase price. The number of sheep to be imported and cattle to be supplied should also be reduced.

Moody offered concessions in the form of land on West Falkland or sixty leagues in the north of East Falkland with a section of West Falkland together with New Island, Weddell Island group and the Jason Islands. This offer was not accepted and Governor Rennie took up the dispute in Montevideo before arriving in the Colony. At this meeting, in June 1848, Lafone requested that his contract be cancelled and that he should be reimbursed the £10,000 purchase price so far paid and costs incurred in settling the area. Lafone argued that his agent, Martinez, who conferred with Moody about the original contract (Lafone himself never visited the Falklands) could not speak English and therefore all the discussions were through an interpreter. At one of these meetings, Lafone asserted, Moody gave his agent to understand that the whole of East Falkland contained 600 leagues, whereas it appeared to be scarcely 300 leagues. Lafone, having estimated the probable number of cattle held on the former area of land, now doubted the number quoted. Finally a new agreement was drawn up dated 9 January 1850 in which Lafone received important concessions. His original purchase price was halved and the remaining balance reduced to £20,000, the annual instalments now being £2,000. Lafone was also allowed to build corrals and buildings to facilitate the catching of cattle in any part of the Falkland Islands. He retained sole rights to such stock, dominion over which was extended to 1 January 1856 and later to 1 January 1860.

Rennie reported bitterly of the manner in which Lafone's manager Williams carried out operations. Intending settlers were continually obstructed and Rennie wrote :

> The progress which I have had the satisfaction from time to time to report to your Lordship, of the advancement of the Colony, has been entirely independent of any aid or assistance from the quarter which Your Lordship and I fully calculated on, and it may perhaps appear extraordinary that although Mr. Lafone has now been in possession of a territory equal in extent to two moderate sized counties for five years, not one single immigrant has been settled on it. The system of feudal dependency to which he would subject every intending settler prevents his terms being listened to by any respectable colonist, and not even his Spaniards will remain on the Islands.

Lafone's agreement to supply beef and cattle to settlers and Government was a continual source of dispute. Supplies were insufficient and irregular. Cattle driven to Stanley by Williams' gauchos were often so wild that the settlers, unaccustomed to handling such creatures, lost them and the beasts reverted to Lafone's domain.

The Falkland Islands Company

By 1849, Lafone had become heavily in debt to Ricketts Boutcher and Company, merchants of the City of London who had financed his project, and in 1851 his brother, Alexander Ross Lafone, issued a prospectus of the 'Royal Falkland Land, Cattle, Seal and Whale Fishery Company' in a bid to sell interests in Lafone's business in the Falklands.

In January 1851, a committee met in London to form a company with a view to buying Lafone's rights and interests in the islands. On April 24 1851, the first meeting of the newly-formed Falkland Islands Company was held in the City of London. The Company was incorporated and was granted a Royal Charter by Queen Victoria on January 20 1852.

Through his manager, Lafone continued to operate the concern for the Falkland Islands Company (Lafone held 200 of the 1,000 shares) and in July 1852, the Company's first Colonial Manager, John Pownall Dale, a brother-in-law of Lafone's, arrived in the islands.

The following year the directors wrote to Lafone that the business was not up to their expectations. The company's managing director, Mr Cripps, wrote:

> The great distance of the Falkland Islands from England having induced the Company to accept the preferred services of the sellers who resided at Montevideo to control the Island manager and to be the medium of all his correspondence with the directors, the true character of the concern was easily concealed until the capital invested and the arrangements involved in it had become too large to be retracted.

The Company attempted to obtain further concessions but Governor Moore held them to their contract, their difficulties being due entirely to 'their own blind confidence'. The Falkland Islands Company was essentially a trading company and soon after Dale had arrived, a store was established in Stanley on their site at Crozier Place.

When the Company took over Lafonia the main settlement was at Hope Place. They found this unsuitable and in 1859 the settlement was moved to Darwin Harbour on the isthmus joining Lafonia with the northern section of East Falkland. At this time sheep farming operations were becoming of increasing importance and by 1862 they held 9,453 sheep. In the next ten years the number rose to 48,500.

In 1922, the nearby site of Goose Green was chosen for improving sheep-handling facilities. New wool sheds were built and a

85

suspension bridge was constructed to enable sheep to be driven from the Walker Creek area. In 1979, 100,598 sheep were shorn at Goose Green.

The company own the freehold of 43 per cent of all farming land in the Falklands, and has almost a monopoly of the trade of the islands. A very large percentage of the farms sell their wool, hides and skins through the Company which acts as agent for this purpose; and they buy a large amount of farm requisites and other stores through this business.

In communications, the Company plays an indispensable part, supplying mail and cargo services with their coastal vessel MV *Monsunen* and a charter vessel (see Chapter Five). The Company owns the only large general store in the Islands.

RELIGIOUS HISTORY

An Early Church

When Governor Moody moved to Port William, the Colony was without a church or chaplain. Services led by Moody himself were held in a 'dockyard' building and a bell post was constructed from an old ship's spar some 35ft high. On top was placed a frame supporting a large ship's bell. This was used to call people to service and during the week was an alarm and work-bell (a work-bell still hangs in the dockyard today). A bell ringer was paid the handsome salary of 6d for each day he was required to ring. The usual annual cost of this service was £7 10s.

In 1844 Moody wrote to England asking for a large folio bible, two cassocks, a crimson cover for a communion table, plated flagon with cup and salver and plate for use in a chapel. That year his brother, James Leith Moody, was appointed as Colonial chaplain, arriving in the Falklands on 23 October 1845. Two years later the estimates allowed £100 for the construction of a church.

In October 1847, a wooden building 60ft by 18ft 'appropriated entirely for the purpose of the church and school' had been erected on the corner between Villiers Street and John Street, now ie site of the Speedwell Store. On Governor Rennie's arrival he ound the building was also used as a dispensary and hospital. inding this 'objectionable', he had the entire building converted or use as a church 'fitted with pulpit'.

he Exchange Building

Rennie considered that a public building or market place iould be constructed close to the water, where the inhabitants ould dispose of their produce to shipping. Exactly when this lan was formed is not clear, but in early 1851 he requested a irge 'out of door clock' which was to be fixed 30–40ft above the round for the benefit of the public. The clock was supplied by lessrs E. Simmons of London. In early 1852, the building of the xchange Building was begun, a large stone structure with a entral tower and two wings. The tower, which was 55ft high, ras divided into three sections. The first was an entrance hall with solid mahogany door, the second a turret clock with a 4ft dial nd the top section had the bell which struck from the clock.)ne of the wings was allocated as a commercial meeting place or the colonists and masters of vessels.

The market place was completed in 1854 but soon afterwards became a temporary residence for the Governor. In October 856, however, Governor Moore decided that the east wing should e used as a church and the west wing should accommodate a hool. On 6 November, Havers of the Falkland Islands Com- any offered a five octave organ originally belonging to Captain now of the *Allen Gardiner*. This was accepted by Moore for the hurch.

In April 1860, the Reverend Bull spoke of the need for a new hurch as the present building could hold only 104 people. His equest was rejected and early the following year he asked Govern- ient to transfer the east wing of the Exchange to a senior member f the Church. This suggestion appealed to the government as meant a considerable saving in the upkeep of the building, a fact lso on the minds of the parishioners. When the government greed to the change a petition was forwarded from members of the community declaring that they were unwilling to incur the expense of upkeep. In 1862, disregarding the petition, Governor Moore transferred responsibility for the east wing to the chaplain and church wardens. After further representations to Governor Mackenzie in 1865, the building reverted to the government. From 1862, it was called Holy Trinity Church 'in the County of Ross'.

Holy Trinity Church and Dean Brandon

Eight months after the Rev Stirling had settled among the Yahgans in Ushuaia (see Keppel Island Mission, p 90), the *Allen Gardiner* brought a summons for his return to England for consecration as Bishop of the Falkland Islands. On St Thomas's Day, 21 December 1869, Stirling was made bishop in Westminster Abbey.

The bishop arrived in the Falklands on 11 January 1872 aboard HMS *Cracker* and he was installed as bishop on the 14th by the colonial chaplain, Charles Bull, in the Church of Holy Trinity. Stirling at once made representations to the Governor on 'the incongruity of my position without any jurisdiction over the only ecclesiastical building in the town'. Governor D'Arcy then recommended to the Earl of Kimberly that the building might again be passed to the church. Stirling refused to consecrate the building while half of it was being used as a school, so proposals were made to move the school and thoughts were given to the building of a new church.

In 1876, the Rev Bull completed his term of office and Stirling returned to perform the duties of chaplain for some months. On 19 March 1877, the Rev Lowther E. Brandon arrived to take up office. One of his toughest fights was against intemperance (See Chapter Six). Youth work played a special part in his life and he held two Sunday schools, opened a children's library and started a Penny Savings Bank at the government school. He became as familiar a figure in camp as in Stanley, travelling over incredible distances in all weathers. He made a point of visiting every camp house in the Islands at least once a year, a journey made by horseback and sailing vessel which took at least three months. Brandon made his visits not only as a Minister but also as postman, delivering mail, books, his own Falkland Island Magazine and other matter. He was renowned as an entertainer and his magic lantern, for which he always had room in his saddle bags, became famous among children and adults alike.

Christ Church Cathedral

Services continued in the Exchange Building for 14 years after Stirling's enthronement although in 1882 Brandon was agitating for a proper church, and two years later the government were asked for a grant. In October 1884 Governor Kerr offered three roods of Crown land lying between the public jetty and the Falkland Islands Company jetty for the site of the proposed new church. Work began with the strengthening of the sea wall adjacent to the site, but two years later when the second peat slip occurred (See Chapter Six), the state of affairs changed.

Considerable damage was done to the Exchange Building and it was decided to demolish it. In August 1886 the Church Building Committee asked for the site of the Exchange together with the stone which would result from its demolition. The request was granted, largely because of the government's decision that the site offered by the public jetty would be more suitable for a Customs House. Work began on the new church and on 6 March 1890 the foundation stone was laid by Governor Kerr and Bishop Stirling. Although Stirling had been the originator and prime mover of the scheme it was Dean Brandon who was responsible for the supervision of the work. This was no easy task.

On 21 February 1892 the new Christ Church Cathedral was consecrated by Bishop Stirling. The church, named after the church in Canterbury from where such generous help had come, was designed by Sir Arthur Blomfield. The estimated cost had been about £6,000 but by the time the main part was complete, the cost had risen to nearly £9,000 with the tower yet to be built. Austrian stone masons were employed to build the tower in 1902 but they left the job the following year and the plan to construct a 30ft steeple on top of the tower was not carried out.

The cathedral remains the most prominent building in Stanley. It is a rather unorthodox mixture of rough cut stone and red brick topped with a roof of corrugated iron but it has a solid, pleasing appearance which marries well with the surrounding townships and landscape.

Keppel Island Mission

The establishment of the Keppel Island Mission Station began with the inauguration of the Patagonian Missionary Society in 1844 by Commander Allen Gardiner.

Allen Gardiner spent much of his life trying to establish missions among the natives of South America. In 1841 he visited Port Louis with his family to investigate the possibilities of making the Falklands a base from which he could work among the natives of Tierra del Fuego. Although Gardiner considered this feasible, the plan was not put into operation immediately due to lack of funds.

In March 1842 he visited Patagonia and after an abortive attempt to establish a mission there he returned to England to raise funds for a further effort. On 7 September 1850, Gardiner set out once again, sailing from Liverpool on the *Ocean Queen*. With him were a small band of volunteers, two 26ft boats and provisions for six months. December 5 saw them landed at Banner Cove on Picton Island, Tierra del Fuego.

It had been arranged for the Mission in England to re-supply Gardiner some time later and in January 1851 the secretary, the Rev G. P. Despard, made enquiries about sending supplies to Picton Island. The answer from shipping lines was always the same; that no vessel would risk their insurance to drop so small a freight there. Time went by and no word had been received from Gardiner. Eventually in October 1851, HMS *Dido*, bound for the Pacific, was ordered to call at Picton Island and enquire for the missionaries. The *Dido* arrived at the Falkland Islands, on 1 January 1852, but by this time Captain Smyley with his schooner he *John Davison*, had gone in search of the men. On 22 October 851, he discovered the bodies of all the party except Gardiner nd one other missionary.

Searches for the two men were carried out by *Dido*, the *Ocean Queen* and a Falkland Island Vessel. Gardiner and his companion vere found by *Dido* about 19 January, dead of starvation at anner Cove. Smyley at this time was continuing his search in he schooner *Zerviah*. Unaware of *Dido's* discovery, he carried n until mid-April. Later Smyley spoke of the search having cost ,000 dollars, but wished for no return.

Gardiner had hoped that a mission station could be established n one of the islands of the Falklands and in letters written as he vas dying, he commended the South American Mission to the are of his wife and son.

In October 1854 a newly built schooner, *Allen Gardiner*, of ighty-eight tons sailed from Bristol. Commanded by Captain 'arker Snow she had on board four members of the Mission and upplies for a new mission station in the Falkland Islands. Before heir departure permission had been given to settle the station on ne of the West Falkland Islands. On 28 January 1855, the *Allen Gardiner* arrived off Saunders and Keppel Island and, after in-pecting both they finally settled on Keppel on 5 February.

Governor Rennie decided that the island could be rented for ne year for £1. This was changed and 160ac were purchased utright, the remainder being leased in 1856, with the exception f a small government reserve, for 20 years at annual rent f £10. In 1868 this lease was cancelled and the Mission allowed 60-year lease at 'pepper corn rent'.

On 2 September 1856, the Rev G. P. Despard, his wife and amily, Allen W. Gardiner, son of the late commander, and other members of the mission arrived in the Falklands. Despard took harge of the Mission which he found no easy task, due to dis-armony between those responsible for running the mission chooner and those ashore. Despard's own approach, and dis-araging remarks on the inhabitants of the Falklands, were of little elp to the pioneers of the mission.

In June 1858 the *Allen Gardiner* returned from Tierra del Fuego with Jemmy Button, a Fuegian, and his family and later several more Fuegian families were brought to Keppel Island. They were trained in gardening, reading, writing and religion. The mission farm became the first to practise agriculture, producing potatoes and other items which found a ready sale in Stanley. The following year *Allen Gardiner* took 'the discontented families of Fuegians', back to Tierra del Fuego, intending also to continue the building of a mission station at Woollya, Navarin Island.

Receiving no news of the *Allen Gardiner* from Woollya, Despard requested Captain Smyley to search for them as he had done some eight years before. Smyley sailed immediately on the *Nancy*, returning on 9 March 1860 with the sole survivor of the party, Alfred Coles, and the news that the remainder had been massacred by the Indians at Woollya. The tragedy weighed heavily on Despard and he eventually resigned his post in 1861. In 1862 the Rev Waite Hocking Stirling who had worked in England for the Patagonian Mission Society for fifty years, became the new superintendent of the Keppel Mission Station. Stirling, his wife and family and a party of other missionaries, aboard the now much enlarged and refitted *Allen Gardiner*, arrived at Keppel on 30 January 1863.

Stirling found Bartlet, the farm manager, and Thomas Bridges, both of whom had gone to Keppel with Despard. Also at the station was a family of Yahgan* Indians who had returned with Smyley to Keppel from Woollya. The presence of these Indians proved important as through them Thomas Bridges became sufficiently well versed in their language to converse with the Yahgan tribes of Tierra del Fuego. Bridges at this time was nineteen years of age and during his subsequent work among the Yahgans he produced the Yamana-English Dictionary, containing 32,000 words of the Yahgan language.

Soon after his arrival Stirling, accompanied by Thomas Bridges and the Yahgan Indians, set sail for Woollya. They were naturally apprehensive about the outcome of a meeting with the Indians.

92

All worries were allayed, however, when Bridges was able to talk with the Yahgans in their own tongue, explaining that the missionaries wished only to help.

Many of the Fuegians wished to visit Keppel Island and in the next few years fifty made the trip to the station. Although a new mission station was set up by Stirling at Ushuaia in the heart of Yahgan territory in January 1869, the Keppel station remained the headquarters of the Society. In 1871 Governor D'Arcy visited it describing it as 'a little Arcadian settlement'.

In 1874 Keppel was offered for sale, the Society's intention being to move their mission to Tierra del Fuego. With no prospective buyers the island continued its work, eventually developing into an extremely productive farm which became self-supporting. As a training centre for the Yahgans, the station continued until 1898, when Mr Whaits, the last superintendent, took the remaining Fuegians to a new mission station on the South American mainland. Keppel continued to operate as a farm until 1911 when it was sold to Dean Bros, Pebble Island. Today the island is family owned and run.

The Roman Catholic Church

In February 1857 the Catholic members of the community requested that land might be made available for a church. About this time they also opened a subscription towards the building of a church and cost of a resident priest. It was not until November 1875 when the Rev James Foran of the Diocese of Hexham and Newcastle arived that they had their own resident priest. Previously they had been served by the Colonial Chaplains for weddings and burials and the Catholic Bishop of Buenos Aires had allowed a visit by a priest every seven years.

When the Rev Stirling left Buenos Aires in 1872, to be enthroned as Bishop of the Falklands, a young and active Irish priest, the Reverend Father Walsh, was sent from Montevideo by the Roman Catholic Bishop of Buenos Aires to begin the task of gathering together the Catholic population. Walsh requested D'Arcy to loan him a building in which to hold services. A government store, also used by the amateur theatre group, was placed at Walsh's disposal, but the amateur actors put pressure on D'Arcy and the building was granted back to the theatre group.

In D'Arcy the Catholics found a friend. Although not of their faith himself, his wife was Catholic and he felt that the Catholics had not been treated with consideration. If, D'Arcy proposed, the Catholic population could raise sufficient funds to obtain a Chapel of their own, he would provide government labour. Inspired by Walsh's enthusiasm, they at once raised £150 and, selling a freehold acre of town land bought in 1857 as a site for a church, the sum of £265 was raised. A quarter-acre plot of land was then purchased on Dean Street together with materials and in July 1873 a small chapel for 120 persons was opened by Father de Villas, a missionary priest sent from Buenos Aires.

Walsh also submitted to D'Arcy an application for a Government subsidy to help pay the expenses of a Minister. In May 1872, D'Arcy wrote to the Secretary of State suggesting the Church of England minister's pay be reduced, thus allowing a subsidy of £75 each for the Catholic and Presbyterian ministers. D'Arcy estimated that 400 of the population belonged to the Church of England, 250 were Presbyterian and 150 Catholics. A census carried out in 1951 gave similar proportions.

It was not until 1874 that the Governor was directed to pay a salary to the Scottish minister and Catholic priest of £50 a year. As the islands were without a Church of England minister, the payment was not effective until January 1876.

James Foran served the Catholic community (largely Irish emigrants and members of the detachment of pensioners) until 1888. The church was then entrusted to the Salesian order which had extensive missions in South America. In 1900 a new site was secured and the original chapel was moved from Dean Street to the present position on Ross Road.

The Nonconformist Church

In 1871 many shepherds situated on the Falkland Islands Company's main farm at Darwin were of Scottish origin and

embers of the Free Kirk of Scotland. Finding a growing need
or a minister of their own they undertook, with the assistance of
the Company, to employ a minister for Darwin and in 1872 the
Rev Yeoman took up the appointment. In 1873 an iron-
constructed church was brought from England and erected at
Darwin. About this time it was estimated that one third of
the Falklands' population belonged to the Presbyterian
church.

As Stanley grew, the Darwin minister visited the town
occasionally and held services in the infants school.

A great day for the Nonconformists in Stanley came in 1888
when the Rev George M. Harris, a Baptist minister, was sent out
under the personal interest of the famous C. H. Spurgeon, of the
Metropolitan Tabernacle, London. Services were then held in
the 'Speedwell' on John Street, a one-time church and school used
by Chaplain Moody.

Under the second minister from Spurgeon's College, the Rev
F. E. Lawson Good, the ministry was moved to a new and larger
nonconformist tabernacle. This building was brought from
England, and having been erected by members of the church
was opened in 1891 in Barrack Street, remaining today much in
its original form.

Perhaps the most influential minister of recent years was the
Rev W. Forrest McWhan who, apart from his parochial duties,
also published the local magazine *Weekly News* for some years
and wrote a book *The Falkland Islands Today*, published in 1952.
Following his death in 1966, it was decided to name the new
government motor vessel *Forrest* in his memory.

ISLAND REGIMENTS

From the 1830s there was a strong connection between the
Islands and the British military forces, who were responsible
for a great amount of work required in the building of the colony.
The naval superintendents relied almost entirely on detachments
of Marines from which to draw their artisans, and many of their

stone buildings and corrals remain to this day. Many naval men obtained release during their period of service in the Islands, and they carried out local shipping.

Moody's small expedition force was composed largely of men from the Royal Sappers and Miners. Although this detachment was employed by the government they retained their military rank. Employed as both military guard and artificers for government works, they received military pay. The sergeant received 4s 6d a day for his military duties and as Clerk or Foreman of Works. A Corporal received 3s and a Private 1s 6d a day.

In 1847 cavalry gear was sent to the colony followed by a proposal from Whitehall that a small local force should be set up, composed of civilians living in Stanley. Moody replied that he would place the suggestion before his Legislative Council. On October 9 Moody reported that a military force had been set up composed of an Infantry Group and Mounted Corps together with a gun detachment. The infantry, he reported, was composed of a captain, two lieutenants, ensign, sergeant, two corporals and forty-seven privates. The mounted corps was officered in the same way except that there was a cornet instead of an ensign, plus one corporal and eighteen men. Two 12 pound guns had been sent from England, and were operated by a detachment composed of a sergeant, a corporal and eleven men.

Moody's force did not remain in regular training and in November 1848 Governor Rennie called out the militia for a week's drill. In order to make a reasonable presentation of his force, Rennie issued to the thirty men who turned out blue 'Guernsey' frock jackets and Scotch tartan bonnets, at a total cost to the government of £39 13s., the improvised uniforms being returned to the store after each muster.

The drill followed Rennie's discovery of 14 Frenchmen residing in the settlement and he was worried about the 'present troubled state in Europe'. He sent a letter to the Commander-in-Chief of the French naval ships in the South Atlantic, asking if a vessel could call and remove them. Six weeks later a French man-of-war called, but the French in the settlement, learning of its arrival, promptly de-camped, returning to Stanley only when the ship had left.

With the completion of duty by the Royal Sappers and Miners in 1848 the Colony was without any professional military force. In February 1849, however, Rennie received notice from Earl Grey that he was sending a group of military pensioners. Rennie was instructed to pay 'scrupulous attention' to their position and told that the pensioners must be located on the site most advantageous for the 'security of the town of Stanley'. Rennie duly replied that he would select a site for the barracks and houses to make a 'military village'.

The 'pensioners' arrived under the command of Captain Reid and Sergeant-Major Felton. They came fully equipped with their buildings which remain today on Drury Street and Pioneer Row, then known as Upper Row and Lower Row.

Although the pensioners had been sent to establish a stronger core of settlers, military defence had also been considered and for some years the pensioners in their capacity as ex-marines acted as a deterrent against local disturbance. However, they were treated as civilians, subjected to military law only during the twelve day period of military exercise each year.

On 4 March 1855 the Military Guard and Volunteers were established. There was a permanent appointment for a sergeant, corporal and four men, although they were called out only when required for active service. The privates were paid 1s per day for their duties. The Guard had a short life and in February 1857 Governor Moore disbanded the force and in its place appointed two civilian constables (see p 41).

On 12 January 1858 a force of marines arrived to replace the pensioners. Under the charge of Captain Abbott there were 35 men, their wives and 65 children. All were shipped on the *Ealing Grove*. What their impressions were of the new commission is not recorded but Moore reported that furniture was so short that stones and pieces of turf had to be utilised as chairs in the barracks until six dozen chairs were obtained at a cost of £27. Moore made every attempt to produce some comfort for the new garrison and set up a canteen, book club and reading room. On his store list for the canteen, he asked for 500gal of navy rum and 800lb of tobacco!

Being regular soldiers the garrison, named the Falkland Islands Garrison Company, remained under martial law, took part in regular parades and maintained four men on guard in Stanley. During this time there was no local civilian force of Militia or Volunteer Corps in the Islands.

In January 1863 a new detachment of marines arrived to take over from the garrison. In 1877 Governor Callaghan proposed that the need for retaining a military force was now ended. Removing the marine detachment from the Falklands would, he stated, save the Colony £1,066 per year. A police force could be maintained at a much lower cost. On 1 January, following the arrival of a new police force from England, the last detachment of marines left for England.

The Falklands were then without a force of any permanent nature until 1892, although naval vessels were frequent visitors. The small police force was composed largely of ex-military men and, judging from the return of weapons made to Whitehall every year, they were well armed.

In 1892 it was proposed to re-form the Falkland Volunteer Force. The sail loft to the east end of the Ship Hotel had been allocated as a drill hall and on 13 June that year, thirty-seven volunteers were sworn in at Government House, as the first instalment of the new force. A mounted infantry corps was formed about 1900.

At the outbreak of the 1914–18 war, the Volunteers were called out on active service for the first time (Battle of the Falklands) and although they numbered only a few hundred men and their most powerful weapon was a 12 pound field gun, the force reached a high degree of efficiency. In 1919 The Falkland Islands Volunteer Corps stood down and in 1920 was reconstituted as the Falkland Islands Defence Force, keeping this title to the present day.

NAVAL ENGAGEMENTS

Coronel and the Battle of the Falklands

When Great Britain was plunged into war with Germany on
August 1914, the news was received in the Islands with concern
but with no realisation that the Falkland Islanders themselves
would be involved in two naval battles before the war was out.
These battles have been well documented but their effect on the
Falkland Islands is of interest.

In September Rear Admiral Sir Christopher Cradock with his
flagship *Good Hope* and the rest of the squadron, the *Monmouth*,
Glasgow, *Otranto* and later the *Canopus*, visited Port Stanley
before the Battle of Coronel and it was to the Falklands that the
Glasgow and *Canopus* escaped afterwards.

During this time women and children and other non-com-
batants were evacuated to camp settlements and the Volunteers
who had been called to duty at the outbreak of the war were left
to give warning of the approach of enemy vessels, and to make
ready for the evacuation of Stanley. Extra horses were brought
into Stanley so that the entire force might be mounted. Their
heaviest weapons were two Vickers machine guns and one twelve
pound field gun loaned to them by the *Glasgow*. Caches of provisions were hidden in areas outside the town. Official documents,
code books and other valuables were buried at night, to be dug up
each morning.

On the morning of 7 December, when the Falkland Islanders
expected the German fleet under Admiral Von Spee to arrive
and strike another blow, there arrived instead the British Squadron
under Admiral Sturdee with the two battle cruisers *Invincible*
and *Inflexible*, the armoured cruisers *Carnarvon*, *Cornwall* and
Kent, the light cruiser *Bristol*, the familiar *Glasgow* and armed
liner *Orama*. Sturdee had been despatched from England with his
squadron to seek out and destroy the German fleet.

On the morning of 8 December at approximately 7.30 the lookout on duty for *Canopus* saw smoke on the horizon and at about

7.56 the signal that enemy ships were approaching, was passed to the rest of the fleet. Later Mrs Felton of Fitzroy settlement informed Stanley that three enemy ships, colliers and transports, were lying off Port Pleasant. So began the Battle of the Falkland Islands.

On 11 December, Sturdee had his fleet assembled again in Port Stanley. They received a tremendous ovation. Governor Allardyce visited the flagship to congratulate Admiral Sturdee, who thanked the Governor and the Colony for having given his fleet timely warning. Special thanks were conveyed to Chris Andrearson, the lookout on duty who had first sighted the German fleet, and later he was presented with a gold watch from the Admiralty, suitably inscribed. 8 December 1914 became an important date in local history and is commemorated by an annual holiday.

Battle of the River Plate

At the outbreak of World War II, the Falklands had been prepared for some time. A small squadron consisting of the cruisers *Ajax* and *Exeter* had been stationed there and from time to time they made sorties in the surrounding seas looking for German merchantmen and armed raiders.

In December 1939 the two ships were joined by the *Achilles* and under Rear Admiral Harwood they left Port Stanley for a mission which resulted in the Battle of the River Plate.

The *Exeter* was badly damaged and on 16 December barely seaworthy, she limped into Stanley Harbour. Of the original crew of 600, 64 had died, or died later in hospital, and 45 were wounded. So badly was the ship damaged that the entire crew had to be boarded out in Stanley.

On 22 December *Ajax* and *Achilles* rejoined *Exeter* in Stanley harbour.

Following the battle of the River Plate the Admiralty set up a naval office in the Falkland Islands named HMS *Poursuivant*. In 1942 a battalion of the 11th West Yorks Regiment was sent out as a garrison force and this was succeeded in 1944 by a

100

Page 101 Bird Island, West Falkland. Such offshore islands with their formidable coasts are the remaining strongholds of a large percentage of the islands' bird life. A mixed colony of Rockhopper penguins and King shags nest in the foreground, petrels and Black-browed albatross nest on the steep slopes in the background

Page 102 (above) Drury Street, Stanley, showing the original Pensioners Cottages with the Barrack building at the end of the row. Built in 1849–50 the cottages and barracks were shipped out from England to form a 'military village'; *(below)* shipping unpressed wool bales by small island vessel

detachment of Royal Scots who remained in the Islands until the end of the war.

The Falkland Islanders are proud of the position they held in these battles and to this day the original telegrams of congratulation sent from England are displayed in the Churchill Wing of the K.E.M. hospital.

4

AGRICULTURE

INTRODUCTION OF STOCK

IN 1764 de Bougainville brought to Port Louis seven heifers and two bulls which were the basis for what became one of the finest herds of cattle in the southern hemisphere. Additions to his few pigs and sheep, three horses and a goat were made during the Spanish occupation and in 1785 Ramon Clairac recorded that flocks of domestic animals numbered 7,774 head.

From time to time the British brought animals to the islands, and when McBride settled at Port Egmont in January 1766, he landed a few sheep at Saunders Island. Sealers placed goats and pigs on various islands as a source of fresh meat, although after the islands were abandoned they resorted to the cattle herds which had been left to roam wild on East Falkland.

In 1838, when Mackinnon, first officer of HMS *Arrow*, surveyed East Falkland, he reported that about 30,000 head of fine cattle roamed the island. To the north the animals were dark in colour, while to the south they were lighter, the extreme southerly tip of East Falkland having almost pure white herds.

The year before Mackinnon's report, Captain Grey of HMS *Cleopatra* reported seeing, near San Carlos, fourteen or fifteen separate herds of cattle, each numbering some forty head, and further stated : 'The wild cattle are now calculated at some 20,000 head. I have no idea how it has been possible to form such an estimate, but even after hearing this I was surprised at the numbers I saw. They are evidently increasing from the number of calves in every flock'. Captain Grey also mentioned wild horses which were, rather incredibly, thought to number some 4,000, and herds of wild hogs. 'The wonderful increase of these animals

104

clearly shows how well adapted the country is for grazing, sheep and goats would without doubt increase in the same manner'.

Until 1839 the cattle had been restricted to East Falkland but Sullivan, then Senior Commander of HM vessels in the South Atlantic, directed their introduction to West Falkland. Charles Melville, master of the schooner *Montgomery*, took from Port Pleasant eleven bulls and fifty-five cows landing them at White Rock Bay, West Falkland. Eighteen years later Governor Moore reported that in the Warrah River area he discovered between 2,000–3,000 head of cattle.

The potential value of these increasing herds had been recognised by about 1823 when the United Provinces Government offered the fishing and cattle rights to Louis Vernet and Jorge Pacheco. Between 1826 and 1831 Vernet established ninety settlers at Port Soledad as a farming community. Cereal crops and vegetables were grown, but Vernet's main income derived from the sale of fish and large quantities of jacked beef, a form of dried meat which he sold in South America. Cattle hides became another source of income, which he claimed were worth 30s each when he attempted, in vain, to obtain compensation from the British Government for the loss of his property in 1833.

When the British colonised the islands the cattle were regarded as Crown property. Sealers had become accustomed to helping themselves to the cattle and arrived at the beginning of the season with salt and barrels for laying in stocks of meat for the journey south, and controversy reigned over the rights to the wild herds. Britain and the United States engaged in prolonged diplomatic wrangling arising from an incident over the killing of cattle and pigs. (See p 69ff, case of *Hudson* and *Washington*.)

From 1833–42, cattle were regarded as a form of currency at Port Louis. In 1834 Lt Smith unable to pay Antonina Roxa for her services in taming cattle, agreed that she should receive every other calf from every cow tamed for milking. Contracts between the British Naval Superintendents and employees included articles which read:

105

> We recognise and acknowledge, that all which the Falkland Islands produces, as well as what may be found on them, is the property of the Queen of Great Britain, and what may be paid to us is for our labour and not for the value of any animals, Oxen, Cows or Horses. That none of us can go out and catch cattle without orders from Lt Tyssen or his Capitaz, and also when we shall want hides for lassoos, sinchas or for balls to acquaint the Capitaz and to obtain his order to take them.

Decline of the Wild Cattle

Estimates of the number of wild cattle on East Falkland varied greatly. Tyssen reported 40,000 head in 1840 and two years later Moody gave the same estimate. In 1846, the figure rose to 60,000, a year later to 80,000. The exact number was probably never known, the only real survey being carried out in 1859 by Bailey, the Surveyor General, when 6,611 cattle were counted on East Falkland.

With Lafone's establishment at Hope Place, the future for the wild cattle declined rapidly. Lafone's manager, Williams, embarked on wholesale slaughter largely for the hides and tallow. Across the narrow isthmus between the northern and southern sections of East Falkland, Williams' gauchos built a turf wall to prevent the escape of cattle. To the north the cattle were hunted to such an extent that few remained after five years. In 1860, Government resumed ownership of the wild cattle and issued a public notice that any person hunting, wounding or capturing cattle outside the area of Lafonia, without permission from the Governor, would be fined £20 for each animal taken. The precautions taken by Government in their attempts to retain the remaining herds were, however, insufficient. For sealers, whalers and the settlers themselves cattle killing became most profitable. Government were aware of this and numerous attempts were made to catch the culprits. In March 1862, Moore reported to the Duke of Newcastle that the Falkland Islands Company had been caught salting the hides of 54 freshly killed animals on Crown lands and that the maximum fine was imposed.

The Company argued that the wild cattle were *ferae naturae*,

106

although prior to this they themselves complained of sealers taking cattle. Governor Moore wrote:

> But Your Grace will scarcely credit, that, at this very time, when the company at home are making the most exaggerated representations to Your Grace in respect of sealers killing for consumption a single animal occasionally, I have it on the best authority procurable that the Company's Camp Manager knowingly permits and indeed orders that the Company's servants at their chief establishment some 70 miles distant shall be supplied with fresh beef only from the wild cattle on Crown Lands

Eventually the Privy Council decided in favour of the Company. It was shown that although the Falkland Islands Government had provided penalties against taking wild cattle, it had failed to make clear that the rights of killing were to be held by them on all grants of land. The fate of the wild herds was sealed and although Government raised the fine to £50 for taking the cattle illegally they were slowly destroyed by the settlers.

No records exist to indicate the breed of the Falkland cattle. It is known however, that they were long-haired, had large spreading horns and had the broad fore limbs and small hind quarters of the Spanish fighting breeds. Today a small herd of these distinctive cattle remain on Volunteer Point, East Falkland. It is probable that as this small area of land has been under private ownership since the days of cattle hunting, these animals are direct descendants of the original herds.

Gauchos and Wild Cattle Hunting

Governor Moody reported that cattle hunting in the Falklands was very different from similar operations in the mild climate and on the hard ground of the South American Pampas. The cattle in the islands were much stronger, heavier and wilder than in Argentina. Of the gaucho he wrote:

> It is a life of delightful excitement and of skill and courage in which they may well be proved. The only repose after a day of great bodily exertion is on the bare ground, their saddle gear

serving for bed and pillow and their poncho with the addition of a rug or blanket (and perhaps a strip of painted canvas, if the day's work ends near a corral) to shelter them from every inclementry of the weather.

For these men 'delightful excitement' it may have been, for the horses they rode it was a short, cruel life. They rarely lived for more than three or four years and were generally finished after two summers. They were ridden without rugs and with galled backs. After the day's ride they had to seek their own food and, bathed in sweat, were exposed to cold and often frosty nights. The gaucho used severe bits (the general method still used today), and after the method of breaking them in their jaws were almost broken. The gauchos' spurs had long sharp rowels so the horses' flanks would often be dripping with blood. Tyssen insisted upon the gauchos blunting their spurs.

Cattle killing occurred principally in the summer months, when six or more gauchos progressed round the coast from district to district. They rode together until a herd was sighted then, approaching as close as possible without being observed, the riders dashed into the herd, each man selecting an animal to lasso. One end of the lasso was fastened to the cincha, or girth of the saddle, the other thrown in a noose about the animal's neck. As soon as the animal was thrown the gaucho dismounted, his horse keeping a tight strain on the rope. Approaching from behind, the gaucho cut a sinew or tendon behind the fore shoulder, which at once made the animal helpless. After a day of cutting animals down, the gauchos retraced their steps the following day to kill and skin them.

HISTORY OF SHEEP FARMING

The first main attempt at sheep raising was probably that made by Whitington, who, on his arrival at Port Louis, in October 1840, landed from his brig *Susan* and another vessel, the *Acton*, thirteen sheep and four studs.

At this time, serious thought was being given to sheep farming. Lt Tyssen had received enquiries from residents in Buenos Aires about the prospects of sheep farming in the Falklands, and in 1841 the Colony received a gift of twelve sheep from a Mr P. Sheridan, an English subject who had been raising sheep in Argentina for a number of years.

By 1843, the number of imported sheep was slowly increasing and Governor Moody reported that Whitington had landed a further 198 sheep from Rio Negro, where the best selected stock could be obtained for two or three shillings each. The landed cost in the Falklands was thirteen to fifteen shillings each. Much stock eventually came from Rio Negro and Moody reported that the best horses could also be procured there. The original stock was imported from the King of Spain's own establishment.

Soon after Whitington had imported his flocks they were destroyed by his own dogs. Another settler, Culy, who had imported some 200 sheep from South America, lost them in the more severe climate of the Islands. Moody imported 120 sheep allowing them to stray into the mountain. This, he stated : 'was quite an experiment on my own part and at my own expense and shall attach no importance to its failure'.

Moore, the magistrate, viewed sheep raising in the Falklands as a failure. He reported to London that there were no shepherds to watch the sheep which wandered where they pleased. Rams ran with the ewes at all times, with the result that lambs were born in the colder months. Moore pointed out in 1846 that of the 900 sheep so far imported, only 100 remained, and only two bales of wool had been exported. Moody wrote : 'all these things of course will be altered when sheep farming is adopted by persons proposing to make it their livelihood'.

After these setbacks importation of sheep was discontinued for three years. Moody, however, continued his campaign for making the Falklands an agricultural colony. In 1847 he proposed to Earl Grey that seven farms should be established in the Islands, run by farming families from England. Each one would receive assistance from the home government with rations being allowed in the first year, houses at a cost of £100 each, ploughs and harrows supplied. Lafone, at this time negotiating with the Government over his contract, would have to supply horses and cattle to these farmers. Repayment was to be made by rent, £2 in the first year, rising to a maximum of £10 in the fifth and subsequent years. Moody's scheme did not materialise, and, as the colonisation of the islands by farming families had been mentioned in Lafone's proposals, the idea was discarded.

Lafone's manager, Williams, with 116 other persons, fifteen horses and general stores arrived at Port Louis on 1st May 1847 in the Norwegian vessel *Napoleon*. At the start of Lafone's operations, cattle were the main interest, but in 1850 some 540 sheep were landed at Hope Place. This was probably the largest number to be imported in the Islands up to that time. Losses were high and two years later a further 800 were brought to Hope Place in a bid to maintain stocks.

Also in 1847, Captain R. C. Packe took a lease on farming land on East Falkland and shortly afterwards imported a number of sheep together with a trained shepherd, probably the first to be employed in the Islands. In 1849, Captain Sulivan, who had engaged on survey work in the Falklands, also brought a number of sheep with a view to establishing a farm.

Imports of sheep from South America increased but it was the smaller numbers of pure bred, much hardier animals from England that formed the basis of the Falkland flocks. The first Colonial Manager of the Falkland Islands Company, Mr Dale, brought sixteen Cheviot sheep to the Island in 1852, and shortly afterwards a further 50–60 fine bred sheep were imported at a cost of £11 each. By 1859 there were nearly 8,000 sheep in the colony, composed mainly of Cheviot and Southdown breeds, and by this time the South American breed was dying out. The pastures suited the sheep, and carcases sent into Stanley market averaged 65lb in weight, with fleeces commonly between 10–11lb and averaging 9lb. Wool sent to the London market brought $8\frac{1}{2}$d per pound.

In 1865 the first lease of land for 6,000ac was taken on West Falkland mainland, but was discontinued shortly afterwards. In the same year Governor Robinson received an application from James L. Waldron, a Wiltshire sheep farmer, who had been visiting Australia, New Zealand and parts of South America in search of land on which to establish a sheep farm. Waldron examined West Falkland and requested a lease on 42,000ac, and in June of 1867 West Falkland was officially opened to settlers.

On 24 July 1867, Edward Packe, brother to Captain Packe, leased a section known as 'Many Branch Harbour' and, on 15 November, Waldron took a lease on Port Howard. Waldron arrived there in September, having chartered the barque *Diana*, 223 tons, to convey all his requirements from England. He brought Exmoor sheep from England and also a number of Merino from Montevideo. Wooden sectional buildings originally made for use in the Crimean War, were also off-loaded and a number remain at Port Howard today. By May 1868, Governor Robinson reported to the Duke of Buckingham that all available land on West Falkland had been taken.

A proclamation required West Falkland settlers to meet certain stocking requirements within a period of twelve months. This term would have been amply sufficient had it been possible to obtain sheep from East Falkland, but the only large flockmasters at this time were the Falkland Islands Company who refused to sell, although they were offered up to 40s a head for their sheep. The newly-arrived settler from England, was therefore obliged to turn to the River Plate area for stock. When, in early 1870, many of the West Falkland settlers were on the verge of bankruptcy rents were lowered and the compulsory purchase of land altered from five to ten years. The rights to hunt wild cattle on West Falkland were also given to the settlers.

Sheep Farming Colony

In the years 1871–5, the export of wool from the Islands was 2,075,000lb and, assisted by the Franco-Prussian war, prices of wool rose to a record 1s 6d per pound. Until this time Falkland Islands wool had been sold as River Plate wool. Shortly after 1873 it appeared under its own title. In 1874 the occupation of the colony was returned as 'sheep farming', the number of sheep being given as 170,000. By 1898 the stock returns recorded 807,211 sheep in the Falklands, the highest sheep population the Islands have known. There has been a steady decline over the last seventy years, and the return for the 1978–9 season was 591,388.

In the 1893–4 season, the first steam shearing machine was introduced to the Falkland Islands Company farm at North Arm, but attempts with machine shears were generally unsatisfactory and the hand method continued on most farms until the early 1960s. Hand shearing in 1970–1 was still being practised, but only on one farm.

The pressing of wool has seen a number of improvisations. In the earliest days cider presses were adapted and used for baling. In 1856, when the Falkland Islands Company had 3,140 sheep on their Darwin farm, a hay press was used. Tobacco leaf presses became popular and were much in use about the 1870s. Hydraulic wool presses are now used by the majority of farms, although hand-operated presses are still used on some smaller farms.

From 1900 to 1980

From 1909 to 1913, although there was a decrease in sheep population, the Islands' wool production reached a record level. In 1909 4,869,275lb were exported, more than in 1898 when flocks were at their peak. The introduction of better stock was showing results. Between 1895–1922 a total of 1,380 rams and ewes were imported of which over 68 per cent were Romney Marsh, Lincolns being the second most numerous. Other breeds included Border Leicester, Cheviot, Corriedale, Merino and Shropshire. The largest number of breeding animals were introduced in 1903 when 545 sheep were imported from New Zealand.

From 1917–18 the demand for wool rose, with prices reaching a record of 2s 7½d per pound. In 1933 prices dropped to their lowest, fetching an average of 6d per pound. Before World War II prices steadily increased and during the war years were controlled by the British Ministry of Supply who contracted the islands' entire wool crop at prices of between 7d–8d per pound.

112

With the removal of controls at the end of the war, prices soared from 2s 9d a pound in 1948 to 8s 9d per pound in 1951. Farmers realised profits beyond all expectations, debts and mortgages were paid off and all were prosperous.

In many cases improvements were made to property, housing and other amenities were carried out, but by comparison very little was invested in the land.

THE FARMS

With the exception of about 28,100ac of Crown Land, virtually the whole of the Falkland Islands is owned freehold by a small number of companies and individuals. There are about thirty-six occupied farms owned by not more than twenty-two companies, partnerships or family concerns. Another three farms are leased from the government. In 1970, land on East Falkland was divided into ten estates, with six estates on West Falkland. In 1871 the same number of estates existed on East Falkland, with eight on West Falkland. Farms on offshore islands number fourteen.

Farms vary in size from 850ac to about 30,000ac for offshore island farms while East and West Falkland farms range from 25,000ac to 307,000ac. These figures represent individually managed farms. The largest estate, comprising ten settled farms, is owned by the Falkland Islands Company with a total of 1,330,000ac. This represents 46 per cent of the total farming land in the Falkland Islands (see also Chapter 11).

The total sheep population for the Islands, in the 1980–81 season was 650,130; the total wool clip from 593,889 sheep was 2,112·4 (in '000kg). There were 8,092 head of cattle, 2,301 horses and 52 pigs.

Sheep Farming Practice

Sheep farming in the Falklands is based on slightly varying systems of large scale ranching directed entirely to the production of wool. Although the methods employed may vary within the

113

Islands, all farms are geared to placing the new season's wool on the London market, usually for the first sale of the year which generally occurs in March.

The sheep runs or paddocks on the majority of farms are large. Many are of more than 10,000ac with a number in excess of 20,000ac. Sheep and cattle are often carried on the same pasture for much of the year, this system of set-stocking being employed by more than half the sheep farms. A few farms which have subdivided large paddocks adopt forms of rotational grazing. On some smaller island farms, a modified system of rotational grazing uses the coastal tussac grass plantations. These paddocks of tussac are grazed by sheep during the winter months when the grass lands are poor and for the remainder of the year are closed to stock. With careful management some tussac plantations carry up to fourteen sheep per acre during the winter, and have done so for seventy years or more.

The small island farm supports about one sheep to two and a half acres. On the larger estates the acreage per sheep varies considerably but is more in line with the total Falkland average of four and a half acres per sheep. East Falkland holds slightly fewer sheep per acre than West Falkland.

The few cattle in the Falklands are grazed in much the same manner as sheep, there being very little fodder grown for winter feeding.

The farm's season generally commences about the beginning of October with the main lambing time. On the large farms lamb marking may precede the start of shearing and in the second week of November the ewe flocks are rounded up by mounted shepherds. On the smaller island farm, shearing is usually done before lamb marking. Hoggets—twelve to thirteen months old sheep—are shorn first and their fleeces give the farms the most valuable class of wool. It is general procedure on all farms to prepare this particular wool for the first shipment which generally leaves in January. Two more shipments are made in April and June. From about mid-January the breeding ewes are gathered and while the completion of shearing varies greatly between farms it may con-

114

tinue into February depending upon weather conditions. Lambs and shorn sheep are then dipped from early March onwards, after which the flocks are returned to their runs for wintering. In May, rams are put to the breeding ewes where they remain for some six weeks.

The Wool and Marketing

Many different breeds of sheep were introduced but by the early 1920s Romney blood predominated in the flocks. At about this time Corriedale sheep, developed from crossing Merino and Lincoln, were introduced and produced a finer grade of wool. They became increasingly popular and the majority of Falkland Islands flocks are now either Romneys or Corriedales or a cross between the two.

Most of the wools produced in the Islands are of a cross-bred type, the bulk being 54s in quality, with a few finer classes up to 58s–60s. The whole clip, which has been in the region of 4¾ million pounds weight during the period 1965–70, is exported to England and sold by auction on the London wool market. In 1970, however, the Falkland Islands Company acquired a controlling interest in a British firm of wool processers, and a percentage of their produce is now sold direct by private treaty to this concern.

In the 1971 report, 'The Sheep and Cattle Industries of the Falkland Islands', by the Ministry of Overseas Development advisory team, it was suggested that there should be closer co-operation between the Falkland farmers and the textile industry, on lines similar to those adopted by the Falkland Islands Company. Although the specialist processes of scouring, blending and top-making are not possible in the Islands for economic reasons, it was recommended that farmers should consider joining together to acquire shares in a processing firm which would handle the Falklands wool clip, brand name it and advertise it. The main market for Falkland Islands wool is the high-class woollen trade in the United Kingdom, and it appears to be specially suitable for making hand-knitted garments.

115

AGRICULTURE

Sheep Industry Investigations

By 1900 the quality of the pastures was deteriorating. Farmers blamed the wild geese and it was suggested that their numbers should be reduced (See Chapter Eight). Although the output of wool continued to increase steadily, the industry was no longer expanding as it had done earlier. The annual report produced by Government for 1921 disclosed the depressing state of the industry. Lambing percentages were poor and the decrease in the stock was largely in the younger class of sheep.

Following the 1924 report by Governor Middleton, the principal Director Inspector of the New Zealand Department of Agriculture, Mr Hugh Munro, was engaged to make a thorough investigation. He arrived in the Colony in April 1924 and his report being published in October of that year.

Munro considered that over-stocking and injudicious burning carried out for at least thirty years had done 'very great, if not irreparable damage' to the pastures. This position, he felt, was largely caused by absentee owners and company directors who 'insisted upon a given number of stock being carried'. Munro examined the industry minutely and was critical of the way tussac had been destroyed with other natural pasture. He advised giving more attention to breeding and fencing, to the possibilities of cattle raising, the keeping of records and accounts and the need for more careful handling of stock, especially with dogs.

Mr Munro also recommended that a Government experimental farm should be established. Two years later another New Zealand expert arrived and the Anson Experimental Farm was built close to the original settlement at the head of Berkeley Sound. The farm carried out trials in re-grassing and stock breeding, but in 1928 it closed down on grounds of public economy.

In 1937 William Davies of the Welsh Plant Breeding Station at Aberystwyth investigated the grasslands. Many of his recommendations echoed those of Munro and he reported : 'The present system of grassland farming in the Falkland Islands is nothing short of large scale ranching. Until a methodical and much extended scheme of sub-dividing existing paddocks is brought

116

about, the potentialities for land improvement throughout the Colony will remain all but untapped.' He felt that it should be seriously considered whether the ranching system should continue, or whether there should be a complete change with grassland improvement and a more intensive system of pastural agriculture. Like Munro, he felt that there should be further investigations which could be done under the direction of the Department of Agriculture, formed in the Colony that year.

From 1940–5, the Government Agriculture Department under Dr J. G. Gibbs practised and proved the validity of many suggestions made by these investigators. Dr Gibbs found that many of his experiments met with criticism. Ploughing was an innovation. Although many of his staff were camp men they had never seen a ploughed furrow. According to the returns of 1941, 772ac of land in the Islands was under the plough, less than two acres being near Stanley. By 1945, the acreage in Stanley had increased to 72ac producing a good tonnage of animal fodder, potatoes and other vegetables.

Dr Gibbs made many recommendations including the establishment of Agricultural Education, with an institute and demonstration farm. The Department continued to function but the Sheep-owners Association opposed it and even petitioned the Secretary of State to close it on the grounds that it was unnecessary and redundant. Of the proposed Farm Institute nothing more was heard although in his post-war plans Governor Cardinall, convinced that the Islands had an agricultural future, suggested a similar establishment together with co-operative settlements.

In 1965, a Grasslands Officer ran trials on grassland improvement. In his final report, in 1968, he wrote : 'It will be argued that there is nowadays an upsurge of interest in grassland improvement in the Islands today, but only the next ten years or so will tell if this is a case of bolting the door after the horse has gone. There are at the moment, about fifteen farms involved in some form of land improvement; had this been the case even 20 years ago the present economy would be infinitely healthier'.

117

DIVERSIFICATION OF THE SHEEP INDUSTRY

The disposal of surplus stock has been a recurrent problem since the wool industry started. The first attempt at using surplus stock was made in 1851 when Lafone set up a steaming plant at Hope Place for extracting tallow from cattle. The first tallow works of any size, however, were set up by the Falkland Islands Company at Darwin in 1874. This works dealt with some 15,891 sheep in 1880, indicating the number available. For a short period a market for surplus sheep was found in Patagonia and in 1883 6,000 animals were exported, largely from West Falkland, to stock the newly-formed runs in southern Chile. In 1896, sheep were still being exported but the number had fallen to 3,360 head.

In 1883 a group of farmers formed the Falkland Islands Meat Company Limited and in 1885 an agent of Hoffnung & Co in London visited the Islands to arrange transportation of frozen mutton to England. A contract was drawn up for the sale of carcases having an average weight of 75lb at 12s each. In 1886 a refrigerating ship, the *Selembria* arrived in the Falklands and working from East and West Falkland ports took 28,000 carcases valued at £15,070. This cargo was a loss, fetching only 3d to 4½d per pound. The following year two cargoes were shipped totalling 41,000 sheep, worth £13,882. The first shipment was unprofitable and the second, having been loaded at a time when the sheep were losing condition, was also a total loss. The company, having exhausted all its funds, abandoned the enterprise.

The export of frozen mutton was revived in 1891 and continued until 1895. During this period 67,271 carcases were shipped to London. In 1895 the farmers received 5s 6d each for wethers and 4s 6d for ewes, while New Zealand and Australian mutton was fetching 1s 5d to 1s 6d for 8lb. Dissatisfied with the price the farmers offered no more sheep and the export stopped. The sailing ship *Hengist* of 1,400 tons and fitted with refrigerating machinery had been used as a receiving vessel and the frozen mutton was transferred to Steam Union Company ships calling at the Falklands on their way to England from New Zealand.

118

Page 119 (above) The Falkland Islands Company vessel RMS *Darwin* (withdrawn in 1971) collecting wool bales from a camp station for transhipment from Stanley; *(below)* Falkland Island Fur seal (Arctocephalus australis aust). A sub-adult male on a breeding rookery

Page 120 (above) Small section of an extensive Gentoo penguin colony on the Jason Islands. The site of penguin oiling during the 1800s: *(below)* A Falkland Islands Government Air Service Beaver float aircraft, loading passengers prior to launching from the hangar slipway at Stanley

In March 1896 the steamer *Schleswig* took on 2,278 live sheep from Felton Station at Salvador. The live cargo arrived in England a month later, but not having obtained the required sanitary certificate at the Falklands, it could not be unloaded in London and was, instead, held at Deptford. Here the remaining 2,042 sheep were slaughtered and sold at 30s per head. In the autumn of the same year a number of Pacific Steamers called at Port Howard and took prime wethers to England. Unfortunately the live cargo arrived shortly after a large consignment of River Plate Sheep and so the market for the Falklands' animals was poor. In 1905, and for several years afterwards, the export of live sheep to South America for breeding purposes was revived. The largest number appears to have been 39,003, exported in 1914. A canning factory was opened in 1911 at Goose Green, and was extremely successful for nine years. It absorbed a large proportion of surplus sheep, but during the slump of the post-war years, the concern suffered a serious loss and in 1921 it closed down. During 1913–14 and 1920, occasional shipments of live sheep were made to Argentina for the frozen meat trade. During this period 69,800 sheep, valued at £34,213, were exported.

Encouraged by the success of the shipments to coastal freezers, Governor Middleton suggested building a freezer in the islands. The matter was again raised by Governor Henniker-Heaton in 1939, and in 1947 the Colonial Development Corporation offered finance.

A site was chosen at Ajax Bay on the Falkland Sound, but the scheme met with difficulties from the start. There were building, labour and transport problems. The freezer, started in 1949, was not ready until 1953 and had cost nearly half a million pounds to erect, the original approved capital being £242,000.

Opposition to the scheme was high and in the first season only 14,000 sheep were sent in. Of these, 39 per cent were rejected as unsuitable. The second season (1954) saw 16,000 sheep sent to the freezer. The following year the venture closed down. Today this impressive establishment remains in the quiet and lonely landscape of Ajax Bay. Although many of its administrative build-

121

ings, staff quarters and fittings have been removed, its great freezers, machinery and power house stand much as they were left, but interest has been shown in the idea of bringing to the Islands vessels which could carry out killing, dressing and freezing at such stations.

Experimental Mink Farm

In 1959 the Falkland Islands Company embarked on a fur farming project with a view to utilising a percentage of cull sheep as feed for mink. It is estimated that 35,000 surplus sheep are available annually from Falkland Islands farms and the fur farming project was expected to take between 12,000 and 16,000 sheep per year for the planned capacity of approximately 4,500 mink.

In late 1959 and 1960, two batches of mink totalling ninety-six animals were shipped from England under the care of a manager experienced in mink farming. Although the scheme met with a certain amount of opposition and concern lest the animals escaped and endangered the sheep farming industry, it was given a five years experimental period.

The mink is a northern hemisphere animal, with very precise breeding cycles. With animals brought to the southern hemisphere a re-adjustment period had to be overcome before they would breed. A number of interesting facts were discovered about the breeding of mink in such a southerly position. Hours of daylight were important in the breeding cycle, light being absorbed by the eyes. Animals with lighter coloured eyes, such as the light blue mutations, bred more satisfactorily than animals of the dark breeds.

For the mink to produce good breeding averages and a quality pelt, the diet was critical. Trial disclosed that only 50 per cent of the diet could be composed of mutton because mutton fat, with its high melting point, could not be assimilated by the mink's digestion system. Consequently additional foods had to be found. Costly cereals had to be imported and the whole objective of the scheme was defeated. The project operated for its allotted time during which several hundred pelts were exported to the London fur markets where they were well received. The experiment showed that a large commercial venture was uneconomical; therefore all the stock were pelted, and the farm closed.

Further Investigations

In 1967, Mr C. W. Guillebaud, Emeritus University Reader in Economics, at Cambridge University, England, carried out an economic survey of the Falklands. During March and April of 1967 he made an extensive tour of farms and in October of that year his report was published. It covered the national income, standard of living, public finances and the various aspects of the farming industry.

Mr Guillebaud believed that the sheep farming industry of the Falklands would be 'well-advised' to concentrate on improving the pastures, but that it should also consider the possibility of turning to meat production rather than wool. He quoted reports that some of the large sheep farming enterprises in Australia and New Zealand were moving into cattle rearing on the grounds that beef is not exposed to the threat of synthetic substitutes. He felt that apart from the errors which had ruined the Ajax Bay Freezer project, the scheme had been rather premature because quality and quantity demanded an improvement in the pastures before the development of a frozen meat trade.

He suggested possible ways by which farms which were not actively engaged in improving their pastures might be induced to do so. He recommended that the rate of the Profits Tax, which in 1967 was 2s in the pound should be raised to 4s. In conjunction with this an investment allowance should be introduced to enable capital investment for pasture improvement to be set off against the additional 2s in the pound Profits Tax. The recommendations were approved by the Legislature and in May 1969 the Profits Tax bill was passed.

In September 1969 a five-man advisory team, sponsored by the Ministry of Overseas Development, arrived in the Falklands to look into all aspects of sheep and cattle health and production.

The team also made recommendations on how farmers could best improve the productivity of the sheep industry and advised on the future production of beef cattle. Their report 'The Sheep and Cattle Industries of the Falkland Islands' appeared in February 1971, and in many respects it echoed the findings of previous investigators. They considered labour to be the greatest single item in costs and therefore showed most scope for economies, and it was suggested that a master shearer from Australia or New Zealand should be employed to teach the kind of shearing which maximises wool output per unit of human energy expended.

In the past, thought has been given to the formation of smaller farm units. The Guillebaud Report suggested that the sheep owners should consider establishing tenant farms on their land. The 'Team', however, did not envisage a change in farm structures of smaller units, and it was considered that further investigations into meat production should be carried out by an expert in the wholesale meat trade, to study the processing and marketing of beef. For future agricultural advisory work in the Islands, it was recommended that an Agricultural Experimental Unit in the form of a model farm should be established covering 12,000–20,000ac and carrying 3,000–4,000 sheep. At present more interest is being taken in the ultimate destination of Falkland Islands wool, to give the farmers financial interest in other sections of the wool industry. The Falkland Islands Company have made an important step in this field with the acquisition of shares in a wool processing firm, David Smith & Co of Bradford. In March 1971 the Company's initiative was taken a step further in discussions with representatives of other sections of the wool industry, including a firm which would produce garments exclusively from Falkland Island wool. Today there is one mill producing cloth exclusively from the Islands' wool, with retail outlets for the finished garments bearing the label 'Falkland Island Wool' through Austin Reid of London and Brown Bros. New York.

Surplus Meat Utilisation
The type of sheep used for wool production in the Falklands

124

is generally not suitable for quality meat export. As local requirements are not great there has always been a fairly large meat
surplus. In the 'Team's' 1971 report it was estimated that 1,000
tons of surplus meat were available annually between December
and April. There is no local processing of this surplus, although
in 1980 some 10,601 sheep were exported live to a Chilean processing plant. In mid 1980 Argentina indicated its interest in
the Islands' surplus meat but the 1982 conflict put an end to
plans which were being made to refit a vessel to carry live sheep
to that country.

Research and Diversification

Many reports have now been produced on the sheep farming
systems of the Falkland Islands and an even greater number of
recommendations made for increasing agricultural output, but
such advice has been of limited effect because of the little known
biology of the Islands and the constraints on production imposed
by the environment. In 1975 the Grasslands Trials Unit (GTU)
was set up to carry out investigative work on the vegetation and
livestock, to record its investigations and facts about the Islands'
agriculture, so that any recommended changes in land or sheep
management would be based on scientific information.

The work done by the GTU is extensive and varied. Apart
from studies directly associated with grasslands, research is carried
out on the Upland Goose and its relation to the Islands' agriculture—the team includes a biologist for this specific purpose.
Animal husbandry forms part of the programme and a veterinary
surgeon is employed carrying out work in the eradication of
Hydatidosis and Brucella Ovis in sheep, together with veterinary
research.

Financed by the Ministry of Overseas Development, the team
in April 1982 consisted of seven members recruited in the United
Kingdom and one local employee (see also Chapter 11).

5   COMMUNICATIONS

THE Falkland Islands have always relied on sea communications as the link with the outside world. This will change with air transport, but shipping must inevitably remain very important because the islands are completely dependent upon other countries for many basic necessities.

Lord Anson appreciated the potential of the Falklands for victualling vessels travelling to the south seas. Over 100 years later Governor Moody described the tremendous importance of the colony for those vessels trading on the Cape Horn route. On the establishment of Port Stanley with its good harbour, more vessels put into the islands. The Californian gold rush and the Peruvian guano trade played a part, and for a number of years the port became a major link in the Cape Horn route.

From 1870, fewer vessels called at Port Stanley because of the development of Punta Arenas in Chile. Steam ships were slowly replacing sail so passage through the Straits of Magellan became easier. Vessels could obtain coal at Punta Arenas, this being unobtainable in large quantities or cheaply in Stanley. The Board of Trade issued regulations restricting many ill-found vessels from making the dangerous voyage round the Horn. The development of the overland railway system from the western to eastern coast of North America also had its effect—wheat and other produce, once shipped from San Francisco to New York by way of the Cape Horn route, now travelled by the new overland railway.

In 1876, Governor Callaghan met the Governor of Punta Arenas to make arrangements for the establishment of a steamship service between the two ports, but this came to nothing. Shipping on this route did, however, operate frequently. In the 1880s local vessels were engaged in shipping sheep to the southern regions of Chile to stock the newly-formed ranches there. Large amounts of timber were shipped to the islands from Punta Arenas and this trade, although diminishing, remains to this day.

The British Admiralty attempted making a coaling base in Stanley and work started in 1899 only to be dismantled in 1905. The Admiralty decided that the Falklands were too far south, especially since the South Atlantic fleet had merged with the West African Squadron. That year work started on the Panama Canal, a fact which probably influenced the decision to merge the squadrons and close the base in Stanley. Unable to supply the needs of steam vessels, Stanley's importance as a port declined and the opening of the Panama Canal dealt the final blow.

Present Day Sea Routes

Although ports exist on the South American coast which are much nearer to the islands, the main shipping route has been between Montevideo in Uruguay and Port Stanley. This route provided the main passenger and mail connection with other countries until 1971, when RMS *Darwin* was withdrawn. RMS *Darwin* was owned by a subsidiary of the Falkland Islands Company.

The Falklands' main exports and imports depend on a direct link with Great Britain. This link is currently maintained by the Danish vessel MV *A.E.S.*, which makes a visit to the Islands four times annually, on a voyage lasting about thirty days. In accordance with the 1971 Communications Agreement between Great Britain and Argentina, sea communications existed for some ten years between Argentine ports and Port Stanley. Calls were made several times a year by vessels carrying sundry freight, fuel and small numbers of Argentine tourists. MV *Monsunen* made an average of two trips per year to Punta Arenas, Chile for dry docking; since the 1982 conflict she has voyaged to Montevideo, Uruguay for the purpose.

British Antarctic Survey vessels RRS *John Biscoe* and RRS *Bransfield* and a Naval ice patrol ship, HMS *Endurance*, also

127

make Stanley a port of call on their way to and from the Antarctic. These calls bring increased activity to the port during the summer season.

Inter-island shipping is carried out by MV *Monsunen.* Prior to the 1982 conflict, the MV *Forrest,* which is owned by the Falkland Islands Government, was chartered by the Ministry of Defence for use by the detachment of Royal Marines which used to be stationed in the Islands.

SHIPPING

Early coastal vessels

Not until 1850 were serious attempts made to obtain local vessels. That year Governor Rennie reported that James Phillips and a Mr Williams had requested local registration for their vessel the *Hydra,* the first such request to be made. At that time, however, Rennie had not yet the power to grant registration. By 1858 six vessels had been registered in the colony. Three were temporary, subsequently being transferred to other countries.

Many earlier schooners operating from the Falklands were owned by the Falkland Islands Company. One of the first was the *Victoria,* a schooner of 72 tons. She was officially registered on 21 July 1854.

On 31 July 1854 another schooner of the Company's arrived in Port Stanley, the 104 ton *Fairy* purchased in 1853 from J. H. Snyder of New York. Built at Baltimore in 1850 for, it was generally thought, the slave trade, she ran mail between Stanley and Montevideo until 1865 and was also used to keep an unofficial eye on the seal fisheries. From 1868–76 she was owned by W. Bertrand and J. Switzer, settlers on West Falkland. She was then re-purchased by the company. Until 1889, when her registry was finally closed, she was used extensively for coastal work with the occasional sealing trips to Patagonia. Her final work was that of a lighter. Beyond repair in 1932, she was eventually broken up after seventy-eight years in the colony.

Another coastal vessel owned by the Company was the *Perseverance* which arrived in the Falklands on 25 April 1854 and registered on 5 August 1854. A ketch of 35 tons she was built in 1847 at Christchurch, Southampton. She was wrecked on the Tyssen Patch in the Falkland Sound on 18 September 1905.

Lafonia became a popular name for local vessels and on 14 December 1904 the first of that name arrived in Stanley. Formerly the *George Holt* she had been the last of the Mersey Pilot cutters before being bought by the Company. She was built by Phillips & Co of Dartmouth in 1892.

On 16 November 1906, in the shipyard of Messrs Ferguson & Son, Connah's Quay, Liverpool, another vessel was launched for the Falkland Islands Company. She was the first of a new type working the coastal waters and was named the *Malvina*. She was an 80 tons auxiliary schooner fitted with a four cylinder Gardiner engine of 65hp using paraffin or petroleum as a fuel. She had a two bladed screw and developed a speed of five knots. This was the first vessel registered in the colony which was powered by an oil engine. Her life in the islands was short and on 9 May 1910, while returning from West Falkland with a full load of wool she was wrecked in Reef Channel near Saunders Island.

Shipping after 1910

In 1913 the Company, with Lowden Connel & Co of Liverpool, formed the Falkland Islands Transport Co Ltd and purchased the steamship *Wheatsheaf*, renamed *Falkland*. Built in 1906 by the Ailsa Shipbuilding Co Ltd and having a gross tonnage of 452, she arrived in January 1914 and made her first local voyage under Captain Thomas on 18 February. She was a speedy vessel for that time, being capable of fourteen knots. She traded regularly around the colony until 1932 and was then sold to Chile in 1935.

In 1930 the Company resumed a regular shipping service between Stanley and Montevideo. In 1931 the second *Lafonia* was built at Leith, Scotland. A steamship of 345 tons, she was registered in Port Stanley on 15 March 1932 and re-named

129

Fitzroy. She became particularly important during World War II when she was the only vessel to maintain communications with the islands. She was also used in the establishment of the Falkland Islands Dependencies Survey's Antarctic bases from 1945, undertaking this successful charter under the code name 'Operation Tabarin'.

In 1948 *Fitzroy* was converted to oil burning and lengthened to increase her cargo carrying capacity by twenty per cent. She left the colony in 1957 for a breaker's yard in England.

In 1936, on the decision to maintain a larger passenger service operating a monthly service with Punta Arenas and Montevideo the SS *Southern Coast* was purchased and re-named *Lafonia*. She operated from the end of 1936 until 1941, when she was requisitioned for the war effort. She was sunk in the North Sea in 1942 after a collision.

Yet another vessel bore the name *Lafonia*. This was the SS *Perth* which during the war worked as a rescue ship in the North Atlantic. Her life in the Falklands was short. Purchased by the Company in 1946 the fourth *Lafonia* was re-sold in February 1950.

In 1957 the Company took delivery of a new vessel, the 1,792 ton steamship *Darwin*, built at a cost of over £250,000 by the Goole Shipbuilding & Repair Co. Her engines are reciprocating triple expansion low pressure steam type, built by Charles D. Holmes Ltd.

Operating mainly between Stanley and Montevideo her most important task has been to carry passengers and mail. Some 1,000 tons of freight can be carried but her cargo shipping is largely restricted to wool lifting from camp stations for trans-shipment from Stanley. In 1968 the total approximate amount of cargo carried from Montevideo to Stanley was 2,500 tons. The cargo northbound from Stanley to Montevideo is negligible.

On 11 February 1948 a Government coastal vessel, MV *Philomel* arrived in the colony. She was an ex-admiralty motor fishing vessel built in 1945 with an overall length of 75$\frac{1}{2}$ft and beam of just over 19ft. Mainly of timber construction with a cargo

130

capacity of 40 tons she was powered by a 140hp Blackstone Lister diesel engine. For nearly twenty years she worked around the Falklands carrying cargo and mails, the first successful motor vessel operated by the government.

In 1966 the Government decided to replace *Philomel* with a more modern vessel capable of carrying larger cargoes. On 25 May 1967 the *Forrest* was launched at Wivenhoe, Essex, England. She was named after Dr W. Forrest McWhan, Minister of the islands' Tabernacle (United Free Church) from 1934 to 1965.

Forrest was built by James W. Cook & Co at an approximate cost of £60,000 of which £27,000 was a grant from the Colonial Development and Welfare Fund. She is 86ft long with a beam of 22ft. She weighs over 144 tons gross and is powered by a Kelvin TSMB eight cylinder, four stroke single acting diesel developing 320bhp. The new vessel arrived in the Falklands on 8 November 1968, after a voyage from England which had taken thirty-seven days. MV *Philomel's* more modern replacement was registered in Port Stanley on 1 December 1968.

Antarctic Vessels

Captain Scott's ship *Discovery* was registered in Port Stanley on 7 October 1925 and, more recently, the Falkland Islands shipping register has entered two other well known vessels associated with the Antarctic, RRS *Shackleton* and RRS *John Biscoe*. The former, a motor vessel of 1,102 tons, was built in Sweden in 1954 for work in the Baltic Sea. Soon afterwards she was purchased for the Falkland Islands Dependencies Survey—now British Antarctic Survey—and registered in Port Stanley on 16 April 1956. For nearly thirteen years her seasonal arrival in Port Stanley was an important one, for a proportion of her crew were always Falkland Islanders. On 17 January 1969, *Shackleton* was transferred to the Natural Environment Research Council.

On 27 January 1971 a new vessel arrived in Stanley, the RRS *Bransfield*, built for the Natural Environment Research Council for use by the British Antarctic Survey. The *Bransfield*,

131

built as an ice breaker, replaces RRS *Shackleton* and the supply vessel chartered by BAS each year. She is 305 feet in length with a net tonnage of 1,576·91. Built by Messrs Robb Caledon Shipbuilders Ltd at Leith, Scotland, she is powered by two International Combustion Driven Generators and single propulsion motors by GEC Electric Projects. These drive a single shaft with a net horsepower of 1,020. She has a helicopter landing deck on the stern and a crow's nest fitted as a second bridge for controlling the vessel in ice. She was registered in Port Stanley on 30 January 1971.

CUSTOMS AND HARBOUR DEPARTMENTS

The Early Pilot

A local pilot was available at Port Louis and, in the early years, at Stanley for vessels requiring assistance, and he was the forerunner of the present department. Probably the first pilot was John Dowdle, a member of Lt Smith's boat crew. Employed by Captain Grey during his voyages round the Islands in 1837, Dowdle was paid one dollar a day.

Charles Melville first came to the Falklands as coxswain for Lt Smith's boat crew in 1834 aged twenty-eight. After his service Melville remained at Port Louis as master and part owner of the sixty-three ton schooner *Montgomery*, which he worked as a sealing vessel. Melville was acquainted with every port in the islands, and became, in the words of Lt Lowcay, 'a most excellent Pilot'. When not engaged in sealing Melville was employed as pilot by visiting naval vessels, receiving one and a half dollars per day. In 1843 Moody employed Melville and his boat crew for piloting vessels in Berkeley Sound, a service which Moody considered would encourage shipping. No charges were levied by the government for this service, although £1 was paid to the pilot by vessels accepting assistance. Pilotage was considered an unnecessary expense by London and the service under the government terminated.

In June 1846 the position of Boarding Officer, Harbour

Master and Pilot was created, and James Phillips, formerly mate of the wrecked vessel *Mary Grey*, was appointed. Thirty pounds a year was paid for the work, as the amount of shipping requiring attention was limited. In his free time Phillips was contracted to build roads for the government.

On 1 August 1848 Melville was appointed Government Boat Keeper at salary of £60 per annum. About this time Melville again became pilot and a charge was made on vessels requiring his services. In 1853 pilot charges were fixed at £2 per vessel. That year William Rutter was appointed as second pilot and Melville graduated to chief pilot, a post he retained until near his death on 25 October 1876.

Today requests for a pilot are received by the Government Wireless Station. A small Government launch will lead a ship into Port William or, if required, place the pilot on board if the ship requests entry to Port Stanley. (See also Chapter 11.)

Customs

In 1842 a tax of 20s per gallon was imposed by Moody on imported spirits. A bond was formed in the Government store at Port Louis and Charles Melville became temporary Excise Officer. In the early 1850s a permanent post of Customs Officer was formed, becoming the responsibility of the Colonial Secretary, with the Police force acting as Excise Officers. Wrecks with cargoes of liquor, became the subject of great attention and the story of *Whisky Galore* was re-enacted many times in the Falklands.

In 1883 Fox Bay was established as port of entry for West Falkland and the first entries were made at the port in 1884. In that year dues paid for pilotage, warehouse rent and imports, were £2,628 17s 8d. For some years Fox Bay was engaged in the export of West Falkland produce direct to other countries. Compared with Port Stanley, it was a minor port and one police constable, who was also customs officer, could handle all the work. In 1895, a Stipendiary Magistrate was appointed to Fox Bay and he became Deputy Collector of Customs. In 1916, the importance of Fox Bay as a port came to an end. Today the

COMMUNICATIONS

Government Officer retained at Fox Bay East issues clearances when required by vessels entering from abroad. For many years this has not been necessary. In Port Stanley, customs clearance and harbour master are the duties of one government officer. In 1979 a total of 208 vessels were cleared, of which over 180 were Polish and Russian trawlers. By the end of August 1980, a total of 226 had entered for that year, some 200 of which were trawlers. Harbour dues charged on ships clearing in 1979–80 brought in revenue of £60,000, with an estimated revenue of £80,000 for 1980–81. For the period 1975–8 the average number of vessels clearing was 47. Customs duties for the year 1979–80 totalled £132,500 on wines, spirits and tobacco.

LIGHTHOUSE AND NAVIGATIONAL AIDS

The first written reference to any form of navigational aid was made by Governor Rennie in a despatch dated 1850. Erected on Cape Pembroke at the entrance to Port William in 1849, it was a simple affair consisting of a beacon and a wooden tower surmounted by a flagstaff and cost £118. Another beacon was referred to as not sufficiently conspicuous so it appears that there was an even earlier one which was probably built during the period of evacuation from Port Louis.

In November 1853, a Captain Vetch reported to the Admiralty about the erection of a lighthouse on Cape Pembroke and in January 1854, the Surveyor-General of the Falklands was instructed to commence work on the foundation for a new lighthouse with a tower to be built of timber and iron. The building was completed by the end of January 1855 at a cost of £656.

On 1 July 1855, the first lighthouse keeper was appointed, by Trinity House, England under whose direction the lighthouse has remained to this day. William Creed was the first keeper appointed at an annual salary of £150. Creed arrived with his family on 6 November on the British ship *Frowning Beauty*, and the light came into operation for the first time on 1 December 1855.

There was a fixed light visible over a distance of fourteen miles. The light source was produced from eighteen oil lamps, in two rows of nine each, with 12in reflectors, all made and fitted by Wilkins of London. Rape seed oil was used to feed the lights, an oil which, according to one of the earlier keepers, froze like dripping in severe weather. The average consumption of each lamp was one and a half pints per night. This fuel was an expensive item and on Governor Moore's instructions, in 1856, locally procured seal oil was tried as a cheaper substitute. Later these oil lamps were replaced by sixteen Argan lamps with solid silver reflectors.

The lighthouse was re-built in 1906, and 780 tons of material were shipped from England together with a team of contractors. Until April 1982, the 70ft lighthouse tower built over seventy years ago on Cape Pembroke operated in much the same way as when it was first erected. There was a reflected light of 105,000 candle power produced from a paraffin vapour system and beams were produced from four large glass prisms, the whole system being turned on a revolving platform in the turret. The mechanism for turning this platform was the same clockwork system installed in 1907 having to be re-wound by hand every hour of operation. After damage suffered during the occupation, a semi- or fully automatic system is planned.

In addition to the lighthouse on Cape Pembroke and a sister light to mark the other side of Port William, Mengherie Point, there are today two small lights on the Narrows, the entrance into Port Stanley Harbour and a small light to indicate a hazard at the entrance to Fox Bay Harbour, port of entry for West Falkland.

The Cable and Wireless Company wireless station does not operate a special Radio Beacon Navigation system to guide approaching shipping (as used to be maintained by the government wireless station for use on request). Up until the occupation, if vessels approaching the Islands specifically asked for Radio Beacon Navigation, the beacon system used for Stanley Airport was capable of being brought into use for this purpose.

COMMUNICATIONS

From the very early days of Port Stanley until 1912, a cannon was fired from the government dockyard to signal the arrival of a mail boat. With the introduction of wireless a message transmitted from the mail boat would notify its arrival in Stanley. Such messages were posted on the Gazette Board. Today, the arrival of mail is still an important broadcast notice to residents in the town. Days before its arrival the number of bags coming in containing air and surface mail is generally broadcast.

Letters, papers and small packets are sorted and placed in private letter boxes which are rented at a cost of £1 per year. People who do not rent a box ask over the counter for mail. The broadcast announcement that the mail is ready for collection causes a general exodus to the Post Office. Parcels are then sorted and are usually ready one or two days later. (See Chapter 11.)

An Early Contract

No great thought appears to have been given to an established mail service in the early years but by 1850 although the number of persons in the colony did not exceed 500, there was an increasing need for a regular service between the islands and the outside world. Governor Rennie said that they had once not received any mail for eight months.

The situation remained much the same until early 1852 when Captain Smyley said he was about to establish himself as a merchant in the colony and 'proposed to established communication by schooner which shall leave this Port eight times a year and proceed to Montevideo bringing back the mails the times of arrival and departure being regulated by the steamers to and from England'. He added:

> The terms on which I propose to your Excellency to undertake this communication are £540 sterling per annum. This I believe is less than any Government vessel would cost, but as I am about to embark in a store here I should be able to import my stores by

the same opportunity and thus partly pay my expense of such a vessel.

Governor Rennie forwarded Smyley's proposal to Earl Grey saying he knew of no other person 'who from his intimate knowledge of the navigation of these seas, able seamanship and energetic character, is so well qualified for this undertaking'.

About this time, however, moves were being made by the government in England. The Falkland Islands Company had been incorporated and one of their objectives was to establish a regular mail contact with the Islands. They had bought their first schooner, the 180-ton *Amelia* and sailed for the Falklands. On 1 July 1852 the schooner arrived in Stanley. Mr John Dale, the Company's first Colonial Manager, travelled on her and the ship also bore a mail contract worth £700. Thus the 'Mail Packet' service started and the charge for mail between England and the colony was reduced from 2s 7d to 1s per half ounce.

This mail contract soon proved to be 'disadvantageous' and early in 1854 the company proposed to abandon it. This caused great concern among the principal merchants and employees in the colony and a petition, signed by seventeen of them, was sent to the Duke of Newcastle. But the contract was abandoned that year and mail services became irregular. From time to time contracts were made but they never developed into a regular service. Eventually, in 1862, the UK government bought for the Falkland Islands government the schooner *Foam*, a 71-ton vessel, fourteen years old, which had formerly belonged to Lord Dufferin. She arrived in Stanley with mail on 22 December 1863 and made her first voyage from the Falklands on 26 January 1864. Until 1873 *Foam* made regular mail runs between Stanley and Montevideo but proved too expensive to operate and was sold to a local farmer, Andrez Pitaluga.

There was a transformation in the Islands' external mail service in 1880 when a contract was signed with the Kosmos Steamship Co of Hamburg. This was the first satisfactory and regular mail service. The Kosmos Line operated through the Straits of Magellan from Europe to Valparaiso and the contract required them to call at Port Stanley once a month. The initial subsidy was £1,800 but during the last few years of operation it was raised to £2,500. Having run for twenty years, this mail contract was terminated in 1900. A contract was then made with the Pacific Steam Navigation Co, for which the Falkland Islands Company had the agency. The shippers were to provide a four-weekly service for an annual subsidy of £5,000. However, the mail service continued to have its ups and downs.

In 1930 the Falkland Islands Company re-opened a regular service to Montevideo. Now a new mail contract was negotiated and, with the operation of RMS *Darwin*, twelve mails a year were brought to the Colony. Since 1971, when RMS *Darwin* was withdrawn, about six sea mails a year have been brought into the Colony direct from Britain by MV *A.E.S.* and British Antarctic Survey vessels. While an external air service existed between Comodoro Rivadavia, in Argentina, and Stanley, the Colony had a regular air-mail service carried twice a week by LADE. By the Communications Agreement, air mail from Britain was routed direct through Argentina and forwarded to the Colony bearing a special Communication Agreement frank. A similar frank was applied by the Stanley Post Office to mail leaving the Islands for Argentina. (See also Chapter 11.)

Today most inter-island mail is delivered by the Government Air Service, although the cargo-delivering voyages of MV *Monsunen* and MV *Forrest* are also used for the carriage of mail.

Post Offices and Postal Charges

There is one post office in Stanley. It bears the typical Royal Cipher and has a red pillar box at its entrance. A number of other post boxes exist in Stanley for the collection of mail but there is no delivery service.

One officer is retained at Fox Bay and serves as both post-master and communications officer. Small as this office is, it remains a busy centre of communications for the West. With a population on West Falkland of around 300, stamp sales amounted to almost £4,000 in 1981 and to £3,000 in the months of January, June, October and November 1982. In the first year of operation, 1899, stamp sales amounted to £1 19s 5d, of which the main sale was of 1d stamps. Fox Bay has its own postmark.

With the opening of a whaling factory on New Island in 1908 the island became a Port of Entry. A small sub post office was established, in August 1909, to handle mail and issue money and postal orders, but it closed in 1917, a year after the whaling station.

In 1983, postage rates from the Falklands were charged at 17p per 5 grammes for first-class airmail, irrespective of distance. Postcards were 13p and aerogrammes 14p and 16p. The internal rate is 5p. Surface letter mail sent direct to London continues to be charged at one of the cheapest of all international postal rates—the minimum charge is 12p. (See also Chapter 11.)

Stamps and Stamp Issues

The pre-payment of letters between the Colony and the United Kingdom was approved by the General Post Office in 1861 and became effective from 1 August of that year, with the first such mail arriving in England on the *Oneida* on 1 October 1861. It is not known how the pre-payment was indicated when the scheme first came into operation, but from January 1869 to the autumn of 1876, a small rectangular metal stamp, with the words 'Falkland Islands Paid', was applied in black to each envelope and from then until postage stamps were introduced on 19 June 1878 a circular metal stamp was used with the same words but creating a red impression. The first stamps were 1d and 6d values, followed in the autumn of 1878 by a 1/- value and in September 1879 by a 4d value. Further additional printings and values followed as required by changes in postal rates and monarchs. The first commemorative issue of stamps took place in 1933 to celebrate the centenary of British administration and are considered classics of their type.

Since then the Falkland Islands have adopted a conservative stamp policy under the guidance of the Crown Agents, who handle sales outside the Islands. A permanent local Philatelic Bureau was established in mid 1978 and in the years to 1980–81 dealt with some 9,300 overseas orders with a value of £119,000. The Bureau now offers a standing-order new-issue service for stamps and other philatelic items from the Falkland Islands, Falkland Island Dependencies and British Antarctic Territory.

Stamp sales have now become the second largest source of income for the Islands, with single issues like the Queen's Silver Jubilee issue of 1977 realising £196,066 and the Coronation Anniversary issue of June 1978 realising £170,099. Issues of both definitive and commemorative stamps are linked where possible to local subjects and a recent issue (1983), commemorating 150 years of British administration, like a number of other recent issues, has been designed by local artists. On 13 September 1982 following the liberation of the Islands after the Argentine invasion a special £1 stamp was put on sale for £2, the additional £1 surcharge being donated for the Falkland Islands Re-building Fund.

In addition to stamps, the Islands have issued postal stationery, the first being 1½d postcards in 1883. These were followed by further postcards, reply-paid cards, envelopes, letter cards, registered envelopes and aerogrammes. In 1977 the first stamp booklets were issued containing the Silver Jubilee stamps to the value of £2. These have since been followed by four further booklets each containing current definitive stamps to the value of £1.

AIR SERVICES

Domestic

The domestic service was inaugurated in 1948 using an Auster land plane. Up to the 1982 conflict, FIGAS, the Falkland Islands Government Air Service, operated two de Havilland DHC2 Beaver seaplanes and a Britten-Norman 'Islander' land aircraft. The latter was introduced in October 1979 (see Chapter 11).

During the first year in which the domestic air service was in operation twenty-eight passengers were carried. Eight were

140

private passengers and the balance consisted of government officers on duty. In 1958 the service carried 560 passengers, while in 1980–81 the number of passengers transported rose to 3,369. Today four pilots and a ground staff of six are normally employed by FIGAS. The service provided by the two types of aircraft, 'land' and 'float', varies a little. The Beaver flies no regular route; instead it leaves its base in Stanley, picking up and putting down passengers and freight according to the bookings made for that particular day. These flights might be termed 'short hauls', for although it may happen that the aircraft circumnavigates the entire Falkland archipelago in the course of a day's operation, the average flight between settlements takes only twenty to twenty-five minutes. The 'Islanders' operate from Stanley Airport and, in contrast to the Beaver, fly a number of fixed routes scheduled for certain days of each week. Load-carrying capabilities and other factors probably make the land plane the most suitable for future operations. However not all settlements have landing strip facilities. This means that the phasing out of the float aircraft operation will probably not take place for a number of years.

A feature of the FIGAS operation is the 'mail drops' system. On the arrival of airmail into the Colony, camp airmail is literally dropped to settlements from the air. Both the Beaver and the Islander aircraft are used for this unconventional form of mail delivery.

In 1980–81 expenditure for FIGAS amounted to £324,644 with revenue of £72,733.07. Between July 1980 and June 1981 freight carried amounted to 12,599lb, with a value accrued of £2,320.39.

External Air Link

History was made in 1952 when the first direct flight was made to the Falkland Islands. This was a survey flight by a seaplane of Aquila Airways Ltd., leaving Southampton on 21 April 1952 for Port Stanley. It made the flight via Madeira, Cape Verde Islands, Brazil and Montevideo and arrived on 28 April 1952 with both mail and passengers. She started the return flight on 2

May 1952 and arrived back in Southampton on 8 May 1952. This flight was the first and last of its kind to date.

A small number of other incidental flights have been made into the Colony since this, but it was not until February 1971 that any form of regular external air link was established. The occasion for the formation of the link was when an 'Albatross' amphibian aircraft of the Argentine Navy flew in to evacuate a lighthouse keeper, who was seriously ill, and to transport him to an emergency operation in Buenos Aires. The Argentine 'Albatross' maintained the link thus established between Comodoro Rivadavia and Stanley, carrying passengers and mail on the basis of two flights per month, until November 1972. The 'Albatross' connection ceased when a temporary landing strip was completed. The strip was constructed of aluminium plates and was built under the terms of the Communications Agreement between Argentina and Britain. The task of building the strip was undertaken by an Argentine Air Force construction team. Once the strip was completed, a Fokker Friendship F27 came into service and there were weekly flights from Comodoro Rivadavia.

In 1974 work was started on the construction of the permanent airfield which was to be Stanley Airport. It was built by Britain at a cost of some £4½ million and was opened in December 1977. Until the 1982 conflict there were two flights a week operated by the Argentine development line Lineas Aereas del Estado (LADE). Flights were operated between Comodoro Rivadavia and Stanley using F27 turbo-prop and F28 jet aircraft. (See also Chapter 11.)

OVERLAND ROUTES

The original routes laid out by early settlers still exist and are the foundation of camp tracks today. Broadly speaking there are two main tracks, the one on East Falkland running as a main artery from the south-west of the island to the north-east extremity from which several branch routes run to different points. On West Falkland the track system is much the same.

There are no paved roads outside Stanley. Generally speaking tracks vary between two extremes: sections which run over predominantly peaty ground and others routed over higher, rocky areas. The upper layers of peat consist of a mass of intertwined roots which form a natural carpet over the humified peat several inches below and is capable of bearing quite heavy loads. During the winter and in wet seasons, this ground reaches saturation point and presents a problem for traffic which, at the best of times, is restricted to tractors and Land-Rover type vehicles. In parts the peat layer has been stripped off to expose the clay subsoil on which the tracks have been formed. On these tracks travelling conditions are relatively good, but still suffer from poor drainage and little maintenance. All tracks have numerous bridges, usually simple constructions crossing streams. There is one notable exception to this, the suspension bridge which crosses Bodie Creek, in Lafonia. It has a clear span of 400ft with an 8ft clear roadway. Supplied by David Rowell & Co of Westminster it was erected by local men and given its situation it is a remarkable feat of construction. The bridge was built in 1924–5 to reduce the otherwise long route around the creek and to the southern area of Lafonia.

Fences also intersect routes with gates leading from one property or section to another. As there are, in many parts, no defined roadways to which a traveller is restricted, tracks often wander about the immediate countryside avoiding the more boggy areas and sections of the route ripped up by other vehicles.

A survey carried out in 1963 examined the feasibility of building two gravel roads in East and West Falkland, but the estimated cost of £1½ million, with annual maintenance costs of up to £30,000, ruled out their construction. However in 1979 a scheme to link Stanley and Darwin with 60 miles of gravel type road was commenced with the ultimate aim being to produce a network on both East and West Falkland.

Overland Transport

Horses are used extensively by shepherds and where sheep

farming is the basic industry it is unlikely that they will ever disappear completely. However, a dramatic change has taken place over the last ten years. The Land-Rover and motor cycle are taking the place of the horse for transport between settlements and never again will it be recorded that 300 horses were gathered together at a sports meeting held at Darwin, as was the case in 1891.

Probably the first motor transport was a Ford car introduced into the colony in 1923. Since then a wide variety of motor vehicles have been employed in the islands including ex-Army Bren gun carriers which were left behind by the troops after World War II. In 1969 the number of vehicles registered in the islands totalled 764, nearly half this number being Land-Rovers. The proportion of vehicles to population is one of the highest in the world.

In October 1967 a Royal Naval SRN6 Hovercraft moved across Stanley Harbour for the first time. Until its withdrawal in 1972, this form of transport operated extensively around the islands and made two circumnavigational journeys around the archipelago, demonstrating its potential in the Falklands over land and sea. Transport communications within the islands may still look towards air-cushioned vehicles in future.

RADIO AND TELEPHONE COMMUNICATIONS

In 1890 the Falkland Islands Company made proposals for linking Stanley with their main farm at Darwin by telephone. It was not, however, until 1897 that the first telephone came into operation. This was a single line between Cape Pembroke Lighthouse and Stanley—a distance of seven miles. On the night of Sunday 21 February the first official message came through informing the chief of police, who was in charge of the thirty line magneto telephone exchange, that HMS *Acorn* had anchored in Port William. The chief of police had some knowledge of telephone work and the constables under him, having little to do apart from arresting delinquents, were given the somewhat more

144

onerous task of climbing telephone poles on a windy day to repair broken wires.

The exchange was built next to the chief's residence at the police station, and he had a night alarm bell near his bedroom. This was a convenient arrangement for urgent calls and was at the same time a deterrent to public subscribers foolish enough to ring in the middle of the night for no good reason.

Telephone communication with the lighthouse was installed to report on shipping, especially ships attempting to make for Port William and requiring assistance. Port Stanley, screened by low lying hills from the entrance to Port William, was often unaware of ships in difficulty and before this telephone line was installed the lighthouse keeper, or his assistants, had to make the long ride into Stanley to alert a pilot or the tug *Samson*.

The next telephone line to be installed was the Stanley-Darwin line. Work began in 1906 when the *Consort* was engaged in landing telephone posts at different points along the coast.

The Company brought an electrical engineer from England to supervise the installation of their telephone line. Mishaps occurred including breakages in the wires, which were popularly supposed to be caused by wild geese flying into the wires but on one occasion a fault was caused by a length of sheep's entrails hanging over the wire and earthing it, probably owing to a gull dropping his find at the wrong moment. The Darwin line was in working order by the end of 1907 and measured $49\frac{1}{2}$ miles. The telephone system was solely for the use of the business houses in Stanley although calls could be made by the public at certain times and rates.

On 21 September 1906, the Telephone Exchange in Stanley was officially opened. Government House was the scene of the ceremony and, after experimenting, the Governor's office, the lighthouse, the Falkland Islands Company's offices, the Colonial Secretary's office and the Central Station (situated in the jail and under the charge of Mrs Sulivan, the Chief Constable's wife) were linked. Other lines were soon erected on East Falkland and Mr Homer, the electrical engineer, was engaged by other farms to

145

supervise new lines. In 1911 there was a telephone from Stanley to Port Louis. This line stretched eighteen miles, three men taking five weeks to complete its erection over some of the most difficult terrain in the islands.

Stanley was soon bristling with telephone poles and a public exchange was constructed. In June 1912 all Government buildings, business houses and some private residences were wired. The service came under the supervision of the postmaster and the public were allowed to subscribe to it. The charge was £8 a year or £5 5s for a three-year subscription. Non-subscribers were allowed to use the phones from a public call room built at the exchange. The fee was 2d per three minutes, long distance lines being charged at 6d per five minute call.

The 30-line board was enlarged in stages and in recent months after the events of 1982 the 480-line capacity has been stretched to maximum levels with party lines and other arrangements in an attempt to cope with the extraordinary increased demand. The magneto-type telephone is still the system used and it is necessary to 'turn a handle' to call the exchange. (See also Chapter 11.)

As a result of the conflict, the 'Darwin line' connecting an area of East Falkland with Stanley is no longer operational. It would seem that improved radio communications coupled to the difficulties involved in repairing and subsequently maintaining this line—some of it going across minefields—will make its replacement unlikely. Lines to the northern settlements on the East are still in use.

Broadcasting Service

In 1927 the Telephone and Telegraphic Department was established but it soon developed into something more than its name suggested for it introduced the colony's first broadcasting service.

This was a rediffusion system connected by land line from a government studio to loudspeakers in the houses and benefited not only residents in Stanley but also those in the camps. On East Falkland, the service was carried by telephone line to the stations, a method probably used nowhere else in the world.

146

There were no transcriptions and programmes were restricted to records and talks by local people. The 'Box', the name given to the receiver, was until very recently a common-place item of equipment in practically every house in Stanley.

The rediffusion system would relay programmes from the Falkland Islands Broadcasting Studio, plus announcements of interest to residents. It was general practice to keep the loud-speaker switched on at all times, even when there was no broadcasting, for announcements were made to the public in Stanley at any time of the day or night. These included arrival and departure of vessels, mail notices, 'for sale' notices and, on occasions, the alert for fire brigade members.

In 1942 it was decided to convert an amateur's home-made 100-watt transmitter because the department could not acquire a commercial transmitter. The owner of the set originated from Australia and broadcasting began with a voice with an Australian accent sending out a 'News-Letter', a special item of broadcasting which until recently occurred every Friday evening. This service continued uninterrupted for some years until it was replaced by a commercial quarter kilowatt transmitter. In 1954 a more powerful transmitter was installed at the Government wireless station to provide a broadcasting service in the evenings.

The Broadcasting Service now operates as a government department yet on an independent management basis under a local officer. After the 1982 conflict and with the presence of a garrison on the Islands, BFBS (British Forces Broadcasting Service) programmes were introduced, and the hours of broadcasting extended from the previous two hours in the mornings and four to six hours in the evenings, to a schedule which commences with a 'Breakfast Show' at 0600 hours then runs through till 14.30. There is a two-hour break before afternoon programmes start, taking transmission through until 22.30 in the evening, daily, throughout the Islands. BFBS announcers at present operate through the FIBS (F.I. Broadcasting Station) and the combined service provides many interesting features. These include the local, increasingly popular and important 'News Magazine' most evenings, figuring items of local interest, interviews and snippets of information; full coverage of visits, meetings and other outstanding events are presented regularly. Extensive use is made of BBC transcription material, and BBC World Service News and sports bulletins are re-transmitted from the studio on their FM and SW frequencies. Record request programmes are on the increase to include members of the Forces posted on the Islands—all considerable changes from the day, in 1920, when an operator at the Stanley wireless station tuned in to a programme from South America and, realising he was listening to something new, rang people up on the telephone system to let them hear it over the line.

There are very few television aerials; sets have been brought into the Islands in the hope of picking up South American stations but with little success. During the short-lived Argentine occupation of the islands in 1982 a number of colour sets were introduced and offered for sale to the public at low cost, and programmes were shown daily for a time using a transmitter brought by the Argentines and installed three days after the invasion!

Radio Telephone Service

The most important form of internal radio communication is the government operated radio telephone service. At one time respectfully code-named 'Radio Edith' after an operator who held the post for many years, there is a network of approximately 40 radio transmitters. Every settlement is netted to the main control in Stanley. This service started in 1950 and for some remote places is the only form of communication.

In 1938 several stations had private radio-transmitters of low power used for local communications. In 1922 Mr George Dean of Pebble Island installed a small station and thus maintained contact with Stanley. Power for this station was from a hand-turned generator and after some diligent practice, the operator acquired the knack of turning the generator handle with one hand whilst using the other to operate the morse key.

148

Since the start of the present system, the traffic handled by the R/T service has grown every year and can probably be related to the comparatively swift rate at which the general standard of living has risen in the settlements. Mail communications being rather erratic, the service is used regularly for ordering stores from Stanley.

In 1968 7,693 telegrams were received and sent over the system. This does not, however, give an accurate picture of the actual use of the R/T, for apart from telegrams, a preliminary daily schedule is held with every station, some giving a regular daily weather report for the air service and meteorological station. Many general enquiries and requests are made over the R/T, such traffic far exceeding the total number of telegrams. The service operates daily for twelve hours and a 'listening watch' is kept overnight. It is also used by medical officers to give advice to patients in the camps. For a charge, individuals wishing to communicate direct with a settlement may use the service.

Wireless Telegraphy

The loss of shipping around the Falkland Islands undoubtedly had some bearing on the installation of wireless communications with the outside world. Vessels stranded on these coasts had no means of contacting their agents, relying on other shipping to inform them of their fate. Lloyd's were severely handicapped and although they had established an agency within the islands the need for some swifter form of communication with this outpost was called for. A station was established by the Marconi Wireless Telegraph Co. some three miles out of Stanley, capable of reaching Buenos Aires and Montevideo. There being no electrical power available, power was supplied to the spark-type transmitter by a $15\frac{1}{2}$hp oil engine driving the five kilowatt generator. The station was equipped with two sets of receivers and most of the operation was carried out at night. Messages were telegraphed over the telephone line from the lighthouse, which ran past the station. The first tappings were heard on 18 September 1912 and on the night of 23 October 1912 the first official communication was made by the Governor to the Commanding Officer of HMS *Active*, at that time in Montevideo. A congratulatory message was also forwarded to the King at the same time.

Submarine Cable

A submarine cable was laid in 1915 to link the islands with Montevideo, a distance of some 1,200 miles. But the wireless link proved to be the more enduring. Not long after the cable was laid, it broke at some point between the islands and Montevideo. Repaired by the cable-laying vessel *Colonia* it operated until 1921, when it broke again and was closed down by its operators, the Western Telegraph Co. Today the only reminder of its existence is a small cottage tenanted by one of the medical officers. This building was the terminating point of the cable and is still called 'Cable Cottage'.

Other Transmitters

During the latter part of World War I, the Admiralty installed a powerful spark transmitter at Stanley with an array of high aerials which dominated the horizon to the west of the town. It is difficult to ascertain just how much power was applied to the system at the time of the first trial transmission but many miles of wiring were burnt out as if struck by lightning. Modifications had to be made before this new monster transmitter was eventually tamed. Such was its power that on one occasion the signals transmitted were picked up by a sloop of the United States Navy on patrol in the North Sea.

The wireless station had not been in commission for many years before the invention of the wireless valve made it obsolete and the costly installation with its large electric generators was never used again. Today much of the original installation stands as a memorial to naval activity in the days of the Cape Horn route. It stands like a blot on the Falklands' landscape but it would be too costly to remove it.

During 1928 a great improvement to the wireless telegraph

150

service was achieved by operators at Stanley and South Georgia, when they constructed and wired up components of their own making to convert the existing transmitter to short wave service. Direct radio contact was first established with Norway and then England, resulting in reduction in the cost of telegrams to England. This contact with Norway was also an important step, for whaling activities in South Georgia were at their peak and a large percentage of the personnel were Norwegian. Telegrams were passed via the Falklands and resulted in considerable revenue for the Colony.

Modern Communications System

With the erection of a satellite tracking station by the European Space Research Organisation (ESRO) in 1968 and increased activity by the Radio and Space Research Station, it was recognised that there was a need for a more modernised system of international communications. In 1966 four $7\frac{1}{2}$ kilowatt transmitters were installed at the existing wireless station, together with rhombic aerials beamed on London.

ESRO also needed a private teleprinter circuit between Stanley and their centre at Darmstadt in West Germany; so a multichannel teleprinter circuit was installed, working to the United Kingdom. Private circuits were also leased to SRC/RSRS and the British Antarctic Survey was provided with an immediate link between the BAS bases and their headquarters in London. There was also a public telegram channel and a public overseas telephone service. In late 1973 the ESRO station closed down, although the British Antarctic Survey still has its circuit between BAS bases and their headquarters in Cambridge.

In 1974 the handling of external communications was taken over by Cable & Wireless Ltd. In 1975 this company introduced a Telex service which at the present time operates ten hours per day. Since the commencement of Telex its increasing popularity world-wide has also spread to the Falklands, where there is a growing demand from the public sector for this service. There is also the public telegram channel, which operates for ten hours a day and the public overseas telephone service to London which was opened on 4 December 1968. The circuit operates for two hours per day and handles calls to most parts of the world, via London. (For alterations since the 1982 conflict, see Chapter 11.)

As part of the Communications Agreement between Great Britain and Argentina a direct public telephone service between Stanley and Buenos Aires was opened on 18 April 1972. The service operated for three hours per day. Special 'internal' rates were charged for calls to Buenos Aires.

Up to the 1982 conflict, Stanley Airport had its own communications equipment, operating two 5kW HF transmitters. There were two non-directional navigation beacons, one of which was for use by aircraft navigating to the Islands, the other a low-powered unit for airstrip location. The latter was an independent unit powered by a wind generator. Stanley Airport had an airport approach system, known as a Visual Approach Slope Indicator (VASI).

In the operation of their Fokker aircraft, Lineas Aereas del Estado (LADE) had their own wireless communications. Operating from their Stanley office, the 'station' was part of the general LADE network in Argentina.

Amateur Radio

The amateur radio operator has his own niche in the communications system of the Falkland Islands. The VP8 call sign from the Islands and British Antarctic territories is much in demand as a contact by other amateurs. The amateur has played an important part in the communications history of the Falklands, with amateur radio sets being used when official circuits have failed. In the past, it was often the 'ham' who was the first to receive incidental news.

In 1979 a change in the Wireless Telegraphy Regulations permitted part of the 2m amateur band to be used for social, commercial and limited business purposes in addition to normal amateur use. This led to a large investment in amateur VHF equipment and the establishment of an extensive private communications network, especially in the camp. The total number of current amateur licences is well over 300, a figure representing

Page 153 (above) The MV *Forrest* offloading supplies at a settlement jetty: (below) Stanley Airport in pre-war days showing airport control tower and terminal building. The aircraft is a Fokker 28 operated by LADE

Page 154 The SS *Great Britain* lying in Sparrow Cove prior to her salvage

one sixth of the estimated total population of the Falkland Islands. The majority of these operate only in the 2m band.

SHIPWRECKS AND DISASTERS

The Great Britain

In 1843, when the *Great Britain* was first floated at Bristol, she was the largest ship in the world and considered to be a tremendous feat of engineering. Of nearly 3,500 tons she was one of the first ships to be constructed of iron and one of the earliest ships to be driven by propeller. Designed by the famous engineer Isambard Brunel in 1838 as a paddle steamer, she was re-designed during her construction for screw propulsion. She was the first iron-built, screw-driven vessel to cross the Atlantic.

For many years she operated on the Australian run between Liverpool and Melbourne but in 1875 her Australian voyages ended and she was sold in 1881 to be re-sold in 1882 to A. Biggs & Sons & Co. She reappeared as a sailing ship, her iron hull sheathed in wood and on 6 February 1886 she sailed for Panama with a cargo of coal. Off the Horn she, like many before her, suffered a gale and she was partially dismasted. She ran for Port Stanley for repairs but on her arrival was condemned and sold to the Falkland Islands Company as a hulk.

Until 1933 she was used for storage purposes, then abandoned. In 1936, Governor Henniker-Heaton proposed plans for her restoration and preservation and an appeal was made to the citizens of Bristol for the required funds, estimated at £10,000. The project was abandoned, however, and the vessel was eventually beached in a cove outside Stanley. In 1966 interest in her restoration was taken by the San Francisco Maritime Museum and associates, and in 1969 she was the subject of a BBC feature film. An appeal was launched by the Brunel Society requesting £150,000 for her return and restoration to England.

Early in 1970 the Anglo-German consortium of Risdon Beazley Ulrich Harms Ltd was contracted to carry out salvage operations using a submersible pontoon. On March 25 1970 the German salvage vessels *Varius II*, a tug of 724 tons gross, and the pontoon

Mulus III of 2,667 tons gross arrived in Port Stanley and on 24 April the tow to England began, a journey which took eight weeks. The *Great Britain* was returned to her original dry dock at Bristol, 127 years to the day after her launching.

The Fennia

A steel masted barque of 3,200 tons, the *Fennia* was built in France and registered in Le Havre as the *Champigny* in 1902. In 1921 she was sold to the Finnish Government and renamed, and in 1927 she left Cardiff with a cargo of coal briquettes, and was dismasted off Cape Horn in a severe gale. She turned for the Falklands and the Captain anchored outside Port William while negotiations were conducted with the Falkland Islands Company for a tow into port. The Captain of the vessel, who feared his ship would be condemned, would only accept the tow because of the fifty young cadets he had on board and not as a salvage case. However, *Fennia* remained in Stanley with her vast cargo which eventually became the property of the Company.

In 1967, *Fennia* was purchased from the Company and on 25 November 1967, towed by the Dutch tug *Ocean*, she began a voyage to the famous San Francisco waterfront. In 1982 she was reported to be still in Montevideo, Uruguay.

The Thetis *disaster*

On 22 June, 1893, the *Thetis* was launched from the shipyard of McMillan & Sons, Dumbarton, Scotland. A steel barquentine of 130ft long, she was constructed for the Falkland Islands Company. For eight years she operated in Falklands waters without serious mishap. On 27 July 1901, under Captain Thomas, she sailed out of Port Stanley for Salvador in the north of East Falkland. She carried a cargo of 170 tons deadweight, and on deck, lashed to the mast was a large iron 'sheep-dip'. This was unwelcome and was the cause of considerable concern. As though aware of impending danger, Captain Thomas forbade his wife to travel with him on this voyage, something she often did. As the ship passed through the Narrows that winter's morning, watchers saw r flag halyard suddenly break and her flag drop to the deck.

Another local vessel *Fair Rosamund*, passed *Thetis* on the
lowing day and later reported that she appeared to be making
avy going. She never arrived at her destination. On 3 August
e Falklands experienced one of the worst gales in memory. West
int Island reported that the seas rose thirty feet above normal
gh water mark, and huge rocks which a dozen men could not
t were swept into coast paddocks.

The *Richard Williams* went in search of *Thetis* but found
thing. It was reported, however, that the shores of islands to
e north-west were littered with small pieces of wreckage more
less intermingled with wool.

On 5 August sealers on Elephant Jason Island discovered large
nounts of wreckage. On another island further to the west more
eckage was picked up. The theory was that *Thetis* must have
ne down in the Jason Island area over 120 miles off her course.
xty-five years later, part of a ship's wheel and wheel box bearing
e letters 'THE' were discovered on a remote beach in the north-
stern extremity of East Falkland. If this belonged to *Thetis*,
nat of the wreckage found 120 miles away?

ss of the City of Philadelphia

On 13 May 1896, a three-masted, full-rigged ship was seen
aking for the entrance to Port William. She was flying a signal
questing a pilot. Being rather old and slow, the pilot ship
ictoria was unable to approach the vessel through rough sea
nditions and as night was falling she returned to Port
anley.

Very early on the morning of 14 May, Arthur Hardy, an
sistant lighthouse keeper at Cape Pembroke Lighthouse, rode
to Stanley to raise the alarm that a ship was in distress on the
lly Rock. Immediately, two vessels went to the scene of the
saster through darkness and storm. *Sissie*, a steam and sail
unch owned by the Falkland Islands Company, was first out
ith *Result*, a sailing vessel, following. Although both vessels drew
ose to the wreck, it was impossible to make a rescue attempt.

157

It was so dark that it was not possible even to make out the detail of the vessel. Her shape was very briefly exposed as the beam from the lighthouse caught her.

In an effort at one more rescue attempt *Sissie* returned to the entrance of Port Stanley for a ship's lifeboat. With this it was hoped they could close on the stranded ship. On *Sissie*'s return, however, the wreck was gone, nothing remained to be seen, and the vessel's identity was unknown. Local feeling ran high about the failure to rescue those on board but every attempt had been made with the means available to execute a rescue.

A week later, the Falkland Islands Government employed divers to investigate the Billy Rock in an attempt to discover the identity of the vessel. The work was dangerous, but the divers found that a vessel still lay beneath the water. Several articles were recovered and on their final dive the body of a woman was found in the rigging. From the articles recovered, enquiries were initiated. On 28 July 1896, a letter from the Board of Underwriters, New York, stated that from the evidence of goods salvaged, the ship was the *City of Philadelphia*, a wooden vessel of 1,384 tons belonging to W. F. Hogan & Co, Philadelphia. The vessel had been voyaging between New York and San Francisco and on board were thirty-one persons, including the Captain's wife, the only woman. It was later established that the ship had requested assistance when the weather endangered the vessel, so the Captain had decided to risk entering Port William.

The disaster came to the notice of shipping journal *Fair Play* which conveyed the feelings of mariners who for some years had been concerned about the lack of certain facilities in Port Stanley. A powerful steam tug was required, for although there were many kind hearts and willing hands, the disaster had demonstrated how powerless they were without a suitable vessel. Four years later the Falkland Islands Company purchased the 95-ton steam tug *Samson* which was built at Hull in 1888 and arrived in the Falklands on July 20 1900.

6   THE PEOPLE

WITH a population of just over 1,000 people Stanley has the proportions of a village with capital city status. Workers are mainly connected with administration, trading and construction. These last live on the outskirts of the town. The largest general store belongs to the Falkland Islands Company but there is also a 'Stanley Co-op' and several smaller shops which are privately owned. There are no cleaners or shoe menders and at present there is no bakery. (See 'Service Businesses', Chapter 11.)

Life in the Camp

Falkland Islanders never use the word 'countryside'. All the area beyond Stanley town boundaries is called the 'Camp' from the Spanish word 'campos'. If a person from Stanley goes on holiday to a farm settlement he goes 'to camp'. A travelling teacher is called a 'camp teacher', likewise there are 'Camp dentists' and 'Camp doctors'.

Each settlement forms its own tiny village with the houses grouped together and a small store which is sometimes open only on certain days of the week, although this system is very elastic.

There is a quietness about settlement life, quite different from Stanley, and although the camp is the hub of industry and there is a time limit on each season's work, settlement life has not been caught up in the rush of clock-watching. Although their individual jobs may differ, all work is aimed at wool production and this has produced a tight communal spirit.

In Stanley the communal spirit has a tendency to be divided

between the 'Kelper', the name given to those born and bred in the islands, and the ex-patriates who are basically a floating population. However, the two groups benefit from each other's experiences and knowledge which are readily and willingly accepted by both parties. The air service has done much to dispel the isolation felt on camp settlements and radio also helps to integrate the two forms of life just as the daily broadcasts inform the population of latest events in Stanley and the camp.

With the lack of sophisticated shops and general shortage of varied provisions, Falkland Islanders and newcomers to the islands must be prepared to experiment with various jobs which, in other circumstances, they might not attempt. There are many expert breadmakers and dinner parties with imaginative cooking become a popular form of entertainment. One of the greatest challenges to a newcomer is the correct use of the peat stoves which are used for heating the house and water and for cooking, although oil-fired appliances are now more widespread.

All households must be prepared to work efficient vegetable gardens and potatoes, root crops and greens are generally grown. Very small amounts of fresh vegetables are available locally but in general, if one does not work a garden one must resort to tinned or dried vegetables. Some fresh fruit is imported sporadically from Britain.

The chores of camp life have seen many changes. A major job over fifty years ago, was that of candle making. Candles were made from the web fat of sheep, sometimes with the addition of Sperm whale oil. This oil was collected from dead whale found on the beaches or picked up from the wrecked cargo of a whaling vessel. Such oil was eagerly sought after as when it was mixed with tallow, it made a better product. Later, paraffin lamps replaced candles and in more recent times small generators have supplied light and power to even the most remote shepherds' houses.

With the major introduction of shepherds from Scotland and the outer Isles, which began about 1852, there was probably a slight influence on the making of homespun clothing, with

160

atural dyes being produced from lichens and mosses found owing about the camp. Although not a common practice the t is kept alive by a Spinners and Weavers Guild which has embers both in the camp and in Stanley.

An important job of the man in camp, which developed into a inter pastime and recreational art, was gear-making from raw de. From the style and naming of the various pieces of horse-ar produced, this appears to be an art left behind by the Spanish aucho. Gear-making was one of the many arts which indicated e adaptability of the Kelper. It survives today, although it is not e common occupation that it once was.

Many Falkland Islanders are talented amateur painters, others re self-taught musicians. In the past, men who had never made cartwheel before set to and produced a master wheelwright's oduct. Perhaps, where the Kelper has trailed behind in academic elds, he has gained an order of merit in other directions.

beech and Dress

The Kelper has developed over the years an accent not unlike at developed in other English emigrant territories. Although not broad as the Australian accent, a percentage of the Kelpers do ave an accent which is akin to that of the Australian. The South merican continent has little influence and very few people speak panish.

Dress, both in Stanley and the camp, has followed the pattern English dress of the day. Rennie remarked in 1855 on the uality of dress, saying that any stranger seeing the people on olidays with their families might doubt if there were any working ass in the Islands. (Modifications of English dress to suit the pe of work and climate were adopted in the camp.) However, e Spanish gaucho's outfit of poncho, wide-brimmed hat, riding ots and wide-legged trousers (bombachas), were also popular. oday, jeans and anoraks are perhaps the most popular form of ress. There is an ever-increasing use of English mail order cata-gues and fashions remain abreast of the outside world.

161

THE PEOPLE

Holidays

Many people in the islands work on contract or conditions which allow them a holiday abroad every $2\frac{1}{2}$, 3, 5 or 7 years. These 'leaves' are passage-paid with full salary for the duration, usually three to five months. Most people choose to take these holidays in England although in rarer cases people have travelled further afield, paying the difference in travelling expenses themselves.

Ex-patriates working on contract usually try to make contact with people of similar interests living in camp, allowing them to see camp life when on holiday from work in Stanley. It has been said many times that one hasn't seen the Falklands until one has visited camp. Without doubt visits to camp settlements are also an attraction as a break from normal routine and the more adventurous have their own tent equipment. Workers on sheep stations, of course, like to spend holidays in Stanley and they also visit other settlements for annual sports meetings.

EDUCATION

The Falkland Islands Government is responsible for education throughout the colony. Schooling is free and it is compulsory for children in Stanley to attend school from the age of five to fifteen years. In the camp school attendance is compulsory for children of between five and fifteen years living within one mile of a settlement school and for children between seven and fifteen years living within two miles of a school.

There are two schools in Stanley, one for infants and juniors and the other for seniors. The main block of the senior school was opened on 9 October 1907 but was refitted after the interior had been destroyed by fire in 1970. It includes a laboratory/woodwork/metalwork block.

The present infant/junior school has a main building which was opened in 1955, and an additional wing with two classrooms opened in 1968. In 1983 200 children were receiving education

162

in Stanley schools. The figure of 200 was exceeded for the first time in 1968.

Camp Education

For children living in outlying houses and some island settlements, teaching remains the responsibility of a travelling camp teacher who is assigned a number of stations to look after. The system generally results in one group or family of children receiving two weeks' schooling from a teacher, with a lapse of about four weeks before his return. During the interim period the children have to rely on the use of correspondence work prepared by the Camp Education Office team and sent out in ten-day batches. Video has now been introduced to camp education, subjects of educational value being recorded in Great Britain and sent out for despatch to the camp. The system does however still rely on the availability of private video sets on the settlements. In 1983 a total of 135 children were receiving education in settlement schools or camp houses.

Darwin Boarding School

In 1951 as a gift to the Colony, and to mark their centenary year, the Falkland Islands Company offered to build a school at their main station. In 1956 the Darwin Boarding School was opened. It could accommodate forty boarders, received from all camp stations of the Falklands, and also catered for a number of day pupils. The school operated as a boarding school until 1980. It was destroyed by fire during the action to re-take the Darwin-Goose Green area from Argentine occupation, in May 1982. (For present and future developments and the school hostel in Stanley see also Chapter 11.)

In 1956, J. L. Waldron Ltd built a similar but smaller school at their Port Howard Station. At present the school has no boarders.

Teaching Staff

The staff of the Islands' education department at present

consists mainly of certificated teachers, numbers in 1983 being 19 certificated and one uncertificated. There is a Superintendent of Education who is responsible for general administration, with camp education coming under a Camp Education Supervisor plus a staff of three. In 1983 five of the teaching staff were itinerant camp teachers. Furthermore, there are some ten 'farm teachers' whose main responsibility is the educational welfare of the individual farms on which they work. Farms employing such teachers receive a subsidy and material assistance from the Falkland Islands government. It has often been the practice for farms to employ a teacher/book-keeper, although the dual role is slowly being discontinued.

Qualified teaching staff and camp teachers are recruited in Britain by the Ministry of Overseas Development. Such staff usually have contracts for two or three years' service.

Overseas Education

Within the framework of the Communications Agreement between Britain and Argentina of August 1971, the Argentine government offered unlimited places in schools in that country with scholarships provided. This arrangement commenced in 1972, since when some thirty children have received schooling in Argentina at five different schools in Buenos Aires and Cordoba. Under a recent scheme financed by the British Council a limited number of students from the Islands are receiving higher education in England. The scheme commenced in 1979 and a small number of students have attended a Sixth Form at a school in Rye, Sussex.

History of Education

The first qualified teacher was George A. Clarke, who was appointed in London on 9 November 1859. He arrived in Stanley with his wife early in 1860. The salary of the schoolmaster was then made up of £44 from the government, £12 from the War Office for the schooling of children of the marine detachment

d a further supplement from the settlers who paid 1s per month
r each of their children attending. The children of the soldiers
id 1½d. per month. In 1860 a girl's school run by Mrs Clarke
s opened. Remuneration came solely from fees paid by the
rents and in 1861 £8 per year was paid by the Colonial
overnment. In 1861 the number of children attending the two
ools was 117.

In 1882 the school became completely separate from the church
d although it had been Dean Brandon who put education in
e Falklands on a firm footing, the colonial chaplain no longer
d any influence in the day-to-day operation of the schools.

Although attendance had grown, the total number of children
eiving tuition represented only a proportion of those eligible
r school, and it was not until 1891 that education for Stanley
ildren between the ages of 5–13 was made compulsory.

HEALTH

ith the introduction of immunisation, most dangers of serious
idemic have been removed, although periodically mild epi-
mics of a form of enteritis, locally known as 'Stanley Sickness',
eep through the population as do forms of the common
fluenza virus, brought in from the outside world.

Although sanitation has been a problem in the town and
mained so to some degree until recent times, a high standard
housekeeping was maintained. Most of the womenfolk take
eat pride in their houses which through the entire history of
e islands have maintained a great similarity with the style of
e British home.

The two most important health hazards in the islands appear
have been tuberculosis and hydatid cyst. Tuberculosis is now
rarity in the Falklands but contract workers from England until
cently needed a chest X-ray before leaving for the Islands.

Although hydatid cyst was known to exist in the islands some
ars ago, intensive preventive methods have been undertaken
ly since 1970.

DIET AND GARDENING

Diet today is influenced by a number of factors. Modern forms of packaged foods have given the Islanders a fairly wide choice. Frozen food was practically unknown before the 1960s, but the prices are high for most of it has to be imported from the United Kingdom. With the growth of the sheep industry and the fall of cattle production, the mainstay of beef changed to mutton, which became and still is the main item of food, so much so that it is often referred to as '365'. For many families this forms the basis of the three main meals of the day. In 1844 beef was sold at twopence per pound, and it was delivered to a household in the form of a quarter of an animal. Prices varied little over one hundred years and in 1980 beef was sold at only 16p per pound for hindquarter meat and 14p per pound for forequarter; mutton, which is supplied by the quarter animal, was also sold at 14p per pound.

The indigenous wild Upland Goose remains an important item of food in the Islands and although the live bird is condemned by the sheep industry for the amount of grass it eats, no one condemns the welcome change it makes in the islanders' diet.

Few species of cultivated fruits are successfully grown in the Falklands. Important pollinating insects such as bees, although they have been introduced at different times, can not survive the boisterous climate. However, excellent strawberries, raspberries, gooseberries and redcurrants are grown and wild berries such as diddle dee, tea berries and wild strawberries, are gathered and eaten fresh or turned into preserves. When possible fresh fruit was imported from South America, sometimes by small syndicates, a method adopted to avoid the retail charges. Imported fruit is however not a common form of diet and its distribution is regrettably largely restricted to Stanley.

Unfortunately, camp people can maintain supplies of milk and butter only for their own use and large quantities of tinned and dried milk, butter and cheese are imported. The small dairy in

166

Stanley has difficulty at present to supply the needs of the town owing to numerous problems. (See 'Agricultural Enclave', Chapter 11.)

Penguin eggs played a very important part in the diet of the settlers. Although the consumption of 'wild eggs' has decreased of late years, they continue to be eaten. Probably de Bougainville's party were the first to find penguin eggs and their search for geese eggs is mentioned.

Cooking Methods

Various methods of cooking have been used according to the means of the individual. The Spanish gaucho adopted those suited to his life in the open camp and cooking was often over roughly-made grates in the open. Governor Moody referred to the Suffolk Grate which, he said, answered best for peat fires.

An interesting system adopted in the Islands, although the origin of its name is obscure, was the use of the 'shadro'. This was a large-capacity iron pot with a heavy, close fitting lid. Also named a 'camp-oven', it was used for all cooking whether it was bread, biscuit, roast or stew. Originally the 'shadro' was employed with an outside fire and the pot was buried in the hot ashes and left to cook the contents slowly. The 'shadro' remained in use for many years and is still used by some shepherds when they are away from their settlement. When grates were built of stone or brick they were constructed to accommodate the 'shadro'. Beneath the grate was a large aperture to receive the hot ashes which were raked down on to the cooking pot and baking and roasting continued to be carried out in this manner. Some 'shadros' were fitted with small iron legs and the system of removing the heavy iron pot from beneath the grate was improved with the fitting of two iron runners in which the legs rested. The pot was then easily withdrawn and replaced by pulling or pushing the utensil with an iron hook along the fixed runners.

HOUSING

Brick buildings are uncommon in the Falklands. Notable excep-

167

tions are the Falkland Islands Company Colonial Manager's House, a section of Government House and a row of terraced houses known as 'Jubilee Villas'. (New housing, see Chapter 11.)

As all building materials must be imported most houses are wooden and galvanised iron has been used since 1847 for roofing. In 1964 several prefabricated houses were imported for the RSRS and ESRO personnel. These are made of concrete and timber sections.

Probably the most outstanding feature of the majority of houses is the glass porch or small conservatory built on the front entrance of most houses. These porches are usually filled with flowering pot plants.

There appeared to be no set pattern in the design of buildings until the late 1800s. Improvisation was very much the order of the day.

There are many examples remaining of the extent to which houses were constructed with material from ship wrecks. Waverley House, Offices of Estate Louis Williams, stands today on a foundation of booms and yards and the store sheds are almost entirely constructed from an array of yards, booms and masts. When this timber could not be utilised in the construction of dwelling houses it was used for peat sheds. Small deck houses were turned into outhouses and hen houses. An interesting feature, common to most boundary fences about the town of Stanley and a reminder of the shipping and wrecking trade, are fence posts cut from the ribs of wooden vessels. Barrel staves were commonly used for fencing battens and also appeared in the construction of stone and mortar walls of some early houses. Barrel furniture can still be seen today.

Hulks of old vessels condemned in the port found a ready use as storehouses. Those which would not remain afloat were beached on the foreshore of the town, to serve as foundations for jetties. A number are still in everyday use in Port Stanley.

Stone Buildings

The present Government House was started soon after Moody

d established the new seat of Government, but it was not until
53 that any number of stone buildings were erected by the
lonists. At this time the controversial Exchange building was
a forward state of construction. In 1862 Governor Moore,
ding the upkeep of wooden buildings costly, had a number of
ne cottages built and at this time laid plans for the construction
a new gaol in stone. This building, Governor D'Arcy remarked,
s the only other dwelling besides Government House which
uld be termed a house.

PEAT

he preparation of this most important fuel of the islands is a
ne-consuming occupation. Most men cut the peat needed for
eir households, with women and children helping with the
ckling'. The peat cutting season marks the coming of summer,
though cutting times vary greatly according to the individual
useholder's requirements. The average amount of peat cut per
usehold is about 150–180 cubic yards in its wet form, but after
veral weeks drying in 'rickles' (small piles of sods on the banks)
e amount carted is reduced considerably.

Machinery has been used for cutting but because of the situa-
on and formation of the peat banks, the conventional spade with
s sharpened edge and the small hole drilled in the blade to
duce suction by the wet sod, is still accepted to be the only satis-
ctory tool and is used by more than 99 per cent of those who
t peat.

ther Fuels

Diddle dee bush was undoubtedly used as a fuel by gauchos
hile working the interior, and was described in Captain Grey's
urnal and reports of 1837 as an important and useful fuel.
ven today, although it is not used a great deal, more than one
eat shed in the camp will produce a pile of this shrub for kindling
peat fire.

Coal has been imported from the very earliest times and today
gh grade coals are still imported into the Falklands in small

169

quantities. With the establishment of the Yacimientos Petroliferos Fiscales (YPF) fuel depot in 1976, natural gas and kerosene have now become fairly popular fuels for use in the home. The prices of coal and oil are still high and peat remains the most economical fuel and the only one of importance yet discovered in the Falklands. (See also Chapter 11.)

The Peat Slip

The poor tracks and the problems of carting naturally induced the early settlers to cut their peat as close to the town as possible. The system, was, however, rather haphazard and little attention was paid to draining off the water from the peat workings. They were situated on the brow of the hill with little firm ground to hold back the accumulated water and were an unforeseen threat to the settlement on the lower slope of the hill.

Just after midnight on Friday 29 November 1878, one of the inhabitants was awakened by the continuous barking of his dog. He discovered that his house was surrounded by a mass of semi-liquid peat several feet deep, that was moving down the hill at the rate of about four to five miles per hour.

At daybreak it was discovered that the water in the old peat workings had weakened the uncut sections. The whole mass had broken through and had been carried down the slope. In his report to the Governor, Arthur Bailey, Surveyor-General, described how the affected houses were completely shut off from communication with the rest of the town. Communication between the east and west ends of the town were severed except by boats. The peat lay about in confused heaps from the peat banks to the brow of the hill, a distance of about 250yds. At the top of the bog Bailey found a depression extending over an area of 9–10ac, the edges of which were cracking and filling up with water and threatening another accident. He immediately called upon the inhabitants to cut a trench at the back of the hill to drain off the water.

Page 171 (above) Carting peat about 1890–1900. Beaver Island settlement showing a typical camp house at that period; *(below)* peat carting today on the Stanley peat banks. The stack being carted would have been cut the previous summer, and left in this form over winter. Note the ex-WD vehicle, commonly used in the islands for such work

Page 172 (above) Meat delivery in Stanley. Mutton is still the most common form of meat and usually delivered by the quarter; (below) a camp shepherd on East Falkland. The horse gear is hand made and typical of that used in the Islands. Covering the saddle is a Cojinillo made from sheepskin

A Second Peat Slip

Drainage of the peat workings remained a problem and on the night of 2 June 1886 a second peat slip occurred, with more disastrous results. Arthur Barkly, the Governor, reported the peat slip as being similar to the previous one, but having taken place some two hundred yards further westward.

> A stream of half liquified peat over a hundred yards in width and four or five feet deep. It flowed suddenly through the town into the harbour, blocking up the streets, as to completely imprison the inhabitants. Fortunately as the night was wet and stormy almost everyone was indoors, and the few who were in the wrecked houses escaped in time. One child was unfortunately smothered in the peat, whose body has been recovered, but no other casualties are known to have occurred. An old man is however, reported to be missing this morning, and it is feared he may also have perished, as part of his house is almost filled with peat.

In this disastrous peat slip two persons died and much damage was done to property, including the Exchange Building, the clock tower of which was discovered to be three feet out of perpendicular.

LOCAL CUSTOMS

The annual collection of wild bird eggs, particularly penguin and albatross eggs, developed into an important event very early in the Colony's history. Today it is regarded as a traditional custom.

Until recently the school children were allowed a semi-official holiday on one day of the year to go 'egging'. To a degree this is still carried out in some camp areas. Egging week, as it became popularly known was an event for most settlers, and a day was usually fixed about November 9, to coincide with Lord Mayor's Day in England, for egging and a picnic combined. In the camp, egging may still take the form of a picnic for members of a settlement, but this now depends on when the birds start to lay.

The season was marked for people in Stanley by the arrival of local cutters bringing in large quantities of eggs from the outlying islands. At the public jetty the unloading and sale of a hold full of eggs was an event in itself. Often the eggs would have been placed loose in the holds and such was the weight placed on the lower layers that the bottom of the boat would be swimming in smashed and cracked eggs. It then became the work of the youngsters to descend into the holds to gather what they could for free.

Following the collection of eggs another important event is 'Gosling Hunting'. This is the taking of young Upland Geese which may start in November and go on into the New Year. For many camp people the young birds and lamb replace the Christmas turkey and other domestic fowl.

The collection of wild berries is often a family event for camp and town people. Berry picking generally starts in mid-January with the gathering of wild strawberries, followed by diddle-dee, ending in April when the tea berries are ripe.

Sports

Sports weeks which are usually held during the Christmas holiday in Stanley and sometime after the end of shearing in the camp, remain big events every year for Falkland Islanders and ex-patriates alike.

The date of the first race meeting is not known, although by 1875, Goose Green, Stanley had been specially levelled and drained for the purpose of holding horse races. Later the meetings were held in an area known as Whale Bone Bay. The first official sports meeting held at Stanley by the Stanley Social Club and Mutual Improvement Society, took place on 9 November 1889. In 1898 the meeting was again moved and held on the sands of Cape Pembroke but eventually in 1909 the 'Sports' found a permanent home in Stanley. At a cost of £70, a new race course was formed at the West end of the town.

Horse racing has remained the major attraction, with meetings held annually in Stanley and at Darwin. Meetings are also held each year on the West Falkland, most stations taking turn at playing host. In the earlier meetings, foot events were important and for a number of years a marathon was run. The course for this

174

event was between Stanley and the Cape Pembroke Lighthouse and back, an overall run of thirteen miles. Today, foot events are not so ambitious, being restricted to the race course.

Dances follow the sports meetings and another custom, 'The Two Nighter' has developed. Dances are held on two consecutive nights with race meetings held during the day. Dancing is very popular in the Islands and is a regular event on even the smaller camp stations. Weddings are generally a social occasion for many people. Receptions usually develop into well-attended dances.

Football, rugby and indoor sports are popular but probably the most outstanding for its long history of popularity is rifle shooting. Competition rifle shooting against visiting naval ships goes back to the 1800s. The Stanley Rifle Club started in 1887 and the Falkland Islands Volunteers formed their club in 1900. Other rifle clubs then followed in camp settlements both on the East and West Falklands.

The Stanley Rifle Club has continued to thrive in association with the Falkland Islands Defence Force and members regularly take part, not only in local competitions but in postal shoots with teams overseas. Besides a local Bisley meeting which has been held annually since 1928, the Falklands are represented yearly at the British Bisley Competition. Major successes of the club in this competition have been the winning of the Junior Kolapore Imperial Challenge Cup in the years 1930, 1934, 1947 and 1957 and the 'Barnett' Junior Mackinnon Imperial Challenge Cup in the years 1937, 1947 and 1948.

A further success for the club occurred in 1980 when its team won the Junior Mackinnon Trophy and came second in the Junior Overseas and Junior Kolapore. This notable success also secured the Nobel Prize for attaining the highest aggregate in the three junior team events.

A most memorable occasion for the Rifle Club however, and indeed for the Falklands, occurred in 1982 when a two-man team represented the Islands in the full-bore target-shooting event at the XII Commonwealth Games held in Brisbane, Australia.

THE PEOPLE

Entertainment

Amateur dramatics were flourishing in 1873. At this time the Government Store was used to stage the shows. In 1916 the Town Hall was opened and was proclaimed one of the finest pieces of local architecture of its day. Complete with stage and sprung floor dance hall, the building was the pride of the Islands. In 1944 the building was completely destroyed by fire. Its replacement stands today, but being constructed largely from concrete it has not the character of the former wooden building.

Although video is becoming increasingly popular, with no television network yet available, the cinema plays a leading role in entertainment in the Falklands as a whole. The first cinema came to the islands after enterprising efforts by a local Roman Catholic Priest, Father Migone, who started the operation in 1913 on the premises of St Mary's Church. At first the projector was operated from a bank of batteries charged from one of the Islands' first electric power plants. This had also been introduced on the initiative of Father Migone. The present system allows for a weekly showing of films in the Town Hall and Parish Hall of Stanley. Both are private concerns and many camp settlements have their own small cinemas. Films that are received in the Colony are either hired privately or loaned through the government central film library (See Chapter Two).

There are a number of Social Clubs in Stanley and the camp thus providing facilities for a variety of activities. All follow a style similar to that of a small English community. The first of these clubs was the Working Men's Social Club, in Stanley, which was formally opened in October 1970. Whist drives and darts matches take place regularly and when snow makes it possible sledging is enjoyed in winter by people of all ages, especially down the long, steep Philomel Hill.

Youth Organisations

In 1911 Governor Allardyce promised the youth of Stanley that a scout movement would be started and in the following November the Boy Scouts held their first meeting. One of their

176

first notable achievements, was the raising of funds for the *Titanic* Relief Fund in 1912.

The Boys Life Brigade was formed in 1944 by Captain McCubbing and men of the Royal Scots Regiment, who were stationed in the Falklands and, together with the Girls Brigade still operates today. The Girls Brigade started as a girls club in 1952, becoming a member of the Brigade in December 1953. A Youth Club was formed in 1966 for the older children of the community.

Military Parades

Small as the population of Stanley is, military parades continue to be well attended and it is customary to hold ceremonial parades on the Queen's Birthday,. Remembrance Sunday and on the anniversary of the Battle of the Falkland Islands.

War Contribution

The Falkland Islands contribution to the British war effort in the two world wars was remarkable. It gives an indication of how close and loyal are the ties with Britain.

During World War I, the colony contributed an aircraft to the Royal Flying Corps, together with substantial sums of money to various relief and other war funds. In 1916 as a contribution to the Imperial Loans a sum equal to ten per cent of the annual Customs revenue was voted, and was donated for a period of ten years.

In World War II, the Colony contributed gifts to the United Kingdom valued at over £70,000, including £20,000 for war charities. Ten Spitfires were bought and flew into action bearing the name 'Falkland Islands'. Considerable sums were also raised for the London Relief Fund, King George Fund and others. Private companies and individuals gave interest free loans to the war effort.

CRIME

An analysis of crimes committed over the period 1964 to 1969 shows that offences against local ordinances such as Licensing and Road Traffic are the highest (with some offences against property). Most crime has been traced to over-indulgence in drink and serious crime in the islands today is practically unknown.

Crime in the Past

The problems of 130 years ago could largely be traced to the floating population of sealers and whalers. Captain George Grey reported that the officer in charge of the British settlement at Port Louis, Lt Smith, had little means of making these men respect the British flag. The sealers were little better than pirates and it was only the frequent visits of British naval ships which prevented them from fighting amongst themselves for the different seal rookeries. One such sealing group consisted of some thirteen to twenty men all armed with rifles and having several whale boats. After an unsuccessful sealing or whaling voyage it would not be unlikely that they would become pirates. Grey feared that in the event of the Islands being again abandoned, they would become a haven for runaway seamen, and Merchant ships which touched at the Islands would run considerable risks.

Governor Moody reported on April 8 1845 on a case of mutiny aboard the British Brig *Camoena* as an illustration of the state of the Colony at that time.

Two sailors who were drunk had excited the crew of the *Camoena* to mutiny. The two men were convicted and sentenced to fourteen days in the jail, a small wooden building which was also used as a hospital. Governor Moody then received a letter from the acting Chief Constable, reporting on the riotous behaviour of these prisoners. He also stated that a man of the Detachment, confined that day for being drunk had since obtained more liquor. Two other prisoners from the Detachment, sentenced to confinement with hard labour, had also obtained drink and as they had refused to work he had been obliged to place them in irons.

Corporal Watts, whom the Magistrate had sworn in as a constable, declared that he could not by himself, ensure the safety

178

of the prisoners in the present temporary jail. Surrounded as it was by so many drunken and disorderly people, he feared that the prisoners would break out and murder someone or burn the place.

Moody described the disorderly section of the community as being chiefly composed of men, formerly seamen in whale ships, sealers, foreigners and Spanish gauchos, who had been 'more or less accustomed to a reckless life' and who had influence over some others in the little township.

This influence continued and in 1846, when the population was about 270, Moody estimated that 106, mainly Spanish Indians, had been imported by Mr Lafone for his establishment in the East Falkland. By 1852, the entry of Spanish Indians from the River Plate was causing some alarm, largely from the irresponsible actions of Lafone's agent in the Islands, Mr Williams. The Indians imported as gauchos were employed during the summer months, but as soon as weather conditions became unsuitable for hunting wild cattle, Mr Williams discharged them, usually destitute. The consequence was that they flocked to the town, half-clothed and physically in a poor state, spending much of their time in the public houses.

Governor Rennie requested Mr Williams to remove the Indians and suggested that in future he should retain a portion of their salary to use as payment for their passage back to the River Plate area. Williams refused this payment and as a result the Aliens Ordinance was brought in.

On March 18 1834, Rennie reported the first murder which had come to the notice of the authorities. In this case one Spaniard had knifed another. Four more murders took place in the Islands, although only one of these was committed by an English subject living in the Colony. This was Christopher Murry who was sentenced to transportation for fourteen years for the manslaughter of his wife in the year 1858.

Many of the problems could be traced to drink, the requirements of the small population being catered for by eight public houses in 1863. In an effort to curb the amount of liquor imported

179

Moody had, during the early part of his tour, imposed a Spirits Tax amounting to 20s per gallon. In 1850 an ordinance came the Falkland Islands Company, the only wholesale importers of liquor, were required to take out wholesale licences at a cost of £20 per year. This step brought complaints from the rival merchants as they pointed out that Publicans paid only £5 for their licence and yet were allowed to buy large amounts of spirits direct from the masters of visiting vessels.

In 1877, very soon after his arrival in the colony, Dean Lowther E. Brandon took steps against intemperance by forming the Stanley Total Abstinence Society. The original membership was about seventy but some months later had fallen to about forty.

150th Anniversary of the Falkland Islands: 1833–1983

To commemorate one-and-a-half centuries of continuous settlement, several activities were organised in the Islands. Despite coinciding with the aftermath of the 1982 conflict, it was decided to set aside one week in late February for celebrations to take place in Stanley. A good proportion of camp dwellers travelled to Stanley and a number of VIPs from England made the journey to share in the festivities. These included race meetings and connected events on Stanley Racecourse, rehabilitated after the scars left by the occupation and subsequent action. Concerts, dances, art and philatelic exhibitions together with other competitions and shows were very well attended, and a carnival, the closing event, proved a great success.

On 3 January, 150 years to the day when the Union flag was raised at Port Louis, a set of stamps was released to mark the occasion. The set, comprising eleven stamps, depicts periods, events and places that have played a significant part in the development of the Falklands and its community.

7   FISHERIES

COMMERCIAL fishing has never been developed in the Falklands. The only attempt was a small effort by Vernet from 1826 to 1831. It is recorded that in 1829 Vernet salted down eighty tons of fish which were sold in Brazil for £1,600. A large proportion of the fish caught was Mullet, fished with nets in the shallower tidal creeks about Port Louis but line fishing for Rock Cod also played its part in Vernet's business. After he had left the islands fish salting and curing continued at Port Louis on a scale suited only to the requirements of the diminished population. Vernet's attempt at founding a 'great national fishery' had ended.

In 1841 Whitington set up a new fish-salting establishment close to Port Louis which to this day is known as Salt House Point in Fish Creek. This business, however, did not reach the same proportions as Vernet's efforts.

During the years 1927–28 and 1931–32, trawling surveys were carried out by the *William Scoresby* under the direction of the Discovery Committee. Fish in large enough quantities to form important fisheries are generally found in relatively shallow waters around extensive coasts and particularly where currents meet. For these reasons certain areas close to the Falklands had promise. The Burwood Bank, south of the Falklands and covering an area of nearly 300sq mi, plus the 150,000sq mi stretching west and north-west from the Falklands to the South American coast all had suitable depths for trawling. In 1842 Governor Moody reported that cod fish were found in the latter area where the most comprehensive survey was carried out by the *William Scoresby*. Many edible fish were found, the most important being species of hake, which is already the basis of a trawling industry operating from the Argentine coast. The Burwood Bank was found unsuitable for trawling and although rich in invertebrate fauna, yielded few fish.

From these surveys it was considered that a trawl fishery based at Port Stanley could find a good supply of fish, while a suitable market for wet and dry salted fish could be found in South America.

In 1946 Governor Clifford proposed to the Colonial Office that the fishing industry should be developed. This was reformed into a scheme to supply fresh and cured fish primarily for local consumption. Regrettably, fish is still not a common item of diet for the average inhabitant of the islands. Supplies are dependent on a few individuals operating in much the same way as the early Colonists. In camp settlements 'fish walls' are used extensively, a system which has descended from Vernet's operations. These are rough stone constructions forming a wall across a tidal creek; on a rising tide fish come over the wall and are trapped behind it as the tide recedes. During those seasons when the species such as mullet and smelt tend to frequent the shallower waters, the 'walls' alone are an effective system of catching fish without the need for nets.

Freshwater Fisheries

Governor Moody reported to Lord Stanley in 1842 that small trout were to be found in the streams and freshwater lakes. These indigenous fish, of which there are three species (Chapter 8), have until recent years been a popular delicacy but with the introduction of an imported Brown trout (*Salmo trutta*) predation of the smaller fish has taken place, resulting in a reduction of the indigenous fish. The Brown trout was first introduced in 1948 to the main rivers on East and West Falklands and almost ten years later they were being caught as good-sized fish. The Brown trout has reverted to sea conditions coming up freshwater rivers to spawn. From a 16½lb specimen examined by the British Museum in 1965 it is evident that conditions are excellent for this species in Falkland waters. Average weights range between six and nine pounds.

Salmon ova have also been introduced, a suggestion once made with the offer of help in 1894 by the Marquess of Exeter. The results of this more recent introduction have yet to be seen but expectations run high for the future of freshwater fishing in the Islands.

SEALING

When Captain Byron anchored at the new-found harbour of Port Egmont, he reported that the beaches were crowded with Fur seal.

In 1767 when Port Egmont was settled, no mention was made of sealing activities, but in 1774 when the British withdrew their settlement, American and French sealers were round the Islands. They were probably not fully engaged in sealing, for in 1778 a French sealer from St Malo reported vast numbers of Fur seal on Saunders Island.

Captain Cook's publication of his discovery of Fur seals on the beaches of South Georgia in 1775 almost certainly led to the major exploitation of the seal in the Falklands. Probably the first large cargo of Fur seal skins, numbering some 13,000, was taken by the American sealing vessel *States* in 1784.

By 1785, sealers were leaving British ports, the Enderby Brothers of London being the first to send their vessels south. Whether they started sealing at the Falklands is not recorded but the following year a British vessel was sealing at Saunders Island, selling her skins to other vessels calling at the Islands. Fur seal skins were still being shipped by the Americans to China where high prices were obtained. Skins shipped to Britain, however, were only of minimum value, being used for tanning purposes. Not until Thomas Chapman of London, in 1796, discovered a method of processing Fur seal skins did the British sealers play a major part in the industry. The price of skins increased and Weddell reported that they brought between five and six dollars.

FISHERIES

By the end of the century an onslaught had started on the vast rookeries of seal at South Georgia. This almost certainly caused a diversion from the smaller and more isolated pockets of Fur seal in the Falklands.

Edmund Fanning made several visits to the Falklands and was probably the most successful sealer. His records illustrate the general trend of sealing in the Islands. He made his first visit in 1792 and recorded that the seal were up in great numbers on some of the outer islands.

Elephant seal hunting, or 'elephanting' as it was known, had also become important. This form of sealing developed along with the early whaling industry, for the elephants were taken for their oil. As with whaling, it is not clear when this form of sealing began in the Falklands, but it probably came with the establishment of de Bougainville's settlement soon after 1764.

During Fanning's first visit he saw forty vessels, mainly American and British, procuring seal around the Islands. Fanning was obviously more interested in the Fur seal but many vessels he mentioned would have been engaged in 'elephanting'. This industry was reaching a peak at that time and for some years remained the more steady form of sealing owing to the slower decline in numbers of the Elephant seal. The reason for this was that remuneration in proportion to labour expended was less.

On Fanning's second visit in 1798, sealing was still in progress, but not on the same scale as elsewhere in the Southern hemisphere. On Masafuera Island, off the Chilean coast, it was reported that year that more than a million skins were taken. Some 1,797 sealers from fourteen ships were engaged on the island taking Fur seal and during a seven year period 3,000,000 skins were taken. The pattern of destruction was similar at South Georgia where, by 1800, sealing became systematic and in 1881, 122,000 seals were killed.

For many years some of the harbours had been used as rendezvous by sealing vessels. New Island, West Point Island and other well protected harbours, mainly on West Falkland, became self-styled 'homes' of sealers. Depredations were extensive and the sealers considered that they had the right to seal as they wished. In 1836 Lt Smith warned American sealers that the Fur seal rookery on Volunteer Rocks belonged to the settlement. This caused a considerable amount of disagreement with the sealing masters, especially when they discovered that they could buy Fur seal skins taken from the rocks by the Port Louis settlers, at eight to ten Spanish dollars each. (A dollar was equal to 4s 4d). Sealing by this time was almost certainly declining. Commander Grey RN, on an extensive journey around the Falklands between December 1836 and January 1837, saw great quantities of 'fine seal' about the Islands, but although he visited several well known sealing areas, he reported few American sealing schooners. He also recorded that only ninety-three Fur seals had been taken from Volunteer Rocks. Considering that these were obtained at the height of the breeding season, his talk of great quantities is somewhat inconsistent.

In 1840 the first licence to seal was issued at a rate of £100 per annum, for the lease of the Fur seal rookery off Volunteer Point. There was a condition that the rookery was to be rested every alternate year, the first attempt at conserving seal stocks in seventy-five years of sealing. But this was for the control of one small rookery, close to Port Louis and under the very eye of authority. Depredations by American vessels continued elsewhere, but as Governor Rennie reported in 1853, he was powerless to carry out his warnings for he had no force to maintain control, which the sealers and whalers knew very well. (Chapter 3 : *Hudson* and *Washington*.)

The American Civil War stopped the sailing of New England sealers and after this war illicit sealing was never repeated on the same scale.

Local sealing

For some years after 1842, local sealing was limited to a few individuals who took out leases for seal rookeries close to Port Stanley. In 1854 only two sealing vessels were registered in the Falklands. But between 1855–60 there was a sudden impetus in local sealing activities. The Fur seals were still scarce (only five skins were obtained from the Volunteer Rocks in 1858), but the main interest was oil and skins from the sea lion, *Otaria byronia*. No restrictions were imposed and wholesale destruction followed. The operation, which lasted until once again there were few seal left, was profitable. A cargo of 650 skins and 1,600 gallons of oil was worth £500 to a vessel's crew of eight.

The years 1860–1 saw a sudden change from local sealing to operations off the Patagonian coast where the Fur seal, undisturbed for a number of years, had increased. At this time, eight vessels were registered in the Islands and those which were large enough to work the Patagonian coasts and Cape Horn regions left the Falklands sealing grounds for the more lucrative prize.

In the Falklands oil was the main interest. In 1862 when the sea lion was low in numbers, oil from seal and whale valued at £2,666 was exported from the Colony. At this point, other sources of oil were drawing attention and in 1863 oil valued at £6,719 left the Falklands, penguins having been added to the source.

In 1870 £3,650 worth of oil was exported, seal oil fetching between 1s 9d and 2s 6d per gallon. Fur seals taken from the Islands made a total export worth £377, skins fetching from 12s 6d to 17s 6d each. The same year, £1,338 worth of sea lion skins were exported. In the following year seals were reported officially as being scarce. Sea elephant was thought to be extinct in the Falklands and sealing around Cape Horn and the Patagonian coast had again almost come to a close.

About 1871 American sealers wandered further south to inspect the old sealing grounds in the South Shetlands. The Fur seal of that area had now been left for some twenty years and had increased to such an extent that further exploitation was again possible. Another rush south took place. The American schooner *Golden West* bound for London, was one of the first to call at Stanley from the South Shetlands with a full cargo of Fur seal skins and oil. During the next eighteen to nineteen years sealing vessels, mostly American, took another 35,000 animals from the

South Shetlands. Again the species was almost exterminated and when Larson, the Norwegian whaler, made a thorough investigation of the Islands in 1908 he was unable to find a single Fur seal. The species was considered extinct and not until Larson made a further trip south in 1929 was the species rediscovered.

In 1881 the Falkland Islands Government attempted to protect their remaining stocks of Fur seal by naming a closed season. During the summer months, naval patrols were maintained around the coasts to ensure protection of the rookeries. In 1889 the first tax was imposed and licences were issued for sealing. For the next ten years local individuals worked as earlier sealers had done. Living in close proximity to rookeries, often for many weeks or months, sealing became a game of waiting. Hauls were small, a sealer's quota of only 100–200 seal rarely being obtained. In 1900 seal-skin exports totalled £1,500.

Pelagic Sealing

In 1901 the exported seal skins brought £1,800. That December Canadian schooners from Halifax, Nova Scotia, arrived in Stanley Harbour. These sealers were engaged in pelagic sealing, the seal being shot at sea from small dories working off the parent schooner. For some years these vessels re-shipped their cargoes, provisioned and sheltered over winter in Stanley and their names became familiar to the residents of the town; the *Markland, Edith R. Balcom, Alice Gertrude* and *Beatrice L. Corkum* were but a few.

Pelagic sealing was most profitable. By 1903, 22,360 Fur seal and skins were shipped through Port Stanley and because they were caught outside the Colony they were not liable to the tax imposed by the Falkland Islands Government.

There was much speculation as to exactly where these large hauls of seal were made. Undoubtedly large numbers of the seal taken by the Nova Scotia schooners were from more northern waters, probably even from the north Pacific and consequently some originating from South America. Poaching, however, was confirmed and a Canadian schooner was caught taking seal from

187

the Falklands. The suspicions of some residents were also confirmed when a log book from one of the schooners was found on the shore of Stanley Harbour. Log entries mentioned seal being taken from the Jason Islands.

Skins trans-shipped through Stanley were exempt from tax, so the Colony lost a considerable amount of revenue, a particularly annoying fact when some of the skins were coming from the Falkland Islands! Governor Grey-Wilson decided to remedy this and in June 1904 a Seal Ordinance was passed levying a charge of 10s on all trans-shipped skins. Notice of the intended tax created considerable consternation among Nova Scotia sealers, and probably caused the added depredations which occurred about this time.

For more than a year no skins were trans-shipped in the Falklands. The sealers maintained that prices of skins had fallen and the tax imposed would render their business unprofitable. For business people in Port Stanley, the now infrequent visits by the Canadian vessels meant that much lucrative trade was lost. Local agitation followed and on 14 May 1906, on advice from the Executive Council, the Order relating to the tax was revoked and duty was put at 1s per skin trans-shipped or exported from the Colony.

A few sealers returned and so did poaching, but this was not entirely the work of the Nova Scotia sealers. Vessels from the coast were now seen amongst the Jason Islands and on one occasion a small steamer, built on the lines of a south sea whaler, with sacking covering her name plate had the effrontery to call at Carcass Islands requesting water. She then left for the Jasons to pick up her crew who had been left sealing. That year the Nova Scotia sealing schooner *Baden Powell* was wrecked on Elephant Jason Island, close to the main Fur seal rookery of the area—that she had been poaching seemed obvious.

After 1908 the Canadian sealers did not have the success of previous years, reporting that the seals were no longer to be found on their original feeding grounds. That year only one local vessel, the *Magellanes*, was engaged in Fur sealing. She also found

Page 189 (above) A pre-war parade being held on HM the Queen's Birthday. His Excellency the Governor of the Falkland Islands Sir Cosmo Haskard, MBE, KCMG, inspecting detachments of the FIDF, Royal Marines and Girls Life Brigade. The parade is being held on Ross Road, Stanley: (below) hand shearing on one of the smaller offshore islands. The system although still adopted is now only used by one or two small farms

Page 190 (above) Immature Elephant seal with Rockhopper penguins. Unlike some other seal species the birds show no fear of this docile type. The tussac grass growth in relation to the shore line is typical of many offshore tussac islands; *(below)* adult and sub-adult male sea lions (Otaria byronia) on a typical boulder beach. Unlike the Elephant seal which is largely reliant on its stomach muscles for movement on land, sea lions utilize fore and hind limbs in a form of walking movement

difficulty in obtaining seals and brought in only seventy-three skins. Again the rookeries had not been allowed to recover before being exploited to a point where it was hardly profitable for local sealers to continue working them.

In 1909 Governor Allardyce said the seal industry was unsatisfactory, estimating that from the four or five remaining rookeries the yearly increase was approximately 1,000 animals. A few seal were taken annually but the Canadians found it unprofitable and eventually left. Poaching continued, however, with South American vessels taking what they could get from the now-diminished stocks. With World War I poaching ceased owing to the protection afforded by British naval vessels. The Fur seal multiplied, but only to the extent that if they were left untouched they might form the basis for herds of the original size.

In 1921 an Ordinance was passed affording complete protection for the Fur seal, a move which had been prompted by the recurrence of poachers from the coast. An Admiralty drifter, *Afterglow*, was purchased as an armed patrol vessel and a guard was maintained for a number of years on Elephant Jason Island overlooking one of the principal Fur seal rookeries.

In 1928 the Falkland Islands and Dependencies Sealing Company was started to extract oil from the apparently numerous sea lions. After its first year the company worked from a land station at Albemarle on West Falkland and it continued operations until the Depression in 1931. Work started again in 1935, continuing until 1940 with a short break in 1938. Some 220 tons of oil were produced in the first year valued at £6,000. The next year production rose to 550 tons but demand was not so great and only 450 tons were sold at £27 per ton. In 1931 prices fell to £15 per ton and from 1935-40 production was very poor. During the total operation, 39,696 seals were taken.

In 1949 the South Atlantic Sealing Company was formed, sponsored by the Colonial Development Corporation. In 1950 they began sealing from the Albemarle station, their aim being to utilise the sea lion fully by taking oil, pelts, meat and bone oil. The first season was a failure, probably owing to faulty equip-

191

ment and inexperience and in the following year the sponsors took over the venture. By the end of 1952 they too failed to make it a success because of technical trouble and a shortage of seals. These operations accounted for a total of 3,045 sea lions.

In 1962 a sealing licence was granted to a local operator to take 1,500 sea lion skins with a view to finding a market in the tanning industry. In 1964, the first year of operation, 37 skins were shipped to London. The licence was renewed but less than 400 skins were taken in 1966. This apparently necessitated the taking of a very large proportion of the seal population from two small off-shore tussac islands where it was alleged the seal were disturbing the natural vegetation.

A New Export

During the early 1960s the capture of live animals, mainly Elephant seal, for export to zoological gardens in Britain and Europe developed significantly. With the facilities afforded by direct shipping between the Falkland Islands and Britain, animal collectors showed increasing interest in this trade. On 10th May 1966 these exports were licensed and a tax was levied. The export of seal and other wildlife was officially called to a halt in 1972, although records show that this embargo was temporarily lifted for one collector in 1979.

WHALING

In 1725, a small fleet of British whaling vessels sailed for the South Seas; whether they worked round the Falklands is not known. Five years later the first fleet of American ocean-going whalers left for the Azores, Cape Verde Islands, the African and Brazilian coasts and is recorded as having probably reached Falkland waters.

Louis de Bougainville was the first recorded exporter of whale oil from the Falklands in 1766 but Pernetty wrote in the same year that between 800-900 seal had been killed in one day, so perhaps seal oil supplemented this product. By 1774 360 ocean-going whaling vessels were sailing out of American ports and when Port Egmont was evacuated, two American whalers, the *Montague* from Boston, and the *Thomas* from Cape Cod were anchored there as the British left.

The number of whalers around the Islands increased, not only availing themselves of the whaling fields but also working the vast herds of seal. The elephant seal was known to yield quantities of oil and the whalers supplemented their main cargo of whale oil with it.

The West Falklands became the principal whaling region where receiving ships from 150–400 tons might lie for months or call at pre-arranged times. The actual fishing was carried out by tender vessels such as schooners. Sperm whale, and the Southern Right whale were the quarry and Governor Moody reported to Lord Stanley in 1842 that there was a large abundance of 'black whales' round the Islands, particularly on the west coast of West Falkland. This was probably the Black Right whale but the small pilot whale was also taken.

Much to the annoyance of the Spanish the whalers continued their activities. American whalers had been much in evidence in the beginning but from 1787–90 a British fishery worked in the west of the Islands. Ramon Clairac, Governor of the Islas Malvinas, reported that 1,385 pipes of oil were obtained during this short period of operation. Largely owing to Clairac's interest the Spanish Government was urged to establish a whaling station in the Falklands, a subsidiary of their large whaling and sealing company at Port Desire on the South American mainland. By 1806, Spanish administration of the Islands had ceased and the Falklands became a haven for the whalers, the same vessels returning year after year to the now familiar grounds. Whalers from the Northern Hemisphere endured cruises lasting eighteen months and often two or even three years. For these long voyages few provisions had to be stowed. Cattle had multiplied on East Falkland and provided fresh meat. Pigs and goats were placed on many small offshore 'tussac' islands, ensuring them of future supplies of fresh meat. The wild Upland Goose afforded a valuable food and a small species of shrub (*Myrteola nummularia*) or tea berry, was used as a substitute for tea. As their supplies of salt meat, biscuit and molasses decreased, they lived almost entirely on geese and pigs for the many months that they lay in the harbours of the Islands.

For fourteen years the islands were left to the sealers and whalers, then in November of 1820 Colonel Daniel Jewitt of the United Provinces arrived to take possession of the Islands. Finding Port Soledad full of whaling and sealing vessels, Jewitt sent a letter to all Masters advising them of his Government's claim to the Islands and stated that whaling and sealing were forbidden. Little attention was paid to these warnings. In 1828 Louis Vernet was appointed Governor of the Islas Malvinas and attempted to set up a whaling industry. Spoliations by foreign whalers and sealers continued to such an extent that Vernet took action in August 1831 when he arrested two American sealing schooners. This move eventually led to the end of Vernet's efforts. (*See* Chapter 3.) Political unrest allowed whalers and sealers to continue their task unmolested and unwatched.

January 1833 saw the British flag raised over the Islands again but the same system of whaling continued. Governor Moody complained of the number of American whalers arriving in Port Stanley and causing disturbances. New Island was the rendezvous of many of these whaling vessels and from its harbours the whalers could be upon good fishing grounds within a few hours. Moody wrote :

> The whales are scarce here, but the assertion is circulated for particular ends, and is disproved by the fact of numbers being caught actually in the bays and vessels quickly filling upon this ground. The fishery is carried on with great secrecy, and very successfully, by many foreign vessels.

Ten years later depredations by whalers were again brought to the notice of the British Government by Governor Rennie who, in a letter to Sir John Pakington dated 1853, reported that whalers lying at New Island caught not only whale but also seals.

Three whalers of 3–4 hundred tons with a tender schooner of 100–150 tons to each vessel, and with aggregate crews of 120–150 men, may be said to gain profitable employment to the prejudice of the Colonists of the Falkland Islands. These vessels pay no regard to established regulations respecting fisheries, but capture whales actually in our harbours.

This apparently occurred when whales came into more sheltered waters to calve. Governor Rennie continued :

When it is calculated that each of these vessels, with its tender, stows at least 400–500 tons of oil, the average price of which is £30 per ton, and the usual time required to obtain it 2–3 years, it will be seen that the coast and harbours of this Colony are robbed to the extent of £10,000 or £15,000 per annum, one of the whalers completing his cargo annually.

But whales were becoming scarce and in 1854 a whaler reported that in the eight months they had been at New Island, only one whale had been caught. Only 200 barrels of oil were procured during their eighteen months of whaling. Sperm and Right whales were still the basis of the industry although it was very largely the Right whale which was hunted around the Falklands, the former species being hunted in warmer waters further north. Whaling was carried out from open boats, the whales being secured by hand-thrown harpoon. Sperm whale hunting was a dangerous occupation and a great loss of life resulted. Hunting the Right whale was comparatively easy but success still depended on the unsuspecting nature of these species. Other species were too wary and not easy to approach by the small hunting vessels. Whalers also discovered that many other species almost immediately sank on being killed.

Whaling slowly declined over the next quarter of a century. Many whalers calling at the Falklands were bound for the Pacific whaling grounds. The ships were a welcome sight for 'it had become customary for whalers to bring large stores and many transactions took place between the masters of whaling vessels and residents of the Colony.

Baleen, or whale bone, which local vessels probably collected

195

from dead or stranded whales found about the coasts of the Islands, was also traded.

A New Pattern in Whaling

In 1892, the Tay Whale Fishing Company, the Dundee whalers, with an expedition fleet of four vessels wintered in the Falklands on their way to the Antarctic in search of the Right whale. The following year Captain C. A. Larson, a Norwegian whaler, came south in his vessel *Jason*, to explore the Weddell Sea. Both expeditions reported that no Right whales were to be found.

But they had seen numerous Rorquals, mainly Sei, Finner and Blue. With the perfection of the harpoon gun invented by Svend Foyn in 1860 and with larger and faster vessels, the hunting of these whales was possible. Larson eventually found the financial backing he required in Buenos Aires and in 1904 the Compania Argentina de Pesca began operations at South Georgia. In 1906 the Company became the first to hold the licence which was now necessary for whaling.

The success of Larson's venture encouraged others and in 1906 Alexander Lange obtained a licence to fish the waters around the Falklands with a base at New Island. In 1908 Salvesen & Co of Leith took over at New Island and established the only Falkland whaling factory. The establishment was small, fishing with three catchers. The annual catch, mainly of Fin and Sei whales, never exceeded 7,000 barrels of oil. In 1916 the station was closed and moved to South Georgia.

So ended the whaling in the Falklands but from 1906 the industry at South Georgia grew; shore stations there ceased to operate in the 1963–64 season.

Penguin Oil Industry

The first attempts at taking penguin oil in the Falklands are attributed to American sealers in the 1820s. The American schooner *General Knox*, lying in the harbour of West Point Island, is thought to have taken penguin oil to top up barrels of seal oil. How long this first attempt lasted is not recorded.

196

Whether this industry reached the same proportions as in South Georgia is doubtful. At South Georgia the elephant seal hunters found the vast rookeries of penguins, probably Gentoos and Macaroni, an easy alternative source of oil and between 500,000 and 700,000 birds were taken annually. The skins of penguins supplied a suitable fuel for firing the try-pots of the elephant oilers.

The height of the penguin oil industry in the Islands was reached in 1864 with seven operating vessels. The rookeries on Bird, Speedwell and Arch Islands were decimated and from 1864 to 1866 an approximate total of 63,000 gallons of penguin oil were brought into Stanley. It is generally accepted that eight Rockhopper penguins produced one gallon of oil but the larger Gentoo penguin was certainly taken from places like Speedwell Island. Statistics for the two species are not defined so one can only give an approximate figure. For the three seasons it is estimated that over half a million birds were rendered down.

In 1866 the law was amended and the killing of penguins prohibited on East Falkland except by permission. West Falkland remained unprotected. The following year Governor Robinson described the profitable employment which penguin oiling gave to a portion of the population, but the Colonial Revenue derived no benefit and Robinson felt that this should be changed. Licensing of the industry was therefore started. On private lands licences were free while those taken out for Crown land were rated at £10 per 8,000 gallons of oil.

During this period of eleven years most of the penguin oiling was carried out by three vessels. Two of these schooners, the 23 ton *Victor* and 51 ton *Enterprise*, were owned by J. Phillips, a local shipbuilder.

The total amount of oil brought into Stanley in this first period was 138,000 gallons. Much larger figures commonly quoted as being exported probably included seal oil. There are no records that foreign vessels exported penguin oil. During the height of the industry the dealers paid 2s 3d per gallon of oil in the Colony. After absorbing freight, insurance, casks and coastage they were able to net 2s 6d per gallon in England. In 1871 the oil brought only 1s 6d per gallon and the industry declined. That year only one cargo was recorded. Governor D'Arcy attributed the decline to the war in France where most of the oil eventually went. He thought the halt was only temporary 'and in the meantime the penguin rookeries would recover'.

From 1876 and 1880 there was a slight revival in the industry and a total of 39,776 gallons of oil were exported, indicating the probable destruction of about 320,000 birds.

Although many more inaccessible rookeries remained untouched, the main rookeries were decimated, some never to recover. The only evidence that such rookeries existed are low stone wall corrals into which the penguins were herded and the deep banks of burnt penguin bones left at the sites of the try-pots.

How many birds were destroyed is not known. The oilers had little interest in statistics, but it is indicated that the oil obtained during the 16 years of intensive operations required approximately $1\frac{3}{4}$ million birds. In practice the rough system of trying out and the use of penguin skins and bodies for firing the pots probably resulted in 2 million to $2\frac{1}{2}$ million birds being killed.

Guano Industry

Guano was first introduced to the Old World and North America about 1840 from the rich guano islands off the Peruvian coast. Its value stimulated search by seafarers and the Falklands drew their share of attention, probably because of the vast rookeries of sea birds.

In a despatch to Earl Grey in 1851 Governor Rennie mentioned having found extensive deposits of guano on New Island. Rennie knew little of the product and sought the advice of a Captain Campbell who was engaged in the Peruvian and African guano trade with his vessel *Levensides*. Captain Campbell viewed deposits of guano on the coast of East Falkland and declared it unsatisfactory. On Rennie's suggestion, Captain Campbell agreed to visit New Island, returning to Stanley three months later with

198

little more than half a cargo. The guano at New Island was, according to Campbell, much better than he had expected and with manpower and horses the *Levensides* returned to New Island to complete her cargo.

Rennie's first intended export of guano however, never left the Falklands. Returning from New Island, *Levensides*, with Rennie as a passenger, struck the then unknown 'Billy Rock' at the entrance to Port William and sank. Although there was no loss of life and the *Levensides* was insured, Rennie lost a considerable amount of government stores and was obliged to support the crew of *Levensides* at a cost of £31 14s 8½d.

Rennie was undaunted and issued a notice to the effect that shippers could obtain this guano at an export price of 5s per ton. At that time the export cost of Peruvian guano, of far superior quality, was £1 per ton. On the London market the product made £5–£6 per ton.

The following year the deposit on New Island was again investigated and reported to be approximately 40–50ac in extent, varying in depth from 9in to 3ft, although one area contained crystals 7ft or more deep.

Two shipments were made from New Island after Rennie offered licences for its collection, then came a temporary halt.

The long-established trading firm of Smith Brothers of the River Plate learnt from Captain Smyley of the deposit on New Island. They requested a lease of the island for the collection of guano and the right to oil and fish on the coasts. Moore offered them a lease amounting to £64 down and £10 a year and shortly after the firm sent their brig *Tigre* to New Island with cattle and families to work the deposits. This effort was short lived and in February 1860 they wrote of their disappointment in finding the New Island guano of no value, and of having had to give 100 tons away to a ship as ballast.

In 1872 Governor D'Arcy attempted to find alternative work for the men laid off from the declining ship repair industry. Investigations were made of the guano deposits on some of the smaller offshore island rookeries and samples were forwarded to London for analysis. They were again found to be inferior in quality so the scheme was abandoned.

Several other investigations have been made but the guano of the Islands is deficient in nitrogen in the form of ammonium oxalate and urate and is not found in sufficiently large quantities to warrant commercial exploitation.

The Kelp Industry

In 1967 the British company Alginate Industries Limited, which was responsible for a survey of the Falkland kelp beds in 1947, took renewed interest in their potential.

Late in 1970 a small pilot plant for the production of dry milled kelp was established. Dry milled kelp was to have been shipped to the United Kingdom for further processing because of the expense of importing into the Colony the chemicals for the extraction of alginates. Unlike the kelp harvested off Scotland, the Falkland species required a new chemical process. The species was also found to have a much lower ratio of alginates to fresh cut weed, being one to thirty-five, the northern kelps having a ratio of one to sixteen. It had been estimated that by 1980 the production of dry milled kelp could have reached an annual total of 30,000 tons. With a ratio of one to twelve for the species *Macrocystis*, the amount of weed harvested would have been some 360,000 tons.

For economic reasons the pilot plant closed down in 1976 and the scheme for full production was shelved.

8   NATURAL HISTORY

THE natural climax vegetation of the Islands is a complex mixture of dwarf shrub, herbs and grasses which, as Skottsberg noted, is in its formation very similar to the Atlantic heath found in areas of Scotland, the Faeroes and Western Norway. One hundred and sixty-three species of native plants have been described, with ninety-two introduced species (Moore 1967). The vegetation can be divided into five main formations, the Feldmark, Oceanic heath, Tussac, Bog and Bush formations, with freshwater sources and shores giving rise to collections of littoral and freshwater plants.

Except for those on the coast the distribution of the main formations differs greatly, often with considerable intergrading of plants found in more than one formation. Most widespread is the oceanic heath formation, commonly dominated by Diddle dee (*Empetrum rubrum*) and White grass (*Cortaderia pilosa*). These form the general colour pattern of the main islands, one of sober buffs interspersed with areas of darker browns.

In the interior of West and East Falkland and some other larger islands with higher elevations, soil layers are thin and often eroded to expose areas of clay and rock rubble about the quartzite ridges. Here, cushion plants such as Balsam bog (*Bolax gummifera*), *Azorella selago* and lichens predominate to give a Feldmark formation. Although such areas are sparse in vegetation, the soft greys of lichens and brilliantly coloured algaes against a backcloth of bright green Balsam present a most pleasing splash of colour to the quartzite ridges. Formations vary greatly and the Feldmark is no exception, such structures also appearing on the higher cliff areas and stacks of the SW and NW regions of West Falkland.

The Oceanic heath develops below the Feldmark and among the lower ridges. On higher slopes where the soils are better drained, the heath is dominated by Diddle dee, Christmas bush (*Baccharis magellanica*), Mountain berry (*Pernettya pumila*) and fern. In many areas the 'fern beds' are extensive, adding their rust-red colour to the landscape. On lighter and better drained soils the Lady's slipper (*Calceolaria fothergillii*) presents one of the Falklands' most colourful species, still locally common.

Among the 'stone runs' which intersect the heath formations, Balsam forms cushions often equal in size to the boulders on which it has established. Growing upon the balsam and soils between the 'runs' Almond flower (*Enargea marginata*) is common. The deep rock crevices afford habitats for some smaller ferns such as the delicate *Hymenophyllum* and *Serphyllopsis* species, while tough mats of the creeping Blechnum penna-marina commonly form dense coverage over the margins of the 'runs'. Associated with Blechnum and Diddle dee formations more delicate flowers seek protection. Scurvy grass (*Oxalis enneaphylla*) is abundant and was at one time a valuable source of vitamin C for the prevention of scurvy. The Vanilla daisy (*Leuceria suaveolens*) commonly inhabits the heath, also some orchids such as *Codonorchis lessonii*.

On lower elevations with poorer drainage the heath associations give way to a dominant coverage of White grass. This plant is the most common to the Islands. Davies, 1939, calculated the total percentage of this species on East and West Falklands as 44·41 per cent with a further 14·81 per cent as a mixture of Diddle dee and White grass. The plain of Lafonia is covered by an almost pure stand of this species.

Falklands' camp is generally referred to as either 'hard' or 'soft'. 'Hard' camp embraces much of the plant formations described. 'Soft' camp covers bog formations which occur where the water table approaches, and in some seasons reaches, the surface. Two plants, *Astelia pumila* and Brown swamp rush (*Rostkovia magellanicus*) are, after White grass, the most common in such

202

areas, generally forming almost pure stands on areas of deep peat with a high saturation point. On the north-east coast of East Falkland the Astelia forms large flat cushions growing with few other plants over acres of land. Such areas are often pitted with shallow pools, only a few feet or even inches in diameter. The mats of Astelia form a firm route for the traveller on foot, horse or even vehicle, but very soft peat lies below the surface.

Associated with Astelia the small insectivorous plant Sundew (*Drosera uniflora*) is common but from its minute size is very often overlooked. During the flowering period in January the plant can often be traced by the rather sickly sweet smell and glistening of its honey-like substance.

Davies gives a figure of 44·88 per cent for the total area of soft camp on West and East Falkland with the remaining 55·12 per cent as 'hard' camp. The Islands have little true mire and fen land. Where such areas occur a small rush (*Juncus scheuzerioides*), sphagnum, swamp rush, mosses and liverworts commonly form the vegetation.

Although the archipelago has large numbers of freshwater ponds and other water sources, a comparatively small number support freshwater vegetation. Ponds, associated with peat and rock ridges, are virtually sterile of any form of life. Native Water-milfoil (*Myriophyllum elatinoides*) is common, frequently forming dense mats over the water's surface. Native Pondweed (*Potamogeton linguatus*) is rare. A number of semi-aquatic and marginal species coming within this formation include Spike rush (*Elcocharis melanostachys*), Marsh marigold (*Caltha sagittata*) and Native Willow herb (*Epilobium cunninghamii*).

Only two native species of plant attain sufficient stature to be classed as bushes—Fachine (*Chiliotrichum diffusum*) and Box-wood (*Hebe elliptica*). Both are evergreen, the former inhabiting sheltered valleys, stream and river banks, while the boxwood is naturally confined to coastal regions of West Falkland and a number of adjacent islands. Today both species are locally common but are not as widespread as they were before the introduction of stock.

The tussac formations are confined to the coastal areas. When the early voyagers sailed the coasts of the Falklands they described the formations of tussac as thickly-wooded areas, as indeed they might have appeared when viewed in certain conditions. Tussac grass can attain a height of two or three metres, each plant forming a fibrous base of varying height and diameter, from the top of which the plant throws a dense crown of leaves. Generally, tussac is confined to a narrow belt on the coasts 100 to 200 metres in width, but on a number of larger offshore islands, stands of tussac grow inland to elevations of over 300 metres. At one time tussac grew along extensive stretches of the East and West Falkland coasts. Unrestricted grazing reduced the tussac and today a large percentage of the remaining stocks are confined to smaller offshore islands, islets and knobs. On some islands tussac forms almost pure stands, of such compact communities that the leaves of adjoining tussacs interlace to make a canopy. In such areas few other plants compete but where sufficient light can enter Wild celery commonly grows to over half a metre in height.

The littoral zones support large formations of Sea Cabbage (*Senecio candicans*) and Marram grass (*Ammophila arenaria*) introduced about 1923 in an attempt to prevent the spreading of sand dunes, while Sea pink (*Colobanthus quitensis*) and Sea stonecrop (*Crassula moschata*) grow in moist sandy and rocky areas immediately above high tide levels.

Marine vegetation

The marine vegetation of the archipelago not only has an important part to play in the ecological chain but, in an indirect manner, affects the physical structure of the Falklands themselves.

The term 'kelp', can refer to several species of seaweed found growing in different zones of the sublittoral fringe. The true 'kelp' or Basket kelp (*Macrocystis pyrifera*) and species of *Lessoniae* inhabit the deeper waters of the sublittoral, forming vast beds commonly hundreds of metres in extent, for which the Falkland Islands are well known. From its presence the Islanders have been given the nickname 'kelper'.

204

Three species of Lessoniae are known, *Lessonia nigrescens*, *flavicans* and *frutescens*, the most common of these species being flavicans. Tree Fern kelp (*Desmarestia Rossii*) inhabits deeper waters.

Growing on the more exposed coastlines in zones immediate to the low tide levels are two species, *Durvillea harveyi* and *antarctica*.

Only the larger and more common species of seaweed have been mentioned. Many more species are known, and belong to three groups, the *Chlorophyceae* (green), *Phaeophyceae* (brown) and *Rhodophyceae* (red) seaweeds. Their description lies in the hands of an algologist and is outside the scope of this book.

AVIAN FAUNA

The present check list of birds breeding in the Falkland Islands lists sixty-three species. Of this number seventeen are regarded as Falklands races. A further eighty-four species have been recorded as non-breeding visitors and vagrants.

Some 70 per cent of the Islands' breeding species depend on the sea for their food and although there is not a great variety of species, there are large populations of birds. The largest colony of Black-browed albatross has been calculated at over two million birds. Estimates of certain Rockhopper penguin rookeries are in excess of this figure and the penguins, family *Spheniscidae*, represent the largest populations of birds in the Falklands. Rockhopper, Magellan and Gentoo penguins are common, with small breeding numbers of King penguin and Macaroni.

The *Procellariiformes* probably take second place in population figures. Of the two families in this order the Falklands have large breeding colonies of one *Diomedeidae*, the Black-browed albatross, and nine or possibly ten *Procellariidae*. Large breeding populations of Thin-billed prion, Wilson's petrel, and Falkland Diving petrel are known in the Islands.

Smaller colonies of Sooty shearwater follow a migratory course to and from the North Atlantic, returning to breed in the Falklands. White-chinned petrels, Grey-backed petrel and the Giant petrel also breed in the Islands. Although very commonly seen about the harbours and coastal regions the numbers of Giant petrel breeding in the Falklands is very small, calculations being made at some 2,500 to 3,000 pairs (1970). Recent investigations have also discovered small breeding colonies of the Fairy prion and Greater shearwater, both species of which are great distances from their previously recorded breeding grounds.

Procellariiformes feed on small octopods, munidae, schooling fishes and euphausians, taken by the albatross and the larger petrels, while small plankton forms are eaten by the diving and storm petrels. The King shag and Rock shag are common to the Islands and generally take small schooling fishes.

Of the family *Laridae*, the Falklands have one species of tern and three gulls which are also greatly dependent on the sea. The South American tern in the Falklands feeds on munidae, small fish and arthropods, the latter secured from beds of kelp. The Islands' most common gull, the Dominican, presents an interesting example of how the local industry of sheep farming has affected the feeding cycle of a percentage of this species. A natural scavenger, the bird has turned to the sheep runs and killing fields for its food.

Birds of the sublittoral fringes and shores present an interesting assemblage of species. The Flightless steamer duck, an endemic species, has a common distribution round the archipelago except on the most remote outliers or where the bird is unable to obtain its variable diet of bivalves, gastropods, shrimps, chitons, mussels and limpets. The Flying steamer duck, although having the same distribution, is, however, uncommon in the Islands. The Night heron and Crested duck are well distributed about the Falklands coasts. The Night heron often forms 'heronries' in a variety of coastal habitats : small offshore knobs where the bird may nest on raised ground; cliff ledges supporting small growths of tussac; abandoned hulks, boxwood bushes and introduced coniferous trees.

Page 207 (above) Breeding group of King penguins with Gentoo penguins on East Falkland; *(below)* a mature Johnny Rook or Striated Caracara (Phalcoboenus australis) *(centre)* with two fully-fledged young at a nest site in tussac grass

Page 208 (above) Mixed colony, of Black-browed albatross and Rockhopper penguins on one of the Falklands' remote outliers; (below) breeding pair of King cormorants at nest site. These birds are commonly found nesting in association with Rockhopper penguins

The Black oystercatcher is exclusively a shore dwelling bird, restricted largely to those zones where mussels and limpets are readily available. The Pied oystercatcher, the more common of the two species, shows a considerable adaptability in both feeding and breeding sites. In some regions fairly large populations nest within a few yards of each other along stretches of sand and shingle beach. These birds commonly feed on tidal mud or sand flats extracting small bivalves and marine worms from below the surface. Other populations are found on rocky coastlines where they adapt to nesting on grassy plains often some distance from the coast. Only occasionally are these populations seen to feed off the shoreline, usually feeding on ground beetles and earthworms in the grasslands.

Kelp geese usually graze on Chlorophyceae, forms of seaweeds of the middle and lower shores, but in some areas the Kelp goose has become a grassland grazer with the sea supplementing its diet.

For habitat much of the Islands' bird life relies on the tussac grass formations, and on the smaller offshore islands to which such formations are now largely restricted. These present a most valuable ecological niche. Thirty-one different species have been recorded as using tussac formations for nesting shelter or for the supply of nesting material and as a feeding area.

The family Procellariidae is an example of a group of birds which, although capable of surviving without tussac formations (except perhaps for the Grey-backed petrel), appears to prefer this habitat. The Falkland diving petrel, Prions, White-chinned petrel and Shearwaters are burrowing species. In some coastal areas there are colonies of the two former species on virtually open terrain with little or no vegetative cover, but the influence on such colonies by erosion, activities by man and predation is greater than in those colonies formed in tussac plantations. There is evidence that the destruction of tussac has resulted in the disappearance of some colonies of shearwaters.

The Turkey vulture and Short-eared owl are commonly found nesting beneath the tussac canopies while species such as the Grass

209

wren, Cobbs wren, Falkland thrush and Siskin may often use the dead leaves of the skirt and crown of the tussac plant. Some populations of Johnny Rook also have a preference for the tussac habitat as do populations of Terns, Dolphin gull and Pink-breasted gulls.

The seed heads of tussac provide food for Siskins and, in some cases, for the Black-throated finch and Yellow-billed teal, but tussac is also rich in invertebrate fauna. Spiders, Flightless Camel crickets and Mites are evident, while the ground about the tussac formations is generally covered with a layer of dead and decaying vegetable and animal matter inhabited by ground beetles and other insect fauna, providing food for several species of bird.

Associated with the coastal regions, low valleys and small areas immediate to freshwater ponds and streams are dense swards known as 'greens'. Many of these mark the old sites of Gentoo penguin rookeries, the birds having been instrumental in their formation. Here are found the grazing species, the wild geese, of which two species are common, the Upland and Ruddy-headed goose and the much rarer Ashy-headed goose. Although fairly widespread the species are largely restricted to coastal stretches and areas adjacent to lagoons and ponds.

During the late summer many populations of geese move to the heath formations and feed on diddle dee berries. The importance of the berry to the geese appears to be considerable, for some grasslands will be completely forsaken by the birds. They may move many miles for their new feed, thus constituting a form of local migration.

Yellow-billed teal, Pampa teal, Chiloe Widgeon and Brown pintail are the main species which inhabit these ponds or streams in the coastal regions. In some areas, Silver grebe and Rolland's grebe are found.

Twelve species may be found inhabiting the heath, feldmark and ridge formations, of which the Ground tyrant, Black-throated finch and Falkland thrush are probably the most widely distributed species and most common to these areas. On the lower and more open heath the Dotterel and Falkland Island plover are more evident, while the Paraguayan snipe appears in a widely varying number of habitats.

Five species of the *Falconiformes* breed regularly in the islands. In the higher regions the Red-backed buzzard may be found, although the species ranges in nesting and feeding from the high ridges of the larger islands to the coastal cliffs. Their main feed is composed of rats, mice and small birds. Hares and rabbits are also taken. Coastal habitats appear to be favoured by the Cassins falcon, a race of Peregrine and certain populations have adapted to feeding largely on prions and petrels, while others take mice, insect life, and other birds.

The remaining Falconiformes are largely carrion-feeding birds. The Turkey vulture and Carancho have a wide distribution over the islands. The sheep runs are an important source of food, and although considered by some farmers to be predators of sheep, their value in keeping the camp clean of dead and decaying sheep outweighs the supposed damage that these two birds do to livestock. Seal rookeries are also favoured, some appearing to have resident populations of Turkey vultures which live on dead seal, afterbirth, and excreta.

The Johnny Rook or Striated Caracara is also a carrion-eating hawk. Besides being one of the Falklands' most interesting species, it is one of the world's rarest birds of prey, being confined to the Falkland Islands and a number of remote islands off Cape Horn. In the Falklands, although fairly common in some regions, populations are isolated and generally confined to the more remote offshore tussac islands. The diet is very variable according to the season. During the winter the bird may feed on marine life, vegetable matter and insects. In the summer the bird plays an important part in the predation of penguin rookeries, taking eggs and young from unwary penguins. The species is commonly associated with penguin grounds, and probably gained its local name of Johnny Rook because of the fact that in early days the bird was described as a 'Rook' often seen standing about the rookeries of 'Johnny' penguins, an early name for the Gentoo penguin.

211

Penguins

Probably no family of birds has been the subject of so much depredation and interest as the penguins. The Islands' populations of penguins are, perhaps, unique.

Rockhoppers are the most abundant and, except for the southern shores of East Falkland, are widely distributed over the archipelago. In the summer 1932–3 Dr Hamilton estimated that there were 3,169,100 Rockhoppers. This figure did not include some of the largest known colonies of today and more recent calculations indicate a population approaching five million birds.

The Magellan penguin (locally called Jackass penguin after the South African species) is probably the next most common species, but from its habit of nesting underground over a wide range of coastal areas and small tussac islands, calculations of the total population are extremely difficult to ascertain. It is conceivable, however, that a figure approaching that of the Rockhopper population might not be too liberal.

The Gentoo penguin forms colonies in a variety of coastal areas. On rocky sites the birds use stones for constructing their nests. In other areas vegetation readily affords building material. Nesting sites are also commonly found several hundreds of yards inland, and in some cases the birds have an overland route of over three miles from landing to their nest sites. A colony may total several thousand birds in an area, with sub-divisions into groups varying in size from a few pairs, but rarely exceeding several hundred pairs.

Dr Hamilton also estimated the number of Gentoos. His total for breeding pairs in the Islands was 116,020. A more recent census carried out by the author between 1965 and 1970 gave a total of 99,360. The results show a remarkable similarity when the figures for two Jason Islands colonies are disregarded, with a rise of 3,040 pairs between the 1932 total and that of 1970. There is reason to believe that Hamilton's figure for the Jason Islands colonies was too liberal.

Records indicate that the Macaroni penguin has always been uncommon. Habitually the bird nests with Rockhoppers and is usually seen as single pairs, although a colony of fifty-five pairs was recorded on an outlier in 1967 and it is possible that others exist.

One of the most interesting and attractive penguins breeding in the Falklands is the King penguin. Unfortunately the breeding numbers are very low although they are thought to have been quite common at the time of early settlement, though very few records actually indicate this. In one of the earliest reports of this bird Pennant, in 1768, speaks of a specimen brought by Captain McBride from the Falklands. McBride described it 'as a very scarce species', though he saw 'multitudes of a lesser kind with which it agreed in the manner of its life'. The 'lesser kind' was probably the Gentoo penguin with which the King penguin often associates. Two years later Erasmus Gower, from the sloop *Swift*, describing colonies of Gentoo penguins wrote, 'Among these, there are few, from their superior bulk and fine plumage, called kings and queens'.

Other records of the species exist but only one in 1867 suggested that the birds bred in any number. It is recorded that a man named Lecomte, collecting specimens for the Zoological Society of London's gardens, discovered a group of about twenty King penguins among a colony of Gentoos. Lecomte secured about a dozen which were shipped to London. He does not mention that the birds were breeding, but from his description the area, if not the actual site, is the same as that used by the main group of breeding birds today.

There were no local records which prove or support the possibility of breeding groups until 1933 when a young bird still in down was found in the same area described by Lecomte. In 1942 a pair of adult birds were discovered with a single egg close to the same site. However, the birds lost their egg and not until 1945 was breeding recorded as successful.

By 1983 there were five known sites where King penguins breed regularly. One of these, occupied by some seventy breeding pairs in the summer of 1982–83, represents the largest colony, while others contain very few pairs.

Visitors and Vagrants

A number of sea birds such as the Wandering Albatross, Grey-headed Albatross, Pintado petrel, Silver-grey Fulmar and Wattled Sheathbill are regular visitors to the Falklands. A common visitor is the White-rumped Sandpiper, and during the summer months large numbers inhabit the coastal regions.

Some vagrants like the Barn Swallow, have become regular annual visitors to the Islands during October and November and the Straw-necked Ibis, Violet-eared Dove, American Egret, Cocoi Heron, Chingola Song Sparrow and Fire-eyed Pepoaza or Chilean Ground Tyrant are often recorded. The last four species have a marked ability to survive in the Islands and it is possible that there might be small resident populations.

MAMMALS

Cetaceans

Eighteen species of *Cetacea*, whale, porpoise and dolphins have been recorded around the Falkland Islands.

At one time whale were very commonly seen and only ten years ago, although these creatures were not then abundant, it was possible to view them at close quarters as they made their way through various island passages, sea-ways which they have used for generations on their migratory routes. On calm nights settlements close by heard them blowing. Today, however, the larger whales such as Fin, Humpback and Sei which were the main species fished by the New Island whaling station are a very rare sight about the Falklands.

It has not yet been discovered what is the most common whale around the island today. Records of stranded whales indicate that the Sperm whale may be more common at certain periods of the year. In February 1968 a pod of eighteen Sperm whales were found stranded on the Pleasant Roads sand beach at Fitzroy. Of these, seventeen were positively identified as male animals.

One of the lesser known families of whale, the *Ziphioids* or Beaked whale, have been recorded from the Falklands and in

1964 specimens of Cuvier's Beaked whale were recovered from Whaler Bay, West Falkland, and Layard's or Strap-toothed whale in the same year from Bleaker Island off East Falkland. An earlier specimen of this species was collected in the same locality by the Challenger Expedition in 1877.

Of the family *Delphinidae*, Porpoises and Dolphins, six species have been recorded of which Commerson's Dolphin is probably the most common. Peale's Dolphin or Porpoise are also quite commonly seen.

The first cetacean mentioned in reports from the Falklands was the Southern Pilot whale or Black-fish, a true Dolphin. Governor Moody indicated that this creature was hunted as in the Faeroes where they are herded and stranded. Schools numbering several hundreds appear off the Islands, and large numbers have been found stranded on the beaches of the Islands. In 1966, 340 Pilot whales stranded themselves on Speedwell Island. They were observed coming ashore, and appeared to be following a single male animal. Even as the tide refloated the creatures, allowing them to swim out into deep water, they returned to join the leader. After three days the entire school was finally stranded.

Another true dolphin is the Killer whale. Indications are that the populations of the Killer whale are on the increase around the archipelago. Large whales, porpoise, seal, penguins and other dolphins are attacked by this animal and its increase in these waters could be a reason for the apparently slow increase in some seal herds of the Falklands.

Seals

The Falklands have four kinds of *pinnipeds*. The Southern Elephant seal (*Mirounga leonina*), South American or Southern Sea Lion (*Otaria byronia*), South American Fur Seal (*Arctocephalus australis*). and Leopard Seal (*Hydrurga leptonyx*). The latter was at one time a fairly common visitor and has bred in the Islands but is now rarely seen.

The Southern Elephant seal is circumpolar in the subantarctic. The South American Sea Lion is widely distributed along both coasts of South America. The Leopard seal is a true Antarctic seal and normally inhabits the pack ice fringes while migrating to the subantarctic regions during the winter. The South American Fur seal is found along the southern coast of South America, with separate races in the Falklands, Galapagos, South Georgia, South Orkney, and South Shetlands.

Southern Sea Lion

The Southern Sea Lion is at present the most common pinniped in the archipelago, forming breeding groups rarely exceeding about two hundred animals. Where strong tides prevail and where kelp grows in profusion, groups gather on nearby islands and coastal areas to form populations of up to one and two thousand animals. Tides play an important part in the availability of food and sea lion can often be seen diving along the edge of kelp beds, returning to the surface with food. Large catches of squid, the mainstay of the animals' diet are brought to the surface, where the seal thrashes it before swallowing it. On calm nights, one is made aware of sea lions feeding with the slap-slap of prey being broken on the surface. Occasionally sea lions are seen patrolling favoured routes of breeding penguins, seizing slow or unwary birds and literally shaking them out of their skins. Evidence of this practice can be found on the beaches where bodies, complete with peeled-off skins, may be seen strewn along the tide line. This practice is carried out usually by old male animals, and although the penguins will sometimes be eaten, evidence suggests that the deed is done usually in malicious play rather than for food.

The breeding season of the Sea lion in the Falklands is between late December and the end of January.

Fur seal

The Fur seal restricts its breeding colonies in the Islands largely to three or four well chosen areas, where a normal approach is difficult. Two of the main rookeries occupy small isolated offshore rocks. Covering a few acres, such breeding areas are thickly populated. On one rookery an estimated two thousand seal are

216

established on little over an acre of rock. Territories are established by breeding bulls in early November with pupping commencing in late November to early December.

The food of the Fur seal varies according to the availability at different periods of the year. Indications are that 'krill', euphausians and particularly munidae are the most important feed. This is evident by the pink and red staining of excreta on the rookeries. Small schooling fish and squid are also eaten. Feeding is largely carried out at night when food supplies rise from the greater depths to the surface layers of the sea. This is apparent when, as evening approaches, there is increased activity on the rookeries and many more seal take to the water and leave for feeding grounds.

Elephant seal

The breeding season of the elephant seal commences in September when adult bulls establish territories. Easily accessible, low lying sand or shingle beaches are preferred on which to establish harems where pupping commences in mid-September with the main pupping during the first few days of October. Mating of the cows follows shortly after pupping. The main moulting period may extend from January to March when there is a tendency for many animals to move further inshore and form wallows. Such wallows can become a fermenting bath of rotting kelp, excreta and water in which they lie during the period of moult. During breeding and moulting these seals adopt the curious habit of sand throwing, the flippers being used to toss sand over their bodies. The reason for this is not clear, but it is a habit adopted at an early age. Pups only a few days old have been observed sand throwing.

The main diet of the elephant seal is composed of *cephalopoids*, (Octopods Cuttlefish and Squid).

Seal Populations

The Elephant seal, which was undoubtedly quite common in the years of early settlement, was hunted to such an extent that it was believed to be extinct in the Falklands by about 1871. In the early 1900s it had returned but was a comparatively rare sight. In 1951 it was estimated that possibly some 1,000 pups were born annually in the Falklands. Since this date the population has risen, this being evident over the last ten years when many more localities, hitherto uninhabited by these animals, have been occupied. The estimated number of pups born in 1971 was between 4,000 to 5,000.

A recent survey of the sea lion has shown a very severe population decline over the last thirty years. Between 1929 and 1937 J. E. Hamilton produced two reports for the British Discovery Committee indicating a total population of 380,000 individuals of which 80,000 were pups.

Between 1928 and 1938 except for a four-year period during the Depression, a total of 39,696 Sea lion were taken for their oil (Chapter Seven). In 1948 the sealing inspector for South Georgia was asked to allocate a quota for sea lions for a new sealing venture. He suggested that 15,000 adult males for the first three years and 10,000 thereafter would be a reasonable kill. Sealing started in 1949 but by 1952 the venture had failed for lack of seals and operational problems. During this period 3,045 sea lions were taken.

In 1962 a licence was granted for 1,500 sea lions to be taken for their pelts. This licence was based on Hamilton's figures as no proper survey had been done since that time.

It was apparent that Hamilton's figures were no longer a correct evaluation and the need for a new census was evident. Initial investigations made before the issue of the 1962 licence had indicated a drastic decline. Intensive investigations of a few of the larger rookeries, followed by an aerial survey of all known sea lion colonies in the Falklands in 1965 and 1966 produced positive evidence of this decline.

The total number of seals counted and estimated during the 1965 survey was 18,876 of which 5,516 were pups and the remaining 13,360 adult and juvenile animals. This figure was supported by the results the following season. Corrections were

218

made to these figures for adult animals not present on the rookeries and pups which may have been born late. With all calculations on the optimistic side, the total of sea lions of all age groups numbered 30,000 animals. Since the 1965 and 1966 surveys, supplementary counts have been made which indicate that the populations have not changed.

The reason for this decline is not yet known. Animal populations tend to fluctuate and it is possible that, at the time of the early survey, the herds were at their peak and now are at their lowest point. Have the complex food chains of our seas changed, causing such marine life as squid, a mainstay in the diet of the sea lion, to become scarce? This seems unlikely owing to the apparent increase in the elephant seal populations. Are such marine predators of the species such as the Killer whale taking a heavy toll, or are the animals of these Islands migrating to South American coasts? Whatever the answer, the sea lion stocks of the Falklands will have to be carefully watched.

The Fur seal of the Islands were also counted in 1965–6. Just less than 14,000 animals were counted, some 6,000 less than in a survey during 1951. The 1951 census however estimated that 6,000 animals existed on Beauchene Island. The later census discovered that there were no Fur seal on that island. Although this has shown a setback 'on paper' the indication is that the Fur seals of the Falklands are stable and although no major recolonisation is evident on the animal's old haunts there is every probability that this could happen in the not too distant future.

Introduced Species

At various times twelve different species of mammal have been introduced. Eight of these remain in the Falklands today.

The introduction of most species is fairly clear. The cattle and their probable descendants have been discussed in Chapter Four. Horses introduced to East Falkland by the French ran wild and in about 1842 were estimated by Moody to number between 2,000 and 3,000. In 1859 the Surveyor General, Bailey, reported eleven

219

horses on the island. Since this date there are no further official records of wild horses.

Although there are no records of their introduction, rats and mice were probably introduced by the early shipping and shipwrecks. Mice were recorded on Saunders Island in 1774 and in 1842 Moody reported rats and mice as being found about the settlement of Port Louis but in no other regions. Today both species are fairly well distributed, with rats locally common about some settlements and on some offshore tussac islands. Mice range over much greater areas of open camp on East and West Falkland with populations on remote islands such as Steeple Jason Island. Specimens collected from East Falkland have been identified as *Mus domesticus*.

In the valleys close to the settlement of Port Louis, Moody wrote of rabbits 'literally in myriads' and of how the settlers had formerly exported their skins. Whitington mentioned the 'immense' numbers of black and grey rabbits. Probably the French were responsible for their introduction with the animals being taken to different islands by the settlers and sealers. The rabbit was introduced to Saunders Island by Byron in 1765. Today the rabbit is locally common and in some populations black remains the dominant colour. The same pattern of distribution also appears with feral cats which, particularly on East Falkland, have made their territories in the open heath of the coasts.

The French also introduced pigs, which developed into semiwild herds in some areas and were probably largely to blame for the destruction of much tussac on East Falkland. Tussac was discovered to be an excellent feed for pigs and it soon became the practice of sealers and whalers to place pairs on some of the offshore tussac islands. Saunders Island, where Byron first introduced them in 1765, became one of the main haunts of wild pigs and many references are made to hunting them. Pigs were also placed by sealers on Beaver Island, New Island, West Point, Speedwell, Bleaker and Quaker Islands. On the latter island it is recorded that the tussac was fired purposely to drive the pigs onto the foreshore, a probable reason why sealers burned other islands. It was also the habit of American sealing and whaling vessels to carry dogs for hunting pigs. How large the population of wild pigs became is not recorded, but in 1838 there is a record of some 3,000 hogs being killed in that year for their skins. The last semi-wild pigs were introduced to Jack's Island off Albemarle on West Falkland about the 1920s. Sightings were last reported in 1952.

Goats were also used by sealers. In 1846 goats were known to have gone wild and inhabited East Falkland mountains and in the 1870s there is a record of goat skins numbering several hundreds being brought from Grand Jason Island. The original population was almost certainly placed there by sealers. There are no goats remaining in the Falklands today.

From 1862 there is an interesting record of guanaco in the Falklands. Animals were probably introduced from South America to East Falkland with a view to exploiting their wool and skins. This venture was first suggested by Moody twenty years earlier, when he discussed the value of Alpaca and Vicuna wools. Moody considered that parts of the Falklands would be suitable for raising such animals because of the similarity that exists both in climate and vegetation. He remarked that the project 'is worthy of the attentive consideration of the enterprising settler'.

For how many years these guanaco were resident in the Islands is not recorded, but in 1871 further mention is made of them in a report concerning a visit by the then Duke of Edinburgh. 'On Monday Captain Packe organised an expedition for the Prince to Mare Harbour fifty miles distant from the settlement to the southward. Here His Royal Highness remained until the following Wednesday evening shooting Guanacos, wild geese, duck and snipe etc.'

In the early 1930s guanaco were once again introduced by the John Hamilton Estate. Hamilton placed a small number of these animals on an island in the Weddell group and eventually they multiplied into a herd of a few hundred. In the years 1956 and 1959 nearly 400 were shot to reduce the population which were in danger of eating themselves out of existence. In 1970 approximately sixty animals were counted which, it is hoped, might be retained not only as an interesting introduction to the Falklands, but as a valuable herd of a species which in its own native areas is slowly being depleted. In 1970 a programme of studies was started and a move made to establish a further herd for study on West Point Island.

Hamilton was responsible for the introduction of a number of South American species to the islands : otters, rhea, skunk, parrots, ibis and patagonian fox were introduced onto small offshore islands off West Falkland. Only the fox and perhaps the otter remain today. This species of otter, originating from the channels of Tierra del Fuego, has not been positively seen for many years. An animal was shot at East Bay, Fox Bay in 1942 and in 1965 evidence of the animal was found in a creek on the south-east coast of East Falkland. Unidentified spoor marks have been found on some beaches so it is possible that some animals remain.

Although the Patagonian fox was confined to a small number of islands, its introduction is viewed with regret. On islands where sheep are run, the fox population affects the lambing. Undoubtedly bird populations were greatly reduced, but probably only when the foxes were first placed on the islands. Observations made of the fox on one island show that the animal feeds very largely off the shore line on limpets, small crab, fish, particularly the species of 'dogfish' (*Harpagifer hispinis*), and other marine life, while in the autumn the animal's diet will consist largely of diddle dee berries. Fairly large populations of ground-nesting birds on the island were apparently affected little by these animals.

No records are available of the introduction of the hare. It has never been recorded from West Falkland or offshore islands of the archipelago but is common on East Falkland. The species is identical in appearance to the European hare (*Lepus europaeus*).

The Falkland Fox or Warrah

The only indigenous quadruped was the Falkland fox (*Dusicyon antarcticus australis*) which became extinct sometime during 1873–6 on West Falkland. The first description of this interesting wolf-like fox, which was locally called 'Warrah', was given by Simson who sailed with Captain Strong in the *Welfare* in 1689–90. He said the animal was a fox twice the size of the English species.

Bougainville called it 'loup-renard'. Byron discovered several foxes on West Falkland and from them named Fox Bay. He said they were as big as middle-sized mastiffs, and according to his men they were 'creatures of great fierceness, resembling wolves'. The early settlers on East Falkland, however, appear to have found them timid creatures. Moody wrote of the 'Warrah' or wolf-fox as 'about the size of an English hound, but slender with long legs. It has always been supposed that they are dangerous, from the fearless manner in which they will venture to approach any person, but I am informed by many well acquainted by their habits, that they will do this more from ignorance of the power of man, and strong curiousity, than from ferocity, and that they may be easily driven away. They will take a piece of meat from the hand, but this habit led to the animal's eventual downfall, for with meat in one hand and knife in the other the gauchos killed many of them.

Charles Darwin named the animal *Canis antarctica* and said it had moderately long fur. The underparts were pale brown, with chest and belly hairs a pale dirty yellow with black tips. The head was wolf-like, the legs shorter than in the true wolf, and the tail had a white tip.

In December 1836 Captain Grey encountered a pair of foxes at Port Edgar on West Falkland. He said they approached him and his dog, barking and howling and open-mouthed as though to attack. A cub was seen with the animals, accounting for their ferocity. Grey shot the two animals which were 'much larger than the English fox and not quite so large as a wolf. In shape they resemble a fox, their colour is much darker than that of our foxes, and fur thicker; they are also longer in proportion in the legs.'

Various reports from the two main islands indicated that the fox of West Falkland was smaller, much redder and darker in colour, and had a finer fur than the East Falkland animal. In 1914 Oldfield Thomas gave some measurements from skulls of the East Falkland and West Falkland animals and decided that there were two species : *Dusicyon darwini* of East Falkland and *Dusicyon antarcticus* of West Falkland although he wrote, 'no certainty is possible'.

The population of the Falkland fox is not known and available records indicate that the species was not common on East or West Falkland. In 1839 a New York fur trader, John Jacob Astor, sent a vessel to the Islands to buy the skins of foxes and 'thousands of foxes were slaughtered' (Crowe 1967).

Origin of the Warrah

Many questions remain unanswered about the Falkland fox, undoubtedly the most puzzling being how did the animal first come to be on the Falkland Islands?

If the theory is accepted that the Falkland Islands were once connected to South Africa, then the suggestion that the animal crossed by a land bridge from South America is invalid. However, the question can be viewed in another way. The Falklands are separated from the South American continent by only 300 miles of sea, making this land mass the most likely source of origin, but how did the animal arrive? The currents which sweep up from South America bring with them timber which has originated from the Straits of Magellan and Tierra del Fuego. This drift-wood is deposited on the southern shores of the Falklands so perhaps our fox arrived aboard this. An even more plausible theory evolves when it is noted that Fuegian Indian canoes have been found on the beaches of the Falkland Islands. It was a habit of these ancient people to carry hunting dogs in their canoes. They were the partially domesticated 'Culpeo' or South American Fox or Jackal (*Dusicyon culpaeolus*), very closely related to the Falkland fox. This could account for the fact that the Falkland species tamed easily. It could also be that the animals were deposited on West and East Falkland at widely varying periods of time, accounting for the different types.

lorhynchus commersoni

lkland Islands 6ᴾ

Falkland Islands

Dusky Dolphin

15ᴾ

Lagenorhynchus obscurus

Falkland

Lagenorhynchus australis

Islands

3ᴾ Peale's Porpoise

Falkland

Phocoena dioptrica

Islands

11ᴾ Spectacled Porpoise

norhynchus cruciger

lkland Islands 7ᴾ

Falkland Islands

Orcinus orca

25ᴾ Killer Whale

Page 225 'Marine Mammals: Dolphins, Porpoises and Whale' stamp issue released 25 February 1980, one of the 'short' or 'commemorative' issued some four times a year

Page 226 (above) Group of adult Magellan penguins at the entrance to a nesting burrow. The only Falkland species of penguin which nests underground; (below) An adult Gentoo penguin feeding its chick by regurgitation

OTHER FAUNA

Marine and Freshwater Fish

Over eighty species of fish have been recorded. The importance of some species has been described in Chapter Seven. Possibly the best known and most common are the mullet (*Eleginops maclovinus*) and two smelt (*Austromenidia smitti* and *nigricans*) while the herring (*Clupea fuegensis*) commonly appears around the coasts at certain times of the year. Eight species of *Notothenia*, locally known as rock cod, have been recorded from the Islands.

One of the most abundant fish found by the *William Scoresby* research party in 1927 was a species of hake (*Merluccius*) while two other important fish were a species of *Macruronus* and *Stromateus*. Species of skate and snoek are not uncommonly discovered stranded on the beaches of the Falklands.

Of the freshwater species endemic to the Falklands the 'local trout' is a name given to three different species all closely related. These are *Galaxias maculatus, Galaxias smithii* and *Aplochiton zebra*, the latter being recognised as the local trout. *Galaxias attenuatus*, locally named smelt, also inhabits fresh water.

Marine Invertebrates

The seas about the Islands are very rich in invertebrate fauna, the scope of which is well beyond these pages although a few of the better known species can be mentioned.

Two species of edible crab have been found in Falklands waters, the *Paralomus*, a species commonly found on the beaches and identified by its rather rough shell and short fat legs, and *Lithodes antarcticas*, the Southern Stone crab or centolla, which in the southern regions of South America is highly prized as food, and is the objective of an important industry there. This species, which has a spiny shell and long legs, was fished by the *William Scoresby* in about fifty fathoms of water a few miles off the Falklands coast.

Clams and mussels are common, while the waters offshore

abound in a variety of sea urchins, starfish and other life. The cephalopods are represented by squids and octopuses.

Perhaps two crustaceans can be regarded as the most abundant and probably the most important. The shrimp-like Euphausia of which there are several species, is collectively known as whale food or 'krill'. Euphausia is the leading species of antarctic zooplankton and is itself the main food of the larger marine animals from fish to the species of baleen whales of which the Blue whale (*Balaenoptera musculus*) is the largest mammal in the world. During the summer the 'krill' reproduce in incalculable numbers, often changing the colour of the seawater. Krill concentrations might be called 'food fields' or 'whale stew' and will attract high numbers of sea birds, whale and seal which may feed on them for days. These Euphausians follow a migratory pattern, some drifting northwards in the surface waters with the microscopic diatoms which constitute the main food of the krill, then descending to the southward moving waters and so back to their original positions.

Many of these migratory patterns undoubtedly pass close to the Falklands, their northward movement coinciding with the main breeding season of the Falkland birds and some mammals. Large 'food fields' appear in certain areas of the archipelago during the summer months and accumulations of krill are stranded on some beaches at this time.

The Munida species or 'lobster krill' follow a similar pattern to the euphausians, appearing in the Islands' waters in dense shoals. On their northward drift they become involved in the upwelling of the Falkland Current as it passes through the group. (Chapter One.) The effect is a natural straining and funnelling of the marine life of which the krills are an important factor. The 'food fields' are more apparent in particular areas of the archipelago, and large populations of birds form colonies close to these areas.

Insecta

The Falklands have no native species of bees, wasps or ants, the insects being largely confined to various flies, beetles, weevils, crickets, moths, spiders, mites and two species of butterfly.

Such a subject is, however, far too diverse for inclusion within the pages of this book, therefore remarks will be confined to only a few.

Although a fairly large variety of butterflies are seen in certain seasons, by far the greatest number of these are vagrants from South America. At one time two species of butterfly were known to breed in the Islands; a small blue species which before the 1900s was quite common, and the species *Brenthis cytheris*, reddish-brown with black spots and veins. The blue species, unidentified, has not been observed for many years and probably no longer exists.

Although Brenthis cytheris is observed in most seasons, it is not common. Many of the older inhabitants, however, speak of large numbers of these butterflies being observed in the camp until the 1920s since when it has slowly declined.

Small species of moth are both abundant and widespread over the Islands, as are spiders and some types of ground beetles.

CONSERVATION

Island ecology is highly vulnerable to foreign influences and therefore is easily damaged. This is particularly apparent on small isolated groups such as the Falklands. The small size of the Islands and their distance from the mainland limit the number of species found there, hence there is less competition between species than on a continental land mass. Even relatively small changes, some natural and some caused by human interference, can have profound general effects, for the buffers of great size and diversity found on a larger land mass are lacking.

How has the ecology of the Falklands changed? Few records exist to indicate how extensive were the original colonies of birds and seals when the Islands were first visited. However, there is sufficient evidence to show that populations were far greater than today. Colonies of Fur seals were known to exist on Saunders

Island, Keppel Island, North and South Fur, Sedge Island, Beauchene Island, Beaver Island and other areas. All disappeared as a result of direct assault by man. Penguin rookeries vanished either from the onslaught of oilers or from excessive egging.

Natural Vegetation Decline

Probably the greatest ecological disaster that has occurred in the islands is the destruction of natural vegetation. The introduction of pigs, goats and cattle onto East Falkland in the 1760s and later to West Falkland and adjacent islands resulted in the destruction of much vegetation. Sealers and whalers burned tussac grass and by the 1840s much of it had been destroyed on East Falkland. When sheep farming started in the 1860s this grass soon disappeared from West Falkland and some other main islands.

Hooker, visiting the Islands in 1847, described many native grasses and other plants as abundant. Blue grass, Cinnamon grass, and Wild celery were all recorded as covering large areas of the main islands. From a description by Herbert Felton, one of the first settlers on West Falkland, it is probable that they saw little change until the introduction of sheep. He wrote :

> The northern part of the West Falkland from Chartres through Roy Cove and Hill Cove to White Rock was covered with grass bogs reaching to a rider's knees, interspersed with fine grass and acres of celery. In many places, because of the growth, the camp was difficult to get through. In those days the white grass camps as we now know them were considered valueless for grazing. Cattle were magnificent, enormously fat and very plentiful. This wealth of good fodder was destroyed during the fine summer of 1871 when it was fired, and the camp was burnt to the soil from Chartres to Port Purvis. It took fifteen years before there was a semblance of recovery, the blue grass pulled up by the sheep as soon as it tried to grow, making the camp look like a hay field. Before this, stock kept fat summer and winter.

Fortunately pure stands of tussac grass survived usually because they were confined to small largely inaccessible islands which had no farming value. Ironically its great value as a fodder and its importance for sheltering stock has been recognised throughout the history of the Falklands. Moody spoke of the need to preserve the grass in 1842. In 1924 Munro wrote in his report :

> The extent to which the large tussock has been destroyed, particularly on the Western Islands, and the total absence of any serious effort to replant the old bogs appears to me to be very regrettable. In view of the fact that this can probably be classed as one of the most nutritious grasses in the world, it is quite remarkable to see it so much neglected in a country where nutritious vegetation of any kind is all too scarce. I can assure Falkland Islands farmers that, had we similar tussock points and islands in our country, we would value them sufficiently to take very good care of them.

In the 1971 report 'The Sheep and Cattle Industries of the Falkland Islands' Munro's words were repeated and it was pointed out that the position has 'changed but little since 1924'. On many large farms it is considered that tussac has no place in the sheep rearing industry, and it is very doubtful that sufficient tussac could be cultivated for the Islands' entire sheep population. However, the above report wondered whether this argument was sufficient reason for having no tussac at all 'and doing nothing about attempting to propagate it'.

There are exceptions where some smaller island farms have made great efforts to preserve the tussac. West Point Island is a notable example where preservation combined with stocking (see p 114) has been continued since sheep farming began. Because of their manurial value to tussac, Magellan penguins are encouraged to nest within the coastal plantations. During the Magellan's breeding season sheep are kept out of the tussac, thus a system operates which benefits man, plant and bird. Early voyagers associated tussac with penguins and the grass became known as 'Penguin Grass'.

It is difficult to assess the remaining tussac stocks, but calculations made of stands on offshore islands, which represent the main bulk, gives an approximate area of 12,000 to 14,000ac.

The present acreage of tussac appears to remain constant, a balance maintained between diminishing acreages in certain areas and natural re-seeding elsewhere. In the past the system of stocking land without any grazing control has been responsible for the loss of many acres of tussac on smaller islands. The system is still carried out but, with the economic decline of the wool industry the practice which brought very high profits, but often resulted in the complete destruction of an island's tussac, is now less popular.

The value of this native grass to stock has been recognised throughout history and this grass also affects the future survival of a very large percentage of the Islands' wild life. It is most regrettable that an intensive programme to increase the acreage of this plant has yet to be started.

The Wild Geese

Throughout most of the history of sheep farming in the Falklands it appears that the farmers have held the wild geese as their scapegoat, declaring that they compete with sheep for grass. In 1903, shortly after the sheep population began to decline, efforts began to reduce the number of geese. Farmers suggested that 150,000 geese be destroyed annually and payment be made at the rate of 15s per 100 beaks. In 1905 the Livestock Ordinance was amended and Government agreed to the payment. This caused great controversy, both within the Islands and outside, especially as the Bill had been passed by only a narrow margin.

Since then the goose has remained a controversial subject and interest is undoubtedly renewed during agricultural investigations. The agricultural team who visited the Islands in 1970 reported that, like other visiting teams, they were unable to study closely the habits of the Upland Goose. They considered that geese were a 'major pest' on newly-seeded areas and arable fields and also on coastal 'greens' but they also felt that the subject should be studied in detail by a pest control-cum-conservation specialist. The team recognised the ornithological value of the bird but felt that numbers could be reduced without endangering the species.

Conservationists agree that wild geese present a problem to farmers at certain times of the year but it is imperative that the

232

bird's habits and relationship with sheep should be studied carefully. The eradication of this bird will not arrest the decline of the wool industry and it has food value. In a world hungry for protein is it not feasible that geese could be farmed and provide a subsidiary industry for the Islands?

It is felt that the conservationist and the farmer could co-operate in solving this problem. The Islands have a regrettable history of depredations—here is an opportunity to prove that the inhabitants today are more far-sighted.

Conservation Measures

After a long history of depredation, the Falklands have made great strides towards fauna conservation in the last twenty years, but the sudden development of commercial fishing in the region could now mean that a new initiative has to be taken. The seas about the Falklands are the life-blood of such a large percentage of the Islands' bird and animal life, that any over-fishing could lead to disaster. It seems that the Falklands on their own can do little to control this new threat and, as for many other regions of the world, the problem has to be an international one.

It would be incorrect to say that nothing was done before to preserve the Islands' natural life. On the contrary; early conservation work was considerable, but it can be said that the need to preserve wildlife on a national scale is a new idea in the Falklands, although now rapidly being taken up by the younger inhabitants.

The most significant step taken in recent years was in 1964 when an Ordinance for the establishment of Nature Reserves was passed by the Legislature. At the same time an existing law which provided for the protection of a short list of wild birds, many being rare vagrants rather than breeding birds, was amended and made more realistic. One of the amendments made provision for the establishment of animal and bird sanctuaries. In the same year a senior representative of the World Wildlife Fund toured the Islands to view conservation measures.

The Reserves ordinance provides the ideal legislation, a brief interpretation being that land should be reserved for the study and research of both flora and fauna and that they should be virtually closed areas. Sanctuaries are considerably different. Fauna on this land is protected from man's direct assault by shooting, trapping etc. but Sanctuaries can be stocked with ruminants, and so no protection is afforded to the vegetation. Consequently the ordinance is anomalous when virgin tussac islands are declared sanctuaries and then stocked. However, the Sanctuaries ordinance does have the merit of presenting private land owners with the opportunity of protecting land against human depredation. The Reserves title may also be used by private land owners, although in this case the right to stock such an area would of course be lost.

By mid 1980, 7 sanctuaries had been formed; 2 of these embrace fairly extensive areas on the northern section of East Falkland island, the remainder being offshore islands. Five sanctuaries are on private land, the remainder belonging to the Crown. The total area covered by the Sanctuary Ordinance is approximately 9,500 acres.

There are now 14 Reserves totalling 4,429 acres, all offshore islands owned by the Crown. In 1970 two islands, Grand and Steeple Jason Islands, with a total acreage of 5,424, were acquired privately as wildlife reserves and remain valuable refuges today. In 1971 New Island was acquired privately and the New Island Preservation Company was formed, with the objective of illustrating a new concept in conservation.

Although run as a wildlife reserve, New Island retains its small sheep farm and encourages limited numbers of wildlife tourists and scientists to visit and work on the island, showing that conservation in the Falklands can be a viable operation. One of the most significant features of the New Island project has been the development of its ideas by others.

The realisation that specialised wildlife tourism can assist both conservation and the economy has brought new developments. A new conservation body, the Falkland Islands Foundation, with offices in London, was created in 1980.

In 1972 the SPNC (Society for Promotion of Nature Conservation) with offices in Lincolnshire, England, extended its interest in obtaining wildlife reserves by acquiring nine small islands. Two of these, the Twins, lie close to the Jason group in the north-west archipelago, and seven are found around New Island in the south-west. Thus the west side of the Falklands, the richest area for wildlife, now has the larger number of wildlife refuges.

Assisted by the World Wildlife Fund programmes of conservation, investigation has been carried out since 1963 by private enterprise. Such programmes receive the interest of the International Union for Conservation (IUCN) and the Falkland Islands Government, although the latter does not employ a biologist or maintain a department of natural sciences. Through these investigation programmes, special attention has been given to islands with no history of stocking or depredations and with a high ecological value. These were recommended for Reserve status. Areas were also classed according to populations and variety of fauna upon them. Any island supporting pairs of Johnny Rook (*Striated Caracara*), a bird which might be classed as an endangered species, had a high priority. Reserves and Sanctuaries have also been established in different regions of the archipelago in order to cover a wide range of habitat.

What of the future for the Islands' wildlife? The Falklands have an asset of vast potential value, not as exploited in the past, but in a new, wider field. The Islands are proving to be a special attraction to wildlife tourists and although the conflict has temporarily halted would-be visitors, the potential for this industry re-gaining lost ground is there. However, a continuing programme of conservation is needed, perhaps even more than before. Suddenly the Islands have become an area that has to be defended. The military are aware of how delicate this environment is and measures have already been taken to reduce conflicts to a minimum. Ultimately the fate of the Falklands and their unique wildlife would seemingly lie in the hands of some sort of agreement that must remove the military threat from the region and control the larger development issues.

9 THE FUTURE AND DEVELOPMENT

WHAT the future might hold for the Falkland Islands is still a subject of much debate and, amongst many, one of concern. Besides the sense of insecurity regarding their future, the Islands are faced with economic problems. With an economy based largely on wool production, one continues to hear the call for diversification. The islanders' discomposure may be related to their political future, or it could be the natural reaction of a very small community which has suddenly lost much of its isolation.

There is growing concern about the drift of population away from the Islands, and there are pleas for this steady disappearance of islanders to be halted. But is the situation any different from that in any other part of the world where better communications have suddenly been presented to a previously isolated community? Better communications with the outside world were wanted; with them has come emigration. But in the same way this could bring immigration. One view is that emigration should be halted by widening the opportunities to those (generally young) people who are leaving, but how is this to be achieved? Also deserving critical examination is the question of what percentage leave through lack of opportunity, and what number leave to seek a new life-style regardless of opportunity. Even in the most advanced communities, the seeking of a new life-style is not uncommon. The Falklands, though, have their own life-style, attractive to many would-be immigrants and perhaps the answer to this problem lies here.

In July 1976 a report was published under the title *Economic*

236

Survey of the Falkland Islands. This followed a survey by members of the Economist Intelligence Unit, led by The Rt Hon Lord Shackleton. The report is generally known as the Shackleton Report. Its terms of reference were, broadly, as follows:

> In the light of the Colony's weakening economy, to examine resources and prospects for economic development with particular reference to agriculture, wool industry, diversification and possible developments in oil, minerals, fisheries and alginates. To examine and advise on improved infrastructure. To assess the financial, manpower and social obligations of any recommended economic strategy, with particular reference to the encouragement of small scale enterprise and scope for local investment.

The report was an exacting and detailed work, leaving little unexamined. It included possibly the first study of social aspects, and on this subject the team felt that 'dependence' was a significant factor in the Islands' development. They reported that:

> . . . the indigenous people have obvious qualities, including honesty, versatility and hardiness; but there is also an apparent lack of enterprise at individual and community levels, and a degree of acceptance of the status quo which verges on apathy. Although they clearly have greater commitments to the Islands than most of the short-stay contract personnel from the United Kingdom, their sense of identity reflects mainly their strong awareness of British origins, and they do not yet seem to have evolved the kind of distinctive local culture which could foster self-confidence. While this situation is partly attributable to factors such as the settlement pattern, the diversity of origins in the United Kingdom, and insecurity caused by the sovereignty dispute, the most important single cause, in our view, is the pattern of dependence.

The Report goes on to say that:

> . . . in the camp there is dependence of people on the companies and resident owners or managers in various important respects. Though this pattern can be convenient and even comfortable in material forms, it does not encourage initiative. There are signs

237

of dissatisfaction with the situation, especially among the young, and this is a factor in migration from the camp. In Stanley there is dependence on the Falkland Islands Government, on the Falkland Islands Company and — for various social and other activities — on the ex-patriate community. For all there is dependence on Britain for most goods, for defence and for identity.

There has been little opportunity for individuals to acquire their own stake in the economy of the Islands — most notably a stake in the land. In all the pattern of dependence seems largely responsible for the inertia evident in certain areas of economic, social and political affairs.

The Green Patch Scheme

In an effort to alleviate this problem of dependence, and notably to offer opportunity to those requiring their own stake in the economy by obtaining land, the Falkland Islands Company sold their Green Patch holding, 72,000 acres situated north of Stanley. This was acquired by the Falkland Islands Government, sub-divided into six separate holdings and in 1980 was leased to applicants, with an option to apply for freehold possession after twenty years.

The scheme has been a bold approach to assist those who want a stake in the land, and all hope for its success. However, considerable patience will probably be required of those who now call for the compulsory purchase of more land for similar schemes.

Roads

The authors of the Shackleton Report considered that there was a strong social need for roads, although on economical grounds it doubted whether even a low-cost network could be justified, except in the long term by virtue of a greater enterprise amongst the Camp dwellers. However, in 1978, supported by a grant of some £1.157 million from the Ministry of Overseas Development, an ambitious project of road construction was commenced. With the plan initially to link Stanley with Darwin 60 miles away, some 8.5km had been laid by mid 1980.

THE FUTURE AND DEVELOPMENT

Tourism

At the time of the Shackleton Report, tourism on a small scale was already showing its potential. Today, although it has not expanded greatly, the position of certain forms of tourism in the Islands' economy is much firmer, and there is a stronger awareness of its potential. At the present time three forms of tourism are in operation. One has developed exclusively from Argentines visiting—from a natural curiosity about the 'Malvinas' and a desire to shop for British goods. This operation accounts for the majority of tourists now entering the Islands but is generally confined to Stanley and is a year-round business. A second form involves a minimal number of tourist vessels which call in at the Islands as part of an Antarctic cruise. These might be termed semi-specialist, and although a percentage of the tourists have a keen desire to see the Falklands, the main attraction is undoubtedly farther south. The future of this form of tourism in the Islands is probably questionable as it involves a considerable diversion from the main Antarctic cruise.

The third form of tourism is a specialised operation involving wildlife enthusiasts. This type of tourism would seem to hold the long-term possibilities. However, even for the ardent wildlife enthusiasts, the Falklands environment can be a constraint, and to balance this out this type of tourism needs to be fostered very carefully. By virtue of their geographical location the Falklands will always be remote and expensive to reach from those areas supplying this type of visitor. Participants are specialists; the majority know what they wish to see and are very mindful of related matters such as conservation. By displaying an understanding of conservation matters to these visitors and not viewing them merely as a commercial undertaking the Islands will assure their return.

Fishing and Oil Resources

The Shackleton Report drew attention to the hydro-carbon prospects in offshore areas about the Falklands. The report was based largely on the conclusions of Professor Griffiths and his

239

Birmingham University team who, in 1975, produced a report on 'The Geology of the region around the Falkland Islands'. The Griffiths team believes the Malvinas Basin to be a geological extension of the Magellan (Austral) Basin which currently produces both oil and natural gas. Seismic data revealed sedimentary thicknesses going up to 3.5km, which is apparently similar to many areas of the North Sea deposits. However, the Shackleton Report concluded its findings on a non-optimistic note with regard to the potential commercial gains from any exploration, but further stated that, 'however, there is no doubt that if political obstacles were removed and exploration blocks were leased/licensed, there would be response from oil companies.'

One of the greatest prospects for development lies in the fisheries about the Falklands. Surveys carried out on a commercial basis indicate that two species, hake and blue whiting, are probably the most important, with a sustainable yield for whiting in the region of 1 million tons per year. Another fisheries resource of even greater potential is krill, that shrimp-like crustacean on which the one-time large populations of whales fed. Some estimate that 150 million tons per year of krill could be taken from waters in the regions around South Georgia. Soviet, Japanese and German fleets are already fishing for krill, which in some cases is rendered into a form of 'shrimp paste' for human consumption, or used as a high-protein animal feed.

The question of the Falkland Islands' role in any fishing industry is the subject of much debate. Modern fishing methods do not require shore-based processing plants. The Islands can offer some services to the fleets, such as sheltered harbour facilities for transferring catches and supplies, and this is currently developing. Harbour dues are being charged to ships entering and in 1979–80 brought in revenue of £60,000. It seems likely that the estimate for the present year, of £80,000, will be exceeded. However, the Falklands only retain a 3 mile limit, which gives no opportunity to license or have any control of fishing.

For the majority of people living in the Falklands who have

witnessed the sudden phenomenal increase in Polish and Russian fishing vessels which are now a daily sight as they transfer catches to freezer vessels in Stanley's Port William, there is both concern and amazement: concern in those who view the possibility of the waters being fished out, amazement in others that Britain is not fishing in her own territory or at least licensing in order to take a better share of this potential.

The problem remains political: to extend the Falklands' limit to 200 miles would involve an overlap with that of Argentina. The present good relationship between the Islands and that country would almost certainly suffer if this issue was insisted upon. There would be little point, either, in taking such a limit unless it could be effectively controlled; this could not be done without the assistance and co-operation of Argentina. The matter was effectively summed up by the Rt Hon Anthony Crosland, Secretary of State for Foreign and Commonwealth Affairs, on 2 February 1977 when he made a statement in the House of Commons regarding the Falkland Islands and the British Government's relations with Argentina. Referring to the Shackleton Report he stated:

> The Survey further recommended certain major capital projects, notably an enlargement of the airport and a pilot fishing project, which would bring the total recommended expenditure' by the UK up to some pounds sterling 13–14 million. The Government, like Lord Shackleton and his colleagues, are in no doubt that the potential for development is there, and they will at the appropriate moment commission the essential preliminary studies to determine whether airport enlargement is likely to be practicable and cost effective.
>
> But for the rest, we cannot at this time accept the more costly recommendations. The overseas aid budget, recently cut in the December public expenditure exercise, would not stand it. There are more urgent claims from much poorer communities. And the right political circumstances do not exist.
>
> In Lord Shackleton's words, 'In any major new developments of the Islands' economy, especially those relating to offshore resources, co-operation with Argentina — even participation — should, if possible, be secured'. The Government agree. Such

241

new developments require a framework of greater political and economic co-operation in the region as a whole. Without such a framework, the prospect of achieving a prosperous and durable future for the Islands is bleak.

Communications Agreement

Probably the largest single step that has been taken in the Falklands' history concerning the very long standing dispute with Argentina over sovereignty was the implementation, on 5 August 1971, of what is generally termed the 'Communications Agreement'. Although the final question of sovereignty may not be resolved for some time yet, the Agreement has unquestionably lifted a veil of uncertainty. There is a better understanding within the public sector, both in the Islands and in Argentina, of each other. Air communication between the Islands and Argentina has brought a large interchange of people. Visitors from the coast are now common in Stanley shops and LADE and YPF personnel living in the Falklands have a place in the community. A comparatively large number of Island children have now received education in Argentina. Trade, mainly in building materials and food from the coast has commenced, although with rising costs in Argentina, this has become a constraint for buyers in the Islands. Argentina is at present viewing the possibility of buying the Falklands' surplus meat, a move which could have economic advantages for the Falklands.

The Argentine state-owned oil company Yacimientos Petroliferos Fiscales (YPF) have a depot in Stanley. Holding stocks for the operation of air communications, the depot also supplies fuels for domestic purposes to the advantage of the islanders. Locally, feelings were strained when the fuel agreement was being proposed, for it was felt it would create dependence on Argentina for one more important commodity. Today the Falklands might consider viewing the YPF agreement as a possible further advancement in their favour. The proposal to offer bunkering service to the fishing fleets will require fuel comparable in price to the present supply on which the vessels must rely from Uruguay!

Page 243 An offshore stack known as the 'Horse Block' lying off Weddell Island in the SW of the archipelago

Page 244 (above) The Britten-Norman Islander land aircraft introduced in October 1979.
Destroyed in the conflict this aircraft has now been replaced by two of the same type,
coming into operation April 1983; *(below)* Occupation by Argentine troops in Stanley.
French-built Panhard armoured cars were brought in by the occupying forces but
fortunately were never used in the final battle for the capital

Certainly no Falkland Islander wishes to take on Argentine nationality or wants British sovereignty to be given up; nor do hundreds of Argentines who have visited the Falklands expect this, for they have seen at first hand how difficult this would be at a human level. Generally their view is one of amazement and compassion for the Islanders' situation, one of the unusual twists brought about by the Communications Agreement.

In the period 22–9 November 1980 the Hon Nicholas Ridley MP, Minister of State at the Foreign Office, visited the Falkland Islands and spoke to the Islanders about how the sovereignty dispute with Argentina might be resolved. The Minister mentioned three options, a con–dominion arrangement, a 'freeze' on the question of sovereignty and a lease-back agreement with Argentina. The Islands' Legislature were asked to discuss these options and report on their findings, in preparation for Anglo-Argentine talks which were held in New York on 23 February 1981 as part of a series of negotiations on the dispute.

For many people, both Falkland Islanders and Argentines, the dispute is very much an emotional one. It was, therefore, probably not surprising that the Legislature rejected any option other than a 'freeze' and that the Argentine delegation at the meeting in New York duly rejected this proposal. It is probable that both the British and Argentine Governments view the lease-back arrangement as the main possibility of bringing the dispute to a close, but this can only be by agreement of the people of the Falkland Islands.

One has to have a certain emotional tie to these Islands to make a home here, but an increasing number are also aware that their homes cannot survive without a sound economical future for the Falkland Islands. It seems that for this to be realised, there has to be a closer link with the Islands' neighbour. Equally, Argentina must realise that, without the present population to run them, the Islands would surely not survive anyway.

10 THE CONFLICT AND OCCUPATION

THE events which caused the Falkland Islands to be on world news headlines for several weeks during the period mid March to mid June 1982 have been extensively documented, particularly from a military and political point of view. This chapter is a chronology of events in parallel with an illustration of happenings and feelings experienced by the author and family who were in Stanley at the time.

> *18 March.* Argentine scrap merchants land at Leith, South Georgia from the ARA *Bahia Buen Suceso* and the Argentine flag raised.
>
> *20 March.* HMS *Endurance* leaves Port Stanley with detachment of Royal Marines for South Georgia.
>
> *22 March.* British Foreign Office inform Buenos Aires that the Argentine landing is illegal.
>
> *26 March.* British Intelligence sources in Argentina report suspicious preparations.
>
> *28 March.* HMS *Endurance* reports the ARA *Bahia Paraiso* stationed off coast of South Georgia. Main Argentine fleet reported to be at sea.
>
> *29 March.* Contingency plans set in hand and orders given by Prime Minister for deployment of nuclear submarine in South Atlantic. Naval planning begins for despatch of a Task Force. The ARA *Veinticinco de Mayo* aircraft carrier sails, and British intelligence received which reflected view of Argentine officials that some form of military action would take place in near future.
>
> *30 March.* British Naval Attaché in Buenos Aires reports to

246

Ministry of Defence that five Argentine warships, including a submarine, were sailing to South Georgia, and another four had left Puerto Belgrano.

31 March. Reports received that virtually all the Argentine fleet at sea and heading for the Falkland Islands. British Cabinet meeting on the crisis. Request sent to United States for intervention with President Galtieri. Report sent to Governor of the Falkland Islands indicating possible invasion. Submarine *Spartan* ordered to the Falklands.

1 April. British Ambassador in Buenos Aires informed by Dr N. Costa Mendez that his government regarded South Georgia incident closed. Britain calls emergency meeting of United Nations Security Council.

2 April. At 0430hrs Argentine forces commence landing near Stanley.

In a matter of hours, dramatic changes took place in the Falklands, particularly in Stanley, the tiny capital town first hit by invading Argentine forces—changes which were later to spread to other locations in the archipelago. In a matter of weeks, if not days, all the inhabitants of these Islands were to experience alterations to their life style which in many cases would prove irreversible. The eyes of much of the world were focussed on the South Atlantic and a new chapter had to be written in the history of the Falkland Islands.

The morning of 2 April 1982 finally dawned after what seemed to us one of the longest nights we could remember. At 2015 hours (local time) the previous evening, His Excellency the Governor, Mr R. M. Hunt, had broadcast the first of several messages that night, the contents of which chilled our hearts and left us dumbly amazed.

Good evening. I have an important announcement to make about the state of affairs between the British and Argentine governments over the Falkland Islands dispute. We have now sought an immediate emergency meeting of the United Nations Security Council on the grounds that there could be a situation which threatens international peace and security.

The Governor went on to describe the events that had led up to this and the refusal of the Argentines to negotiate over the illegal presence of their nationals at South Georgia; he continued by saying that there was 'mounting evidence that the Argentine Armed Forces are preparing to invade the Falkland Islands'. His announcement continued with a listing of various precautions that were being taken that evening in the event of an invasion. Later the Governor made a further announcement saying that information had been received that an Argentine naval force was heading for Port Stanley and at its present speed could be expected off Cape Pembroke (the entrance to the outer harbour of Stanley) at dawn.

Like many, we were convinced up to that time that this was to be a show of strength on the part of the Argentines and that having perhaps made some gesture of a landing they would retire. That thought quickly disappeared from my mind when at about 6am a number of explosions were heard from the direction of Moody Brook, at the head of Stanley harbour; we were to learn later this was an attack being launched on the Marine barracks by the Buzo Tactico (Tactical Frogmen) of the Argentine Special Forces. Firing then broke out in many areas, although all we could see were lines of tracer coming from the high ground behind Government House and going across the harbour.

Throughout the invasion we continued to get information relayed to us by the local broadcasting studio. Much of this information came directly from the Governor, who was under siege at Government House; other details were relayed by residents phoning in to the broadcasting studio.

Our shocked disbelief slowly turned to indignation, not only for the invasion itself but for the very size of the operation. On reflection I believe much of my anger was probably due to my belief that the Argentine regime had acted with impatience and that by this single action they had thrown away many years of work and understanding which had been built up between the people of both countries.

From the information heard over the radio and from what we could see ourselves by mid-morning, the invading force was made up not only of large numbers of men; armoured troop carriers were also being deployed. Despite the size of the force, the taking of the town was to be no easy 'walk in' and the small detachment of Royal Marines and the local Defence Force were to hold up the assailants for some hours before the Governor (as Commander-in-Chief) gave orders to lay down arms.

As the morning wore on, one grim reality after another came home to us. Large numbers of Argentine troops in tactical formation were to be seen spreading through the town, almost as though they expected street fighting. An armoured carrier rumbled to a halt just outside our house and disgorged further numbers of men, at which point I had my first overwhelming thoughts of alliance with countries such as Hungary and Poland. Many times we had heard over the news of some country's radio station being taken over by a new regime, yet never once could we have imagined the same to happen in the Falklands; but now we were listening to our local radio-station manager, clearly under a certain amount of stress, explaining that the station had been taken over and that he was under orders to broadcast instructions from the invading forces. Later we heard the first of many military communiqués, transmitted by the Argentines. Although these were broadcast in both languages often they were insufficiently clear, resulting in confusion over what one could or could not do. The FIBS studio, re-named 'Radio Nacional Islas Malvinas', became an improvised information centre as the local staff, although under pressure by the mere presence of others, played an important liaison role and attempted to keep the civilian population informed.

On that first day, people were ordered to stay in their homes. The point was put to the military that they should understand that some of the islanders needed to go about their daily chores and eventually it was announced that if people required to leave their houses they were to show a white 'flag' outside their doorways; Argentine patrols would be instructed to give what help was needed. Language immediately became a barrier and it angered me that the military in authority could not appreciate this obvious problem. In our particular case the difficulty over language was not so great as my wife is bilingual, which got us out of many misunderstandings, but a majority were not so fortunate. At first I found difficulty in holding back my indignation over the invasion, and over the host of apparently unconsidered problems which it had caused. During the day I had the chance to vent this annoyance on a soldier, when a friend arrived at the door followed closely by an armed guard who waved a rifle about in the direction of the friend's back as though it was nothing more than a walking stick. The *conscripto* immediately got my feelings in no uncertain terms, which brought him close to tears; certainly he was very apologetic, and was to be the first of a number of these young soldiers confronted by me. Conscription into the forces is compulsory for all males of a certain age group in Argentina, the result being that most hated the military and what they stood for. The first one I confronted had been dumbfounded when he was told where he was, having believed that his unit was going on an exercise in southern Argentina. He had received little training, had scant knowledge of the FN rifle he carried, and had not fired one before.

The fact that many had received little training was evident again shortly after, when I was obliged to convey my annoyance to a group, led by a corporal, who chose to make one neighbour's grounds a training area; in the course of their little exercise they let a stream of uncontrolled fire go into an old shed nearby. This terrified the neighbour's children and proved the last straw for me—out I went and told them in no uncertain language where to go. At the least I expected an argument from one of them, but instead they all trooped off without a word. Although I had not thought about it at the time, these two incidents made me realise afterwards how the social structure seen in Argentina passed through into the forces. The *conscriptos* I had faced were no doubt less-educated rural types and although they had been the ones with the guns, my approach had been taken as authority. It was an interesting discovery of the so-called 'pecking order' and it was put to test many times in the ensuing weeks.

> *3 April.* Debate, British House of Commons; support for an operation to recapture the Islands. Argentine force lands on South Georgia; loses two helicopters, damage to ARA *Guerrico* (corvette). UN approves unanimously Resolution 502 calling for Argentina to withdraw and for negotiations on the future of the Falkland Islands.

On the second day, Saturday 3 April, the bewildered inhabi-·tants of Stanley were allowed to carry on 'as usual'. Walking the streets lined with armoured vehicles and under the scrutiny of military patrols, I remember the town looked and felt quite unreal. The blue and white Argentine flag appeared to be hoisted on every available flagstaff, including the most enormous of flags on the Secretariat pole; this was not to remain flying for long, and a few days later—on 7 April, when General Mario B. Menendez was sworn in as Military Governor—a strong wind plus the outsized flag proved too much for the staff, and all came crashing to the ground. Much was made of the incident and the word was quickly passed around that this was a bad omen for the occupying forces.

On that second day of occupation many people gathered in the general store, more for the comfort of talking to one another than for shopping requirements, although most people tried quite early on to stock up on essentials, in view of the uncertain period lying ahead. It was depressing to walk about the town, as it became evident that more and more troops and military equipment were being brought ashore. Armed sentries were posted outside all public buildings. To anyone familiar with Argentina this sort of thing was typical—and perhaps necessary in that country—but in Stanley it was not required and certainly looked ridiculous. The move was treated with a certain amount of contempt and very quickly the realisation got through to the military that it was out of place and as a result the practice was discontinued.

> *5 April.* The Foreign Secretary, Lord Carrington, resigns. Task Force: *Hermes, Invincible* and RFA *Pearleaf* leave for South Atlantic.
> *6 April.* 3 Commando Brigade leaves for the South Atlantic (4,820 men: 40, 42 & 45 Commandos and 3 Parachute Battalion).
> *7 April.* Britain declares a Military Exclusion Zone (MEZ) around the Falklands.

One cannot emphasise enough how important the BBC World Service news bulletins and other current-events programmes were to become in the way of lifelines, as developments unfolded in the crisis. It was through the BBC that we learned about some of the events listed above, and of American Secretary of State Haig's hectic diplomatic shuttle between Washington, Buenos Aires and London. The radio became so important that two sets were available in case the military might confiscate receivers— one to give up and one to hide away. Events as relayed by the BBC unfolded so quickly that it was almost impossible to keep up with the flood of news. Obviously we were cheered by the enormous backing the Islands received, and by the general condemnation of Argentina's action. But deep down our concern grew, for we were sure that whilst Argentina would not withdraw, Britain would not allow the aggression to go unanswered. The result, it seemed, could only mean some form of conflict in the Falklands, and these islands, which I had always claimed would remain one of the few places in the world to be free of war, were ironically, about to become a military 'punch bag'.

Almost immediately following the invasion, the occupying forces established their own heads over such Government departments as the Secretariat, Education, Public Works, Post Office and eventually the Medical Department (although in the case of the latter, an Argentine doctor was inserted to run the hospital alongside one of our own doctors). Certainly in the early days of the occupation the new military authority was anxious to see the system of civil administration continuing as normal, but little by little it was shown that they could not cope with a system as alien to them as theirs was to us. An Argentine Air Force officer who had spent time in the Islands some years previously was appointed head of the Secretariat (ie the administrative authority over government departments). He was well known to many islanders and I believe was respected by many. His excellent command of the English language was probably one of his greatest assets. His position was not an easy one, as he became the buffer on both sides, receiving complaints from the civilian population and attempting to smooth over problems that developed through the military. Throughout the occupation the Commodore was an important liaison officer and many hard discussions were held with him to iron out difficulties. He was clearly concerned about the situation which had developed and although he was never to say so directly, many of us felt that he did not approve of the action of the Junta. The Commodore, like a number of other Argentines, had known the islands and their people before occupation and I believe they realised the move to invade had been totally wrong. As far as they could they attempted to balance the situation but it was an impossible task and the strain was to become very apparent on such men.

> *12 April.* The MEZ comes into effect. Submarine HMS *Spartan* arrives at Port Stanley; sees Argentine vessel laying mines at Port Stanley.

By the middle of April many changes were noticeable about Stanley. The Post Office 'Royal Mail' sign and cypher now had a twin sign in the Spanish language and two rosettes in the blue and white national colours of Argentina were displayed above

253

the entrance. Falkland Island stamps were issued for one or two days but soon replaced by Argentine stamps. Mail services continued to the UK and other parts of the world, but only letters and postcards were accepted (parcels could be sent only to the mainland). Personally we found it difficult to concentrate on writing, added to which we believed anything written would be censored or simply mislaid. I believe it is quite possible that some mail was censored and towards the end of the conflict when large amounts of mail were held up both in the Islands and in Argentina, mail went missing. But fears that stamp stocks and other postal matter would be disposed of proved to be unfounded and in fact the Argentine civilian postal authority who took charge of the Post Office received credit from our own Postmaster for operating so correctly.

I believe that the simple changes annoyed people more than some of the major ones. The order to drive on the right side of the roads, in keeping with the South American system, was one such change. Many drivers simply 'forgot' the order, some pleaded ignorance when stopped, and others stayed on the side of the road they had always used. The result was sometimes chaotic, with Argentine military vehicles weaving down the roads never sure which way to go to avoid local traffic. For the Argentine authorities there was no way out, until in apparent desperation they were obliged to put up signs in English, saying 'Keep Right', and to paint large white arrows on the road surfaces.

Shortly after the invasion I was surprised to see small blue and white stickers resembling the Argentine flag displayed on certain house windows. Each emblem bore the words: *Usted tiene derecho a vivir en libertad*, the translation being 'you have the right to live in freedom', which seemed rather ironic. Why these stickers had been given to some householders and not to others remained a mystery, except that they were part of a census, started but never completed. Military personnel had visited the houses which now displayed these stickers, had queried the number of people living there and requested the occupants to place these emblems on their windows. They might well have

254

been part of some propaganda campaign for the benefit of the media.

The conflict over language extended beyond the spoken word and various notices in Spanish were largely ignored. One which puzzled even people who knew the language was the word MALIMA which appeared on dozens of containers (improvised from oil drums), placed in the streets, sometimes alongside our own litter bins. Neither was very attractive, but the newly prepared bins were half size, painted a less obvious colour (green, ours were red) and they had handles welded on. For days we wondered about the lettering, until a number of small printed cartoons appeared in some public buildings, advertising a 'Keep the "Malvinas" clean' campaign—in Spanish *Mantenga limpia Malvinas*, MA-LI-MA stemming from the first two letters in each word. It was in effect a gesture on the part of the new authorities to demonstrate that they were anxious that their soldiers kept the town clear of litter. This remained the case until late in the conflict, but was not consistent with the basic rules of hygiene ignored by soldiers about their encampment areas, where latrines seemed to be unknown.

It soon became apparent that the Argentine forces were not geared for movement outside their own country, something which was to lead to problems for themselves, the islanders and their property. In Argentina fuel in the form of timber—used in their field kitchens—is generally abundant; yet this important logistical point appeared to have been forgotten when the treeless Falklands were invaded, and almost immediately the main occupation of many *conscriptos* was a continuous gleaning for pieces of wood to fire these cookers or to keep themselves warm in their dug-outs. Initially areas about the outskirts of Stanley were cleared of old fence posts, abandoned hen runs and old sheds, but gradually pressure increased and property fences and even stocks of unused timber were being taken. During the latter days of the occupation, a chain saw could be heard across the town as the hunt for wood turned to the cutting up of an old sailing-ship hulk. Curiously enough, peat was not immediately appreciated as a fuel, and the few groups of soldiers who did learn of its value were to guard their knowledge closely. Outside Stanley wherever troops were building defences, the search for fuel resulted in some farms losing all their fences and gradually the landscape was stripped.

On quiet, still evenings, small plumes of wood smoke rose from the surrounding hills, indicating exactly where troops were entrenched. In Stanley, peat smoke was obscured by that of wood fires and the town took on a smell not only of burning wood but also of hot cooking oil, a familiar smell of many residential areas in Argentina. By degrees, small groups of wood-searching soldiers started to venture into all parts of the town. Our own experience was that direct confrontation accompanied by a bit of shouting often had the effect of making the young *conscriptos* drop their spoils and run off; others were very apologetic. We were not to win, however, for they would wait until curfew and darkness before returning, knowing full well there was little one could do then.

Whether the Military Authority anticipated problems is not known but notices in Spanish (printed by our Government printer) were produced with the words : *Propiedad Privada. Bajo Jurisdiccion Militar Prohibida la Entrada. Los infractores seran penados por Consejo de Guerra de Comando*, and signed *Mario B Menendez, General de Brigada, Gobernador Militar*—the translation being : 'Private Property. Entrance forbidden under military jurisdiction. Trespassers will be court martialled.' For the benefit of the troops these were then attached to gates or doors by residents remaining in the town. I believe the notices may have acted as a deterrent to some troops, but the absence of notices may also have indicated which houses were vacant.

Discipline lapsed in the latter days of the conflict and the numerous wood collectors became only a minor problem compared with the house breakers. Unoccupied houses were being broken into, many to be used for shelter at night. Some had food and warm bedding stolen from them whilst others were being ransacked by soldiers looking for valuables. Although intensive

256

efforts were made to board up empty houses in an attempt to protect them, the task was difficult and the same houses were broken into time and time again. The Argentine forces had their own Military Police and their efforts went a long way to stop the problem, but the officer in charge of the unit admitted to us that they were aware that within the several thousand troops about Stanley, there were known to be some delinquents, who were responsible for similar acts in their own country. He was very concerned and begged us to understand that such men were but a few but that they gave a bad name to the majority of honest soldiers. On the last day of the conflict, when troops ransacked the Stanley Post Office, I saw the same officer close to tears when he came in to view the appalling mess in the building.

The camp, particularly those settlements accessible overland from Stanley, hosted several hundred relatives and friends who sought a safer location for their children. It was generally felt that the more isolated farms and adjacent countryside would stand a better chance of remaining outside the area of conflict and action, if this was to take place. The most notable anticlimax in this context was probably experienced by those people who travelled 60 miles to Goose Green, the largest population centre outside Stanley, with some 80 regular residents. Their particular experiences of occupation and the ensuing battle merit an account on their own, and no doubt this will be recorded one day by those who were there. Within hours of the occupation of Stanley, many residents left the town and this exodus annoyed some whose decision it was to stay. But only the individuals knew how the invasion had affected them and the decision to leave or stay was entirely personal. In our own experience, concern for the well being of many people whom we initially thought might be seriously affected by the situation was totally unfounded, yet others of apparently stronger disposition seemed to suffer more seriously. We did not blame people for leaving the town but believed the correct thing for us to do was to stay. However, we also had our contingency plan, involving two or three families, if a quick evacuation had had to be made : tents, food and other equipment were packed ready in vehicles, although deep down I knew that if that point were reached there would probably be little chance of us getting out of town.

Regular internal communication links between Stanley and the farms and islands were all but severed, as R/T and other radio contact was banned except for a half hour 'doctor's time' each morning. The numerous amateur radio users in the islands had their equipment confiscated early in the occupation, although we realised that one or two operators had managed to avoid detection. For some time it was possible to reach some settlements on East Falkland from Stanley by overland routes, but there came a time when passes were required.

Argentine forces appeared to be everywhere. The schools, Town Hall, gymnasium, government sheds and workshops all held members of troops, while officers immediately occupied many vacant government-owned houses which the military considered theirs. Where there were private houses known to be unoccupied the military offered to lease and in some cases this was done and correct procedures carried out.

One of our neighbours, who chose to leave for the camp and left us in charge of his property, lived in a government-owned house. In order to keep the house free of military occupation, I adopted a ruse and every day went through a varying pattern of deception for the benefit of the many troops who were digging in about the immediate vicinity of the house. Each night lights were switched on in different parts of the house, curtains drawn, then opened each morning; I would be seen speaking or waving to apparent residents as I passed their windows. After entering the house I would come out wearing the neighbour's hat and coat, feed their ducks and hens, then reverse the procedure before leaving. It was a serious yet amusing gamble although at one stage I wondered how long I would keep up the ruse, particularly when one of the Argentine NCOs in the area asked why it was they never saw the people from that house. We explained that they were rather elderly and could not come out! The plan was successful until shortly after the date when black-outs and curfew were imposed; no longer could I carry on the lights-on routine. On the night of 6 May the house was broken into and taken over. We tried arguing with the intruders and made somewhat more diplomatic moves with higher authority but to no avail.

Arising from this episode we were to learn something more of the structure of the Argentine forces. The first occupants of the neighbouring house had been junior NCOs who had seized the opportunity to take the house over. Shortly afterwards, they were ousted by a group of officers and senior NCOs. Before leaving, one of the earlier occupants warned me to be very wary of the newcomers. They were not to be trusted, I was told, and were obviously not liked by those removed. Later on in the conflict I had good reason to believe this.

From many *conscriptos* but also from a few professional soldiers who lived in makeshift shelters about our area, we learned that they were clearly very angry at the disproportionate issue of food and other facilities between themselves and those who occupied the house. Obviously there was a certain element of the 'barrack room complaint' as seen in any army, but had we not witnessed the situation ourselves, we might have put their comments down solely to this. Late in the conflict we even heard the argument put to us by some officers who were also angry at the way many situations had been handled.

16 April. EEC import embargo on Argentine imports becomes effective. Haig's mission continues.

On 16 April we were surprised by a visit to our home by three respectably dressed civilians, who introduced themselves as members of the Anglo-Argentine community in Buenos Aires. Although born in Argentina, their parents had left Britain either to follow businesses in the Argentine or as immigrants to seek a new life style. Two of the visitors were men probably in their fifties, who spoke impeccable English and could to all intents and purposes have been British tourists. A younger girl and man in their twenties presented me with a picture of a new breed of

259

Anglo-Argentine : they had a good knowledge of English, had English looks, but otherwise I believe had closer ties with Argentina than with Britain. It seemed they were part of a six-person delegation who had taken it upon themselves to come from Buenos Aires as representatives of the British community there, their mission being to allay the fears of the islanders about becoming part of the Argentine and perhaps suggest some solution to the situation.

To have been allowed to travel to the Falklands clearly meant that they had friends in high places, perhaps in the Junta itself. But I believe their intentions were all the same quite genuine and that they did believe they could solve the problem and avert the threat of war between Britain and Argentina. Like any member of the British community in Argentina at that time, they were themselves deeply concerned at the likely repercussions against them if fighting was to break out in the Falklands; so in effect this, to me, was a form of plea to the Islanders to accept what had happened and to try and make a new life out of the situation. I remember agreeing with them that perhaps a solution to the problem could have been found before Argentina invaded the Islands, but reminded them that as the situation stood, we had not had a choice. Their own acceptance of Argentine customs, language and politics had been their choice; we had suddenly had this thrust upon us, which was a very different situation indeed. I do not suppose I made them any happier when I said I was certain there would be war, further emphasising my conviction by taking them to a concealed area of the garden, where I had been digging an underground shelter in preparation for such a conflict.

They had only been allowed a few hours in the Islands and although they were given freedom of movement in Stanley, I could not help but think what a hopeless task they had undertaken. However, in the short time available I agreed to walk them around in order to introduce them to a cross-section of the community. On the way across the town a local lad stopped to talk to me. During our brief conversation I noted a certain degree

260

Page 261 (above) In an attempt to bring in a 'drive on the right' policy, the Argentine authorities were obliged to paint direction arrows on the roads and put up 'Keep right' signs; *(below)* Only hours before a cease fire; an unforgettable sight of tired, beaten but perhaps relieved Argentine paras

Page 262 (above) A scene in Stanley following the surrender of Argentine forces. Even though fighting had ceased, fire and the vast numbers of both British and Argentine troops forced into the small town was itself a problem; *(below)* Argentine Pucara aircraft lie abandoned on the Stanley airfield. Stanley is in the background with Mount Tumbledown, Two Sisters and Mount Kent

of bewilderment on the visitors' faces, and I realised they had not understood what had been said. This brought home another point on the question of language; if they could not understand that young man's English, how did they imagine he was coping with Spanish, which was completely alien?

A little later the point was aired again, to an Argentine naval captain who was apparently in charge of the group's visit; he was also our new educational officer. Conversation immediately turned to the subject of the future; the naval-cum-education officer, in his neat, crisp manner, had an immediate answer to my point on the language problem. He considered this no problem whatsoever; with compulsory Spanish taught at school and extra-mural lessons for other inhabitants, within twelve years everybody would use Spanish as a language. His 'textbook answer' I felt was typical of the military mind we were now dealing with, and even the Anglo-Argentine visitors must have raised an eyebrow.

Ironically, at the very time I was discussing solutions for a peaceful outcome to the problem with our Anglo-Argentine visitors, the occupying forces were already laying mines. Later that day we had an urgent call from the hospital for assistance; a soldier had been injured and as our doctor would be sharing the operating theatre with military surgeons, could my wife help by translating. Apart from the guns we had seen being set up, this was the first real indication that the Argentines were preparing to defend the area by more permanent methods. During my attempts to discover where mines were being laid, I was told the accident had been caused by mines laid by the Royal Marines. We knew they had had none! Later it became apparent that more than one Argentine unit must have been laying mines and this had been a case of one unit over-laying another's minefield. The result in this particular instance was that one man was killed and the one on the operating table lost one foot.

In the weeks that followed, the new administration gradually collapsed as a result of the language barrier. Regardless of the ability of some sections to speak each other's language, there were

263

continuous misunderstandings which led ultimately to serious problems and breakdowns. Even the naval man, who was soon to lose his educational officer's 'cap' simply because the schools no longer functioned, succumbed to the problem he had planned to solve. Weeks later the same sharp, crisp man was hardly recognisable as he was seen slowly walking down the middle of a deserted street, somewhat untidy and with bowed head. The misunderstandings—perhaps disputes—did not appear to be confined only to the running of the administration here in the Islands. Problems were obviously being experienced in other quarters, even on the re-naming of Stanley. Initially this was announced as Puerto Rivero, then changed to Puerto Soledad, and yet a third time to Puerto Argentino.

> *21 April.* Transport *Norland* sails with 2 Parachute Battalion. Argentine reconnaissance Boeing 707 intercepted 12 miles from the Task Force and driven away.

On 22 April the word was passed round the town that President Galtieri was to make a visit to the Islands. We certainly felt no excitement about his visit, although we were indeed curious and wondered if there would be some sort of parade through the town. Except for an unusually large number of aircraft flying in formation over Stanley and a message of welcome in Spanish on the Post Office door, we never saw anything to indicate such a visit, and many people remained sceptical that this actually took place.

> *23 April. Hermes*-based Sea King helicopter crashes; one killed, first British operational casualty.

As the Anglo-Argentine visitors could not have gleaned more than a superficial impression of the community here and the problems we faced, I imagined they had returned to Buenos Aires with little hope of taking the matter further.

However, on the evening of 23 April I discovered things had

gone very much further, for the visitors returned, explaining that they had been flown from the mainland in the Argentine President's own aircraft! They explained that they had had a meeting that very day with Galtieri, at which time they had submitted a proposal for a settlement of the issue. Whether the head of the ruling Junta had accepted the proposal we shall probably never know, but here they were with the blessing of the President himself and permission to do more or less what they wanted in order to publicise their 'solution'. This was in written form and I was asked to read it and comment. Although the paper went into a number of matters relating to the islanders and their future with Argentina, the one basic theme which was the core of the proposal was the maintaining of the islanders' 'way of life'. The visitors had seen something of Stanley and a little of how people lived here, and clearly had viewed this as the sole nucleus of this way of life which they had understood from several people was one of the most important things islanders wanted to retain. To keep this way of life they proposed, therefore, that the town should remain just as it was, and that Argentina would build a new town elsewhere, leaving the islanders to choose where they wanted to live! There was also mention of the islanders having their own council to run the town, but as far as I could gather only to the extent of a local town council, which would not be unlike the running of an Argentine provincial town. What, I queried, would happen about our currency, laws, export of our main produce, our stamps and postal system, none of which was mentioned and of course could not remain remotely the same under an Argentine regime. The overall proposal was extremely superficial and I saw why their efforts were being backed by the authority in Buenos Aires, for this was probably how the islanders were viewed, a simple, camp community, which in the eyes of the generals, wanted nothing other than a 'superficial' existence. I still believe this is one reason why, within three days of the invasion, television was being transmitted from our local broadcasting station and the offer of cut-price TV sets was being made. This one simple commodity it was thought would surely win the islanders over to the new 'military authority'. A new supermarket was next on the list of priorities.

The Anglo-Argentine representatives were clearly anxious to make their proposals public and get people's views; they were allowed to do this and even the camp R/T station, which had virtually come to a standstill, was open to the group so that opinions could be obtained from people on the settlements. As I had previously warned the group, I was sure their proposals would not be taken seriously and furthermore, all of us were now tense with concern and suppression and it was my view that people would release this tension on them. It was indeed a sad but expected ending, for feelings were indeed rent upon the group and there were bitter scenes at a public meeting they were allowed to hold in Stanley. I fear the group returned to Buenos Aires bitterly disillusioned.

At about this time of the occupation the broadcasting station (FIBS) was closed early, presumably so that no messages could be slipped out which the British ships might pick up, although there were numbers of tongue-in-cheek remarks and records transmitted apparently without understanding. Shops and offices were open to the public for shorter periods and the telephone exchange was taken over and manned during the evenings by the military. Speculation had it that telephone conversations were being tapped, but the technical advice received indicated that this was difficult. Had this been carried out, those responsible for translating would have been kept very busy for little or no return in information. Being greeted by *numéro* when one lifted the receiver to make a call was sufficient to cause near collapse of the system, for rather than overcome the language difficulties and ask for a number in Spanish, communication by phone, especially for many of the older inhabitants, came virtually to a halt.

   25 April. South Georgia re-taken. No British casualties; 1 submarine (ARA *Santa Fe*) and 137 captured, 1 sailor killed, 1 seriously injured.

Towards the end of April the decision was taken amongst a group of Stanley residents to set up some form of civil-defence unit. This was approved by the Argentines so long as one of their representatives was present at every meeting. The committee first met on 24 April and the unit's purpose was to help and advise those residents left in Stanley on how best to prepare for an eventual conflict. An information pamphlet was drawn up offering advice on how a house could be fortified against shrapnel, bomb blast etc; the town was divided into six sections and members of the unit from different areas given the job of selecting what were to be termed 'safe houses' (usually those built of stone, brick or concrete). These few buildings were then to be marked with a suitable civil-defence sign; the military did not agree to our own format and we were therefore obliged to mark the safe houses with the letters DAP (*Defensa Area Pasiva*=civil defence), and the symbol X within a circle, all to be painted in red. It concerned us somewhat that using this sign could confuse any British forces; would they think these houses were occupied by Argentine troops?

I was confident that units or either the SBS or SAS were already in OPs (observation posts) overlooking Stanley, and in order to assist in the recognition of the DAP sign we fixed ours on a large board high up on the house. A suggestion was made to others showing the sign that they kept as much washing out on their lines as possible, so that the two might be connected with civilian residence. A message was also sent to Britain explaining what the symbol meant but when we did meet up with men who had been watching Stanley for many weeks, we discovered they had known nothing about the signs!

One of the goals set by the civil-defence committee involved finding out exactly how many residents remained in the town, who they were and where they were placed, the idea being to allocate various 'safe houses' where all the people could go for shelter. The Argentines attempted a census but failed simply because people were on the move from house to house and many were leaving daily for the camp. Even for us on the committee there was an element of difficulty, but finally we established that just over 500 people—about half the normal population for Stanley—remained in the town. One matter which I believe demonstrated how naive both sides were when it came to modern warfare concerned the long discussions that were held on the form of signals to be given prior to air raids. I do not believe anybody thought the town itself would be bombed, but it was felt that warnings should be given of any imminent British air attack. After the first low-level bombing attack by a Harrier (of which one had about two seconds' warning), our idea of air-raid warnings went off with the proverbial wind. Many of us smiled at just how naive we had been, for even the crews of some Argentine anti-aircraft guns, with their early-warning radar systems, were left open-mouthed by the surprise and speed of some attacks.

The majority of attacks were probably heard rather than seen, especially as diversionary bombing often preceded low-level attacks. Probably one of the most spectacular and daring attacks —which was seen by many in Stanley—was a very low-level attack by two Harriers which literally skimmed the surface of the harbour's opposite foreshore, thus making it impossible for the Argentine weaponry on both shores to fire for fear of hitting each other. For perhaps a total of ten seconds we watched with concern and fascination as the two aircraft screamed along the foreshore, turned slightly to line up with the airport and then let a terrifying deluge of rocket and other fire open up on the area. Instantly there were balls of fire and smoke issuing from the target and the two aircraft disappeared over the horizon. One was always left in terrible suspense waiting to hear if the aircraft had returned safely to their base.

Aware no doubt that we would be needing as much information as possible, BBC's *Calling the Falklands* programme commenced broadcasting every evening from 27 April (instead of the hitherto once- or twice-weekly programmes). The move was heartily welcomed but most frustrating as the broadcast was deliberately jammed by the Argentines for a time; fortunately BBC introduced additional frequencies which enabled the avid listeners to follow the broadcasts regularly.

On 27 April we were disturbed to hear that eight Stanley residents, some with their children, had suddenly been moved to Fox Bay, on West Falkland. No reasons were given for the arrests, but of the six adults one or two had been leading members of the Falkland Islands Committee, and two were members of the Falkland Islands Defence Force (FIDF). Others detained, including the Senior Medical Officer, were members of the newly formed Civil Defence unit, which made one wonder who might be next! On reflection, however, it became clear that our Senior Medical Officer did pose a problem to the Argentine military, who obviously wanted to use our hospital for their own troops, something the doctor strongly opposed. He was also concerned that the correct behaviour should be observed by the occupying forces towards the civilians, and he had attempted (unsuccessfully) to get a Red Cross representative to the Islands as an observer. Shortly before his removal, the SMO had explained to us his feelings on this matter and expressed a wish that as many people as possible ought to be made aware of their rights under the Geneva Convention. He suggested that relevant sections of the document be copied and distributed amongst the population; this involved actually copying the convention in the Law Office, which had by that time been taken over by the military. By devious means this was finally accomplished, but it was a nerve-racking undertaking and not until I walked out of the building with the copies rolled inside a magazine did I relax a little. Later, in the comparative safety of the house we typed the convention out and this was then duplicated elsewhere. But in much the same way as our 'air-raid warning' idea, the papers were not used as it was decided that the text of the convention was far too complicated for people to understand.

28 April. Britain announces a Total Exclusion Zone (TEZ).

29 April. Soviet Union launches *Cosmos* general reconnaissance satellite with a South Atlantic orbit.

30 April. British TEZ comes into effect. USA announces sanctions against Argentina.

Also on 27 April, coinciding with a curfew and black-out order, we were surprised to see a very large container vessel, the *Formosa,* come into the inner harbour of Port Stanley. Besides fuel, food and ammunition, we wondered what else this vessel had on board for there was considerable secrecy over her unloading. The eighteen or so guard dogs brought in earlier were posted about the jetty and the vicinity was closed off. An almost sinister atmosphere developed with a lot of movement carried on at night. Ammunition boxes appeared in different areas of the town and people became generally concerned for the diminishing neutrality of the town itself. The Argentine forces must have expected some sort of commando attack, perhaps on the *Formosa* herself, for the use of scare depth charges in Stanley harbour and Port William was stepped up and at different times of the night we would feel the shock waves from the explosions as they travelled through the sewer system!

> *1 May.* Task Force moves into the TEZ. Ascension-based Vulcan bombs Port Stanley airfield; Task Force Harriers bomb Goose Green airfield; *Glamorgan, Arrow* and *Alacrity* shell Port Stanley airfield. Special Air Service (SAS) and Special Boat Squadron (SBS) patrols land in the Falklands.

In the early hours of 1 May we were awoken suddenly and violently by an incredible roaring sound which seemed to sweep by, leaving the house shaking. In half sleep my first thought was that a low-flying aircraft was attacking, as a prelude to a landing. Later I was to realise that what we had heard were the shock waves from twenty-one bombs dropped by a Vulcan on Stanley airport. It was our first experience of many attacks—and the last time we slept upstairs for many weeks. Later on the same day we experienced the first naval bombardment, as ships of the Task Force shelled the airport area. Our house shook and shuddered and from our position at the east end of the town we had a particularly clear view of smoking fuel dumps and aircraft that had been hit on Cape Pembroke peninsula, only $2\frac{1}{2}$ miles away.

Following the bombing and shelling there was a noticeable change in the attitude of the Argentine military; I do not believe there was any question of retaliation against us, but one sensed a mood amongst the occupying forces and instinctively we became a little more wary. By this time the airport and approach areas were effectively sealed off from all but the Argentine military so it was impossible to get any idea of how much damage might have been done to the runway. Speculation ran high on the degree of damage which might have been inflicted, and when we saw an Argentine magazine showing a photograph of a badly damaged airport terminal building, we were convinced that the runway, too, ought to have suffered severely. The fact that the Argentines denied this convinced us further. Perhaps this was one of the most satisfactory ploys, for it was correct that the runway had suffered comparatively little damage, and certainly not enough to prevent the Argentine C130s making regular flights in and out with supplies on most days. Although we were part witness to the bombing I do not think the actual significance of it came home to us until a day or two later, when we noticed much activity in the little cemetery nearby. It then became apparent that quite a few men had died, probably more than was shown by the seventeen or so simple wooden crosses which appeared overnight in the cemetery.

On the same day we heard that the airfield at Goose Green had been bombed by Harriers from the Task Force, and although Goose Green lay only some sixty miles away, no news was received direct of this raid, the first information coming from BBC News broadcasts. In normal circumstances we would have listened only to one or two BBC broadcasts each day, but now the radio became like a drug and efforts were made by one of us to listen to every single news programme from 7am local time until 10 or 11pm each day. When reception threatened to be poor there were frantic moves with the radio to different parts of the house, where various aerials had been rigged up.

2 May. Conqueror torpedoes ARA *General Belgrano;* Harriers sink ARA *Com Somellera* and damage ARA *Alferez Sobral;* 3 Mirage, 1 Canberra shot down.

Following the news that the Argentine cruiser *General Belgrano* had been sunk on 2 May with great loss of life, and the Exocet attack on HMS *Sheffield* two days later, the mood locally grew sombre and tension increased: one visibly noted a change in people. In the West Store, which had become a daily meeting place for many Stanley residents, there were still smiles in greeting but it was obvious that many were deeply engrossed in their own thoughts. However, it also became noticeable that many people were being drawn together more and a bond never before seen developed between those in the town.

4 May. Sheffield hit by Exocet: 20 killed, 24 hurt, 242 rescued. Sea Harrier shot down, pilot killed.

On 4 May a Vulcan again bombed the airport area, but we must have been getting used to the detonation of bombs and shells every night, for the impact of the raid was not to us as severe as the first bombing. The following morning we were witness to another aspect of war. A hesitant tap had taken me to the door and there stood the first of many dejected human beings that we were to see in the days to follow. I suppose he might have been eighteen or nineteen years old, he was a *conscripto* and obviously in a state of shock. His face and clothing were black and smelled of smoke and he had difficulty in asking for the drink of water that had compelled him to try our door. All he could explain was that he had come from the airport and that a bomb had killed others who had been in the dug-out with him. He did not seem to know what he was doing in the town but had, he said, no intention of going back to the airport.

Even though the airport seemed to be under attack most days, we were amazed at the number of Argentine Hercules aircraft that appeared each night. What they were actually bringing in was not clear but more and more troops seemed to be everywhere in the town and we watched with growing concern how their positions encroached further into civilian areas. This bothered me for I could eventually see our own underground shelter being taken over, even though I had gone to some length to keep it secret from the hundreds of troops who were now in the immediate vicinity. Within days of the invasion a number of anti-aircraft guns had been set up close by, but then it seemed the defences had stopped growing; now they were on the increase again.

Immediately alongside the cemetery wall was an area of common land which, if taken over, would effectively have meant that we were virtually surrounded. The problem was how to stop it being used. Then one day, seeing a group of officers and NCOs seemingly planning the use of this area, the idea was there. Quickly I interrupted the discussion by explaining that we 'understood' the area to be an old burial ground; being quite superstitious, the idea was promptly abandoned by the Argentines! On at least two other occasions the same ruse worked and the ground was never used, although in one instance we were amazed to see a group of soldiers commence to build a fortification actually inside the cemetery walls. Even though the soldiers engaged in the work were obviously quite superstitious and concerned by what they were doing, their *teniente* had ordered the work and was indifferent. Our calling in of the padre, who intended to take the matter to higher authority, eventually stopped the work, although the officer in question was very reluctant to take any notice.

6 May. British government announces a total of 20 ships chartered; 2 Sea Harriers lost, both pilots believed killed.

7 May. Foreign Minister Pym announces the offer of a ceasefire, coupled with a mutual withdrawal. The British Government announces a blockade of the Argentine coast, outside the 12-mile limit; the United Nations takes over peace negotiations.

With larger numbers of troops in the town the number of individuals who came to the house begging for food increased. We queried this with some military authorities and were told that the troops were getting plenty of food. This I believe was so at certain levels and in some units, but not all. Those requesting food were usually young *conscriptos* and we eventually established that it was mainly these who were short of supplies. Over the weeks of occupation it was not unusual for people to get to know individual soldiers and in some cases this was mutually beneficial. Although we had to be careful, we eventually adopted our 'tame' *conscripto,* who would appear in the shadows of the house often with one or two of his companions. Through these young men we were able to build up a fairly accurate picture of what they did, how they lived, their personal views about being in the army and their thoughts on being in the Islands. As the majority were conscripted into the army they hated the job they were doing and all wanted to pack up and go home.

Our 'tame' soldier had a passion for football and his only concern was that the conflict should be over so that he could be back in Argentina for the World Cup. The fact that Argentina lost a match just prior to the surrender I am convinced had a final demoralising effect on many of their soldiers.

There was obviously a lot of bitterness between different units regarding the distribution of food and the conditions in which a lot of them lived. Although we did not raise any political questions, many of those to whom we spoke openly stated that they felt it had been wrong to invade such a small place. They were surprised to find that the inhabitants did not speak Spanish and that it was not, as they had been led to believe, just an outpost, inhabited solely by people from Britain. Finding an established township amazed them. Many seemed to view the conflict itself with surprising indifference. One day, watching an aircraft with black smoke pouring from it, slowly descend and crash, we were concerned for what we thought might have been a Harrier and its pilot. We queried this with our 'tame' soldier, who immediately broke into a huge grin. 'No, that was an Argentine Mirage which they shot down by mistake,' he said, 'but it's all right, the pilot ejected.' This, to our knowledge, was the second incident of its kind.

9 May. The Argentine intelligence-collection vessel *Narwal* is captured.

10 May. *Sheffield* sunk; *Narwal* sunk.

11 May. *Alacrity* sinks transport *Isla de los Estados* in Falkland Sound.

After six weeks our diary entries record: 'How extraordinary it seems that situations even such as this can grow on one. Bombs, shots, explosions no longer feel as frightening. The UN talks now seem to have gone on for months rather than days or weeks, and faith in the success of a peaceful solution wanes.' News came through the BBC that the luxury liner *Queen Elizabeth 2* (*QE2*) had been hastily converted to a troop carrier and had sailed from Southampton on 12 May with 5 Infantry Brigade. The news that she could be in the South Atlantic in just 11 days I remember surprised us especially as we always thought in terms of some 30 days for our little supply vessel to make the 8,000 mile journey.

12 May. Troopship *QE2* leaves Southampton with 5 Infantry Brigade (2 Battalion Scots Guards, 1 Battalion Welsh Guards, 1/7 Gurkha Rifles).

14 May. British Ambassadors Sir Anthony Parsons (UN), Sir Nicholas Henderson (USA) recalled to London for consultations. Pebble Island raided by SAS with gunfire support from *Glamorgan*: eleven aircraft (Argentine) destroyed.

Daily we waited for news of some landing, placing our bets on Fox Bay. When we heard that Pebble Island had been the scene of a commando-type raid and that eleven aircraft had been destroyed we were most surprised, not so much about the attack itself, but that the Argentines had a base there. Perhaps because

I was aware that such things would now develop I felt for much of the following weeks like a caged lion, with frustration at not being in a better position to help. Instead, all one could do was to complain (to no effect) about troops shooting Steamer ducks in the harbour, board up empty houses, chase wood collectors, and do daily rounds of a handful of the older residents. Like many I found work requiring mental concentration difficult; instead energy had to be spent on practical tasks, even though in restrospect I suppose they were sometimes rather pointless. At the time some matters had greater significance; when the dairyman started to lose cattle to beef-hungry troops a great deal of concerted energy and effort was directed into argument with the Commodore and Military Governor in an effort to persuade them to save the herd. Some cows were saved, but not before the majority of heifers had been taken and slaughtered.

15 May. Soviet Union launches another *Cosmos* reconnaissance satellite.

16 May. Harriers sink *Rio Carcarañá,* damage ARA *Bahia Buen Suceso* transports.

17 May. Ireland and Italy end embargo on Argentina. Troops moved around the fleet in preparation for landings.

It was largely through the Commodore and the few officers working with him on civil matters that the civil-defence unit was able to continue some measure of service, although it had become evident that the military suspected it of other doings. At a late period in the occupation, when it had become clear that a military conflict was inevitable, four of us connected with the activities of the DAP were summoned to the Secretariat by the Military Authority. Although not directly accused, we were asked to control the increasing number of incidents that were taking place against members of the forces. Most incidents were by younger members of the community and were acts of provocation more than anything else. We of course had no control over these acts although an attempt was made to impress on those responsible that such behaviour could lead to serious problems, not just for themselves but for the whole town. One of those responsible for an incident was to have been sent away to Argentina as an 'example' to others; our arguments that this was not the sort of community that would suddenly erupt against the occupying forces I hope went some way in preventing this matter going to that extreme.

At this stage of the occupation everybody was reaching a very high point of tension. Nobody knew what the next move might be. The Argentine troops were noticeably more nervous, especially at night time, and even during the day, when the town was shrouded in mist at times, one took extra care in how one approached certain areas. There were incidents of random shooting and a number of residents had remarkable escapes. Especially on windy nights, a sentry shooting at a shadow or piece of moving grass on the shoreline would cause a repetitive action along the harbour's edge. There was an increase in the fitting up of trip wires, many with simple arrangements of empty tin cans; others, it was discovered later, were not so simple nor so harmless.

> *19 May.* UN Secretary General de Cuellar makes a last attempt to convince Thatcher and Galtieri to stop the war. British *Sea King* crashes in Chile.
>
> *21 May.* San Carlos sea battle begins. Fleet in Falkland Sound. *Ardent* hit: 22 killed, 30 injured. *Canberra* withdraws. 3 Cdo Brigade lands. 2 Gazelle helicopters down; helicopter crash kills 21, 18 of them SAS.
>
> *23 May. Antelope* hit.
>
> *25 May.* Argentine National Day: heavy air raids, casualties heavy. Sea battle ends. *Coventry* bombed, sunk (21 killed, 20 injured); *Atlantic Conveyor* hit by Exocet (12 killed).

The landings and establishment of a bridgehead at San Carlos on 21 May was met with a mixture of excitement and concern, but as we learnt of the air raids and casualties on both sides the atmosphere in Stanley, although tense and expectant, was very quiet. Probably one of the worst situations at this time was not knowing what was actually going on, even a few miles distant. There were moments when we could actually hear the sound of battle, but it was a case of so near yet so far when it came to news of the events. It was ironic that such knowledge was travelling 16,000 miles before we received it, often 24 hours later.

We found the same situation existed with many of the Argentine forces; either they did not know or they were being issued with some unbelievable propaganda. When we approached one of the *conscriptos* and told him about the landing at San Carlos, he told us that they had heard, but the troops who had landed had been re-embarked and that Great Britain was 'calling the whole thing off'. This swapping of information was always treated with considerable reverence and never reached a point where one argued over the widely differing reports that each side was issuing.

When 2 Para took Goose Green on 28 May and reports started to trickle through of the ordeals there and the number of Argentine prisoners taken, the forces around us started to take more notice of our reports than of the ones that they were issued by their own superiors. This stark realisation of the situation was also evident by the sudden interest taken in building better defences, and there was a lot more intense activity.

28 May. 2 Para Battalion capture Goose Green and Darwin : 17 British casualties, 34 wounded. Some 1,400 Argentine prisoners, 250 killed. 45 Cdo ordered to Douglas Station; 3 Para to Teal Inlet.

29 May. Atlantic Conveyor sinks.

30 May. 5 Infantry Brigade lands; 45 Cdo and 3 Para arrive at Douglas and Teal Inlet. Argentines fire three Exocets, no hits. Harrier shot down. *Exeter* repulsed Exocet attack.

When details came through about the treatment of the residents at Goose Green many of us became concerned about what might happen in Stanley; my fears were increased when the

Page 279 (above) Final surrender. Argentine troops being searched for weapons before being boarded on a vessel taking them back to Argentina; (*below*) The 'litter' of war. An array of arms and ammunition belonging to the Argentine forces which littered Stanley at the time of the surrender

Commodore called me in to warn me that he no longer had much influence over the military as regarded civilian matters and that we were to be especially careful. Whether he thought Stanley residents might be confined together I do not know, but I remember impressing on him the practical problems of such a move in Stanley. There were some seemingly absurd contradictions of this nature but it did go to show that there were others with feelings. About this time a *teniente* in charge of a small unit close by came to the house and enquired if we had shelter against the increasing shelling, and that if not we could share their dugout! He was obviously sincere about his offer so I took him round the side of the house to show him our own little underground shelter. He was clearly impressed by the way I had adapted concrete paving slabs, for the next day his entire unit could be seen toiling up and down some slopes nearby, carrying the same type of concrete block to add to the roofs of their own shelters.

31 May. K Company of 42 Cdo is helicopter-lifted to Mt Kent to link with a squadron of 22 SAS Regt.

About this time word was quickly passed around that the military were short of petrol and that they were therefore requisitioning diesel Land-Rovers. Overnight there was a sudden glut of diesel Rovers that no longer worked, batteries went flat, important parts went missing, while other vehicles simply vanished from their normal garages. At the same time, male residents between the ages of 16 and 60 were being issued with identity cards. Although it was said that these were only for heads of families, this was often contradicted and whole families of males were issued cards. When the military arrived at home to issue mine, I raised this point and, having received a conflicting answer, I suggested what the reason really was! My suggestion was not appreciated and for a moment I thought perhaps I had gone too far; but, more to the point, I knew I had been correct.

The same soldiers enquired if I had a vehicle, and what type it was. I gave the correct details, but added that it was out of order. This was true, but I did not add that only hours before it had been working. . . . Obviously my answer was doubted, for on the following day we were visited by no less than six members of a cavalry unit, who wished to look at the Land-Rover. Ironically, when they arrived I was elsewhere in the neighbourhood giving advice on another diesel vehicle. My annoyance at having been recalled was met by apologies from the young officer in charge, who further explained that they had to collect what vehicles they could. If they were cavalry, we asked, what was wrong with their horses? He smiled, but still insisted that his mechanics should look at the Rover. My annoyance must have made them more nervous than I was myself, for having taken no more than a casual glance at the vehicle with its open bonnet and the array of oily tools purposely left out, they offered more apologies for any trouble and left—perhaps—to look at the very vehicle from which I had been called away!

On 30 May a further military communiqué informed people that those houses at the back of Stanley were to be evacuated for the safety of the occupants. It was a worrying time for those who had stayed living in that area, for with little warning they were forced to find alternative accommodation and had the added concern that they stood to lose their property to the military. The word 'evacuation' was one that we and many others feared, especially as a number of suggestions had been made outside the Islands for this to be carried out. Every time a vessel arrived in Stanley harbour, the thought of evacuation caused tension to build up almost to snapping point, for it was at these times that we thought that the possibility really existed.

Some people found comfort in being close together as a group and the largest store in town—constructed partly of stone—had become a second home where many spent the curfew hours; private homes also became gathering places where people spent their days and nights together. Others, like ourselves, felt a much stronger need to be in familiar surroundings and where we had various contingency plans ready.

THE CONFLICT AND OCCUPATION

1 June. Mount Kent captured; Mt Challenger occupied.

On 1 June we learned that the fighting was as close as Mount Kent, which we could see clearly to the west of the town. I think everybody's gaze was fixed on that distant hill, and every plume of smoke or crash of shell had us wondering who was responsible. The following day our 'tame' soldier reported that the British had given them seventy-two hours to quit, and even the *teniente* in charge of the unit felt that something had to be done before too long to stop the fighting.

3 June. Propaganda-leaflet raid on Port Stanley.

On 3 June our diary made special mention that at about 6am a low-flying aircraft had been heard passing over the back of the town under cover of poor visibility. Later we connected this with the information that propaganda leaflets were being dropped over the Argentine positions. These leaflets, in the form of safe-conduct passes, offered the chance for individual troops to surrender. This was one of the mysteries of the conflict, for we never saw one of these leaflets, and have yet to hear of anyone who did. We wonder if they were dropped in some remote region where they still may be found, or whether instead of dispersing they might have landed in bulk and been quickly destroyed.

5 June. 5 Brigade advance party of B Cy 2 Para takes Fitzroy and Bluff Cove.

On 6 June we were encouraged to hear—as always, via the BBC—that areas as close to Stanley as Fitzroy and Bluff Cove had received British troops there the previous day, indicating that the Argentines were surrounded. This was confirmed when we heard of a radio conversation that the Commander British Forces had had with the Commander of the Argentine Forces, asking him that his men lay down their arms. I suppose at that stage most of us had hoped for surrender but the following day we learned almost first hand that this would not be the case. A number of people locally had been listening in to British Forces radio frequencies, and on 8 June, through one of these, we had early news of the strike on the landing ships *Sir Galahad* and *Sir Tristram*; no details were known except that it had been a serious and tragic setback.

> *8 June.* Landing ships *Sir Tristram* and *Sir Galahad* bombed in Fitzroy; 59 killed, 74 injured. Landing craft bombed in Choiseul Sound, 6 killed. *Plymouth* bombed in San Carlos Water.

Although it must seem trivial compared with the shelling, air attacks and battle going on quite close to us, some Stanley residents were fighting a minor battle of their own. Retreating Argentine troops commenced to swell the numbers of men already in Stanley, and wet, hungry and tired groups wandered about the town looking for shelter and food. Keeping soldiers out of empty houses became a full-time occupation for some of us and we personally adopted a rule whereby one of us remained in our own house at all times. Supplies of water had become short, not only from damage to the mains from shelling, but also due to the increased demand. At first we relied on outside water butts but finally we were even compelled to collect from small streams running down the road outside.

On the morning of 10 June there was considerable air activity and a missile was seen to plunge into the harbour, a second one hitting the top of the Police Station. We know now that the target—missed by some ten metres—had been the Town Hall, where it was known that briefings were held by senior Argentine officers. After the incident, one of the more familiar military men who worked alongside Gen Menendez, a man who spoke English, was seen in the main store in argument with numbers of residents who insisted that the missiles had been Argentine! It was amusing to note he was so perplexed by the number of people who insisted that this was so, that I am sure he went away not over convinced that the weapons were in fact British.

11 June. Final assault on Port Stanley begins.
12 June. 3 Para captures Mount Longdon; 45 Cdo takes the
Two Sisters feature and 42 Cdo takes Mount Harriet.
Glamorgan hit by Exocet : 13 killed, 14 wounded.

The night of 11 June and early morning of 12 June was probably
one of the worst experienced, and certainly the first time we felt
the incoming naval shells closing in on the town. In the confusion
it was difficult to say from which direction the bombardment
was coming, but that night we could actually hear the noise of
shells as they came close over the house before exploding. At one
point there was a loud crashing sound on the walls and on the
roof above our position in the house, which I had thought to be
mud, rock and other debris thrown up as a shell hit the road. In
fact it was a large piece of shrapnel that had sliced into the top
of the house, with a smaller piece that must have spun its way
through one of the walls above us, leaving a trail of wood chips
across the floor. From a vantage point in the house I could also
see a great deal of tracer, flares and blinding flashes on the slopes
of the hills to the west of the town, and I realised that the final
push for Stanley was imminent.

As accurate as we believed the naval guns to be, several parts
of the town had been hit during the night and although we had
been disturbed about the near misses we had experienced, there
was deep distress later when we learnt that three members of the
community had been killed by shells fired by our own guns. In
a township so small, where everyone was known, it was not an
easy thing for people to accept or comprehend.

Over the weeks of listening to gunfire we were by this stage
able to distinguish between the different types of gun used, and
naval guns were as distinctive as the Argentine 105mm and
155mm howitzers. Early on 12 June we were suddenly introduced to a new sound. Why, I don't know, but the roaring we
heard that early morning from just above the house, left a cold

chill in the body. There were two such sounds like rockets going off one after the other, followed by an agonising silence from the naval guns, and I remember thinking that whatever had been used had apparently stopped the ships firing. Later we realised that what we had heard were the two Exocet missiles that had been launched from the road above us, one of which had hit HMS *Glamorgan.*

In retrospect I suppose most days brought a glimmer of amusement, and the morning after this particularly nerve-racking night was to be no exception. Although our neighbour's house had been taken over by Argentine forces, I still made daily visits to attend to what remained of their hens and ducks. The house had obviously suffered near misses as well, windows were shattered and all power cables were cut. The new occupants of the house were not amused and when I made some remark about the numbers of shells that must have hit the area, all I got in reply was a remark about the shells having been made in England. I shrugged my shoulders and walked on to the hen house. All the birds were alive but not a window remained and the door had been blown off the shed. However, for the first time during the occupation there were two new-laid eggs! Later that day we made note of a fantastic sunset, red streaks across the sky probably caused by the dust of war; certainly one could smell cordite and other explosives in the air, and in an odd sort of way it passed my mind that this was almost like some warning of what was to come.

13 June. 2 Para Battalion take Wireless Ridge; 2 Scots Guards take Mt Tumbledown.

13 June arrived bright and crisp, very cold but with excellent visibility. There had been a lull in the fighting before dawn, but now everything seemed to be opening up from both sides. Shells were coming in from the British positions and in response the Argentine forces seemed to be throwing back everything they had.

Over the weeks we had built up a particular dislike to the 155mm gun which was positioned no great distance behind our house and with every salvo of shells fired into the area by the navy we had longed for it to be finally silenced. It did survive however and for many hours to come we were to witness the devastating power that this gun had. Following every ear-splitting explosion as it fired one could almost follow the course of its shells as they made a tearing noise through the still air, then seconds later we would see the shell burst on Mount Longdon. A number of fires broke out in the town and we blessed the calm conditions, for had there been any wind, fires could have swept through the entire town.

None of us knew what the situation was in the fighting, but we certainly realised that if this intensity of shell fire was to continue it would only be a matter of hours before the town itself might be in ruins. The first indication of hope was seeing small groups of Argentines walking up the side of Tumbledown actually towards the British lines carrying white flags. That hope however was not to be fulfilled for many hours and throughout the rest of the day and night the pounding of shell fire went on.

Some time during that night, as we lay fully clothed ready for whatever the situation demanded of us, an enormous amount of small-arms fire opened up right alongside the house. This we thought must be a final move by troops attempting a direct raid into the town. It was in fact a raiding party attempting a diversion but in retrospect fortunately not into the town.

14 June. 1/7 Gurkhas take Mount William; 1 Battalion Welsh Guards take Sapper Hill. Gen Menendez surrenders.

The morning of 14 June dawned one of the worst we had experienced weather-wise. It was cold, with wintry showers making everything grey and inhospitable, a complete contrast to the day before. The firing had continued throughout the night and early morning, but shortly after breakfast there was a lull and instead of shots there were voices, hundreds of voices. Outside, crouching against our stone walls, in our doorway, against the sheds, in the yard and opposite, sheltering against the cemetery wall, were some 400 Argentine paras. An unforgettable sight of tired, beaten but perhaps relieved men, wrapped in their overcoats, blankets and ponchos. Some crouched along the side of the house looking half dazed, starving and cold as the icy southerly wind swept down the hills.

At that point in time we had no idea what their intentions were. It flashed through my mind that they might have been preparing to re-group at this the east end of the town, but looking at them again I doubted very much if they had any fight left in them. Seeing such a sight really disturbed me emotionally and I immediately realised that these men were finished and it was therefore time to show some compassion, simply because they were human beings. Opening the door, two blanket-wrapped figures who had been lying against the door slumped into the porch exuding the over-powering stench of smoke. I had to step over these half-sleeping bodies before I could reach outside. A hundred pairs of eyes stared at me through blackened faces, but nothing was said. Quite a number of them we had noted wore bandages. 'Are there any who need injuries seen to?' we asked. 'If so we will have them in the kitchen where there is a bit of warmth.' Heads moved slowly from side to side and the gesture of hands indicated that their wounded had been left somewhere else. Some of the men crouching against the wall were visibly shaking from the cold, so going back indoors, I took an empty 7lb jam tin, filled it with hot water, added the last of our coffee with a lot of sugar and handed it round outside. I will never forget those faces as the communal tin was passed from hand to hand; the majority appreciated it but the two sergeants who bellowed at the men for accepting the drink and talking to us obviously did not. Moments later the group moved on east, leaving behind men who no longer had the physical capability to move.

Huddled in the road was one man obviously in some state of shock and only by enticing him with a hot drink was I able to get him against a lee wall where there was more shelter. We still had no idea what was happening until I noticed a group of men removing the magazines from their FN rifles and then actually taking out the firing pins. Minutes later there was a light tap on the door and standing there was one of the men to whom we had offered coffee. 'For your concern for us, will you please take something from me and the men.' He then handed us a radio that he had brought with him. At first we refused, at which he was to explain that he would not be able to take it back with him to Argentina. A few minutes later we heard that a ceasefire had been called and that surrender was imminent.

The shock, the nervousness and sadness were to continue for many days, but the conflict that had held us in suspense for weeks was over. We saw no celebrations, no cheering amongst those islanders in the town; just a sense of relief. In a similar way, the British soldiers arriving in the town also showed relief plus very evident weariness of body, whereas ours was of the mind. Many people suddenly aged and I believe the conflict was to carry on in the minds of some for a long while after the surrender. The Argentine soldiers mainly showed delight as they knew they were going home. From those who emerged from bunkers near the house we learned of their relief that it was over. We saw no Argentine anger at being the defeated, just a great deal of sadness at all the lives lost and the pointlessness of the war. There was a deepening bitterness as awareness of the true situation sank in, coupled with resentment and in some cases unconcealed anger towards the handful of men in power who had led them into this, as well as the lies and concealed information that had reached the popular level in their country. One man told us he would reveal all they had experienced to 'every single Argentine'. I am sure he was not to be the only one.

11 POST-WAR AND REHABILITATION

Administration

Following the conflict and the subsequent establishment of a large military garrison outnumbering the civil population perhaps four to one, it became necessary to review the form of administration. Military and civilian operations were thrown together thus requiring a great deal of mutual planning. A joint administration was established whereby the former Governor, Sir Rex Hunt CMG, took on the title of HM Civil Commissioner, and the Commander British Forces Falkland Islands (BFFI), Major General David Thorne, became a non-voting member of Council and took on the title of Military Commissioner. He was sworn in at a meeting of Executive Council on 24 August 1982.

Public facilities

It is probable that no part of the government or private sector has remained untouched in the rehabilitation process and the establishment of the garrison. Public facilities operated by government departments, such as water and power plants, which had already suffered during the conflict, could not cope with the extra requirements. Stanley has therefore seen a mammoth co-operation scheme, with the government power station and filtration plant having their capacity boosted by equipment brought in and operated by the Forces.

Medical

Severely handicapped by the immediate problem of suitable accommodation, the Islands' small hospital in Stanley is at this time being used by both the civilian and military personnel. The consequential overload of this facility has highlighted the need for a new hospital. In order to keep the existing facility going, emergency works have been agreed at a cost of £1.25 million. In addition, a sheltered accommodation complex adjacent to the hospital is planned for the elderly, at an estimated cost of £350,000. Following the conflict, the Island of Guernsey made the generous offer of £250,000 towards rehabilitation and asked the Falkland Islands Government to identify a specific project; of the projects identified, sheltered accommodation was the choice of the Guernsey council and it is therefore anticipated that this will be the project financed by Guernsey.

With the loss of specialised medical facilities obtained in Argentina before the invasion, patients requiring special treatment which cannot be handled in Stanley by the military medical specialists stationed here, are evacuated by military aircraft to England via Ascension Island.

Postal

Probably one of the most extensively used departments has been the Post Office. Used throughout the occupation by the Argentine postal service, the facilities are now shared by the British Forces Postal and Courier Troop (Royal Engineers) and the Falkland Islands postal service. Although distinct in their operations, the two post offices share not only the limited facilities of the post-office building, but also the despatch and receipt of mail. Local distribution, such as mail delivery to the camp, is handled by both military transport and the normal operation using the Falkland Islands Government Air Service aircraft. Mail coming in and forwarded out of the Islands is carried on the 'airbridge' via Ascension Island, using Royal Air Force (RAF) Hercules aircraft.

At the present time, eight months after the re-occupation, there is no regularised delivery or despatch, mail for residents of the Islands being carried with Forces mail as and when space and aircraft permit, although in practice this can mean a delivery of mail three times a week. Depending on the sailing of the now large number of vessels between England, Ascension Island and the Falklands, deliveries of surface mail, parcels and paper categories can be fairly frequent, often carried with airmail on the airbridge.

During the early period after the re-occupation, post for residents and Forces was for a time air-dropped by parachute, with some (airletter forms) being picked up by the air-drop aircraft using a 'snatch' system. In this operation, specially prepared sacks of mail were picked up by a low-flying Hercules trailing a grapple hook on a long line, the resulting catch being winched into the aircraft.

Police Force

Severely stretched with more than its usual duties and with local recruiting problems, the Police department had to be strengthened from outside the Colony. Soon after the conflict assistance was obtained from the Metropolitan Police, and a sergeant plus three constables were seconded to the local force for a term of six months. Attached to the local force and using the same facilities, a Military Provost Unit made up of a Provost Marshal and twenty other ranks from the three services have formed a tri-service provost unit with the added title of 'special constables' enabling them to assist the local police force with its duties. The local force is at present composed of a Superintendent, one constable, and one police woman constable.

Public Works

The PWD has been heavily taxed by the present situation; in addition to its normal duties, the department has been affected by rehabilitation, the work of Army engineers assigned to public services, housing development etc, and facilities are being shared with military units applying the same skills. Owing to loss of equipment and shortage of labour, with the added unusually large amount of heavy traffic in Stanley, maintenance of the roads has presented a further work load, to the extent that under a £15 million United Kingdom government rehabilitation scheme, contractors have been acquired to carry out this work. (*See* 'Rehabilitation and Present Development'.)

Air Service

As a result of the invasion on 2 April 1982 the Falkland Islands Government Air Service (FIGAS) was forced to stop its operations. The two Beaver float aircraft were never to fly again and were eventually destroyed in the ensuing hostilities. The one Islander land aircraft, although put into service by the Argentine military for their own use, was only used once or twice for passenger services. This aircraft was also severely damaged during the fighting and has not returned to service.

Following the war, a considerable number of Argentine military Huey helicopters were surrendered and in the interim period while there were no conventional aircraft available for the FIGAS operation, enterprising members of the air service, with some assistance from the military, refurnished one of the helicopters and put it into service for mail and freight. The operation continued for some weeks but finally had to be curtailed owing to technical problems. Although the aircraft is still retained the future of a helicopter service within FIGAS is not known.

Following a decision to build up a new service using the same type of aircraft that had already proved themselves in the Islands, a land Beaver was acquired and converted to floats (in December 1982) and came into operation on 24 January 1983. Two new Islanders were purchased to replace the one lost, and these came into service in April 1983. All aircraft were purchased under rehabilitation funds. Until the new Beaver came into operation, passenger movement between Stanley and the camp settlements had been very largely reliant on military helicopters. Although at times military machines were used extensively for passenger movement, a service so defined was not put into operation, but nevertheless carried a very large number of residents and mail.

Meteorological

The establishment of an RAF station at Stanley Airport and

the increased need for additional weather reports and forecasting for military aircraft brought about the creation of an Air Force Meteorological Office. Having the facilities to receive Polar Orbiting Satellite weather pictures, which were not available to the Government Met Office, forecasting ability has increased. The local government still retain the services of one Met Officer who is responsible for local broadcast forecasts and as forecaster for the FIGAS operation; both stations operate for the assistance of each other.

The 'Airbridge'

Although a military operation, the airbridge is used for transportation of island residents and other civilians where there are special needs, such as medical evacuation and priority cases. Utilising Hercules C130 aircraft of Strike Command the airbridge first came into operation on 24 June 1982 with flights from Ascension Island. With such great distances involved and the added problems of the aircraft being unable to make use of staging posts on the South American mainland, in-flight refuelling for aircraft on their way from Ascension to the Falklands has become routine over the 3,800 mile, 14hr flight. At the present time the operation has some six flights per week. Royal Air Force VC10 aircraft are used for onward flights between Ascension Island and the United Kingdom.

Shipping

The impact of shipping on the Falkland Islands as the garrison has developed is something the Islands have probably never experienced before. Large numbers of freighters now frequent Stanley harbour. Many of these vessels are roll-on roll-off container ships and although the systems for unloading these are improvised, they have demonstrated that this type of ship could be used on a more established basis in the future.

The export of wool and imports are still carried by the chartered Danish vessel MV *A.E.S.* which except for an interruption during the occupation still maintains four annual voyages between the United Kingdom and the Falklands. At the present time there is no shipping link with any South American port. A plan used to bring down dependants of members of the Task Force lost in the war utilising the port of Montevideo in Uruguay as a link with Port Stanley renewed an old route that ended in 1971. There is at present no indication that this will continue, but it would seem to be one of the possibilities for a route through the South American continent in the foreseeable future. At present a limited number of berths are made available for passenger transport between the Falklands and Ascension, the UK section of the 10–12 day trip being operated by the Royal Air Force.

The Customs and Harbour Department maintains control over local imports and the collection of harbour dues. Prior to April 1982 large numbers of Polish trawlers used the port facilities for bunkering and to transfer catches to freezer vessels. This was interrupted for the duration of hostilities but commencing in October 1982 Polish vessels have again been allowed into Berkeley Sound for the same purpose. Between the date of commencement and March 1983, some 50 Polish vessels have used the harbour facilities regularly.

The large amount of shipping, both merchant and naval, necessitated a greater degree of movement control both in Port William and the inner harbour of Port Stanley. Taking the responsibility for this off the local government department, the military have established a Naval unit, headed by the Queen's Harbourmaster (QHM).

Local internal shipping (see p128) is still maintained as before for the delivery of stores and collection of wool from settlements.

Schools and Schooling

In terms of disruption, schools and schooling were probably hit more than any other government service. As a result of the closure of the schools during the Argentine occupation all the buildings used by the Education Department in Stanley including the schools themselves, were taken over and used by the occupying forces. This included the rather controversial new school hostel building that had just reached completion but had yet to be used. Following the conflict and eviction of Argentine forces, it followed that the same buildings were taken over by the British forces. Repairs to these buildings and the replacement of school equipment necessitated the postponement of schooling, and a normal educational programme was unable to recommence until July 1982.

In the case of the hostel, defects in its construction led to the abandoning of the building as a hostel for schoolchildren, so the building has remained in use by the military. To replace this school hostel, designed to accommodate children from the camp, the educational authority for the present time has had to revert to the use of a large residence leased for the purpose from the Falkland Islands Company, together with a number of specially imported mobile homes purchased under the rehabilitation scheme. The sum of £800,000 has been approved for the construction of a new hostel.

Overland routes

Perhaps one of the most significant changes that has taken place directly due to the conflict concerns overland routes into Stanley. These routes and tracks were viewed by Argentine forces as important military objectives to the British forces, and as a result many tracks and immediate areas were heavily mined. Although many tracks and areas have been cleared of mines and booby traps by the Royal Engineers (EOD), large areas of camp in the immediate vicinity of these routes remain 'red' (uncleared), or suspect areas. At March 1983 some 93,315 hectares had been searched and a total of 1,808,346 pieces of ordnance destroyed. Overland travel has been severely hampered, especially in those cases where stock has had to be moved—for example in the case of sheep being driven into Stanley for the butchery. Routes to some surrounding peat banks have also become danger areas and this has resulted in a deficiency of peat fuel. The loss of this form of fuel, together with the loss of other fuels hitherto imported

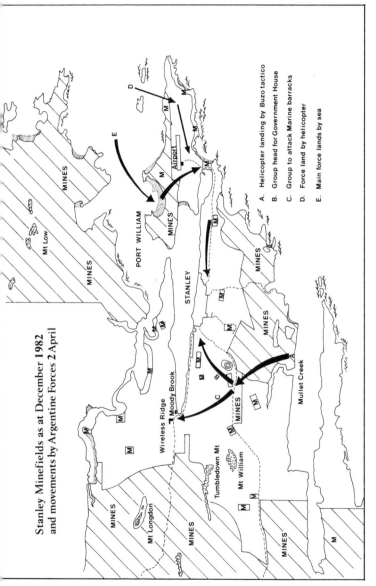

Stanley Minefields as at December 1982
and movements by Argentine Forces 2 April

A. Helicopter landing by Buzo tactico
B. Group head for Government House
C. Group to attack Marine barracks
D. Force land by helicopter
E. Main force lands by sea

Movements by Argentine forces, 2 April 1982, and Stanley
minefields as at December 1982

from Argentina, has meant that solid fuels to replace peat, fuel oil and gas have again been imported from the United Kingdom.

At the end of May 1982 Lord Shackleton was requested by the British Government to up-date his 1976 *Economic Survey of the Falkland Islands*, and in September the new Report was published. Many of the recommendations in this Report remain the same as those in the earlier one. In the 1976 study however a total of £13–14 million was recommended for development, without any indication of the time scale over which the expenditure would fall; the present recommendations involve expenditure of some £30–35 million over a 5-year period, excluding major developments such as exploratory fishing.

Concerning the scope of the new study by Lord Shackleton, the Report has had limitations imposed upon it; the immediate needs of rehabilitation were a separate issue from the future economic prospects and as such had to be analysed separately. The military and political backgrounds have also presented limitations, as Shackleton states in the new Report:

Now despite the *de facto* cessation of hostilities the situation is clearly still fluid, with the future attitude of Argentina to co-operation with the Islands unknown but at the very least unpromising. In the introduction to the 1976 report I emphasised the importance of regional co-operation in any major new developments of the Islands' economy. I believe that logic still applies. We hope particularly that co-operation will be forthcoming from South American countries in one aspect, external communications, because without satisfactory air links the Islands' prospects will be considerably less promising.

In the 1982 Report a number of principal recommendations were made for action seen as necessary to arrest the decline of the internal economy, to diversify the economy, and to explore offshore potential in the area. Some of these were:

1 *A Falkland Islands Development Agency* to be created under the administrative and financial umbrella of the Overseas Development Administration, but based in the Islands, was recommended; its purpose being to act in a similar way to the Highlands and Islands Development Board. The agency would be responsible for the local allocation of development loans and grants for new enterprises, take up shares and in some cases own particular development enterprises and services, and also act as agent for the buying and selling of farms during the recommended ownership transfer of some Falkland Island farms.

2 *Transfer of farm ownership.* In his Report Shackleton considered that urgent steps should be taken to transfer the ownership of absentee-owned farms, with the idea of creating owner-occupied smaller farming units.

3 Under the *development of agriculture*, the Report recommended the expansion of the existing Grasslands Trials Unit, the introduction of farm production and improvement grants and subsidies. The introduction of rural sciences in the school syllabus was also recommended.

4 Under *fisheries* a survey of shellfish fisheries was suggested, support for a salmon-ranching pilot scheme (*see also* 'Salmon Ranching') and the recommendation for a 200-mile fisheries limit around the Falklands, South Georgia and the South Sandwich Islands.

5 On the question of *communications,* the establishment of the external air service was reviewed (*see* 'External Air Service'). On external shipping, it suggested the investigation into the potential benefits of new direct-charter arrangements, such as linking the Falklands to the St Helena/Ascension Island shipping service.

6 The *expansion of the road network,* taking into account the infrastructure needs of the small-farm development, was recommended.

7 The *construction of an all-purpose jetty* in Stanley for the unloading of ships up to 8m draught was listed, and recommendations were made regarding alternative *energy supplies,* including investigation into the use of a 200–250kW wind turbine in Stanley, and smaller (3–10kW) units in the camp.

8 The new garrison and its effects on the civilian community were looked at and recommendations made for the establishment of a Falkland Islands civilian/military liaison unit; this would include the new Chief Executive recommended under proposals for the enlargement of the governmental structure.

In his Report Shackleton commented that 'there can be no avoiding the fact that the public funds required to implement the regeneration of the Falklands economy and to provide the means for investigating and to some extent realising the development potential of the Islands are quite substantial, relative to the size of the population.' Ignoring the finance required for exploratory fishing, which the team believed should be judged in a wider and longer-term context than development of the Islands, a sum of £30.6–35.6 million over five years is estimated, or the equivalent of £3,245–3,786 per islander per year. The Report also stated that the 'Falkland Islands economy is at a critical stage; if funds are not made available now for necessary change and development, the cost of supporting the Islands over a long period of further decline could be considerable. The Falkland Islands do have a resource development potential but much of it may be in the longer rather than the short term. Furthermore, if public money is not to be wasted, it is in this interim period that the commitment of the Islanders will be tested.'

On 8 December 1982, Mr Francis Pym, the Foreign and Commonwealth Secretary, outlined a development plan designed to implement some of the main proposals in the Shackleton Report, at a cost of £31 million, to be spent over a period of six years. He also stated that a further £5 million for rehabilitation was to be added to the £10 million announced in July 1982.

POST-WAR AND REHABILITATION

Under the heading 'Recovery and Rehabilitation' the Island of Jersey was to give £5 million which has gone to Her Majesty's Government; although forming part of the total £15 million earmarked for rehabilitation, the Falkland Islands Government hope to acknowledge this help from Jersey by identifying it with a specific project in the Islands.

REHABILITATION AND PRESENT DEVELOPMENT

Housing and Roads

One of the largest projects under the rehabilitation scheme and one critical to further development has been the acquisition of fifty-four houses (manufactured by Myresjöhus of Sweden), for erection in Stanley. The dwellings are being erected by Brewsters, a contract firm from the United Kingdom, and will form new extensions both to the west and south of the existing town. Besides the functional aspect the new buildings will present a completely new dimension in house design to the Islands, both in appearance and construction.

Another major project under the rehabilitation scheme is the repair and re-construction in concrete of some 10km (6 miles) of roadway in Stanley, and construction of a further 2.2km (1.4 miles) to the west of the town; a sum of £2–2.5 million has been allowed for this work. Under a separate contract the Ministry of Defence (MOD) are to repair with asphalt 6.4km (4 miles) of the road linking Stanley with the airport, at an estimated cost of £3 million. Construction of the Stanley to Darwin road (see page 236), interrupted during the conflict and severely handicapped by the loss of machinery, continues under a £1.6 million grant from the ODA. Some 19km (12 miles) of the all-weather hardcore-type road had been constructed by March 1983.

Infrastructure

Electrical energy and transmission for Stanley, at present being boosted by the inclusion of a military installation, is to be renewed with the introduction of two 1.5 megawatt generators and five transformer sub-stations, under a scheme costing £1.5 million. Repairs to transmission lines caused by war damage are being carried out, at a cost of £100,000. Development of the generating capacity to the year 2000 would be an additional 4 megawatts with extensions to sub-stations and transmission lines; this requirement would exclude the power needed by the British forces in Stanley.

Supply and treatment of water to Stanley : short-term plans are now in hand to repair and make good war damage to the system at an estimated cost of £350,000. In the near future (three–four years) the existing water-treatment plant situated at Moody Brook will have to be replaced along with town mains and added storage facilities to cope with any increased civilian population and development of industry.

With much damage having been done to the existing sewage and drainage facilities in Stanley, the immediate requirement is for the repair, replacement and an extension to the network of drains, septic tanks and harbour outfalls, with a cost of some £110,000.

Deep-water jetty and harbour installations : for some years the need for a deep-water jetty in Stanley has been recognised. While the Communications Agreement existed with Argentina there was much discussion on the proposal to build such a jetty, which would allow the transfer of bulk fuels from vessels to the YPF depot (*see* 'Communications Agreement', page 242). Lord Shackleton in his 1976 and 1982 Reports qualified the need for such a jetty. In March 1983 plans were in hand for consultant engineers to look at the construction of a jetty, at an estimated cost of £7.3 million.

Grasslands Trials Unit

Following the recommendations of the Shackleton Report, the present GTU set up in 1975 (*see* page 125) is in the process of expanding and re-naming. The Falkland Islands Agricultural Research and Development Centre (FIARDC), as it is to be known, will have a budget increase of some £2.5 million over the first phase of the Shackleton recommendation period of six years. Prospects now lie in pasture works and it is hoped that subsidies and grants to farms may lead to relatively substantial increases in output of some classes of stock. Originally staffed by eight Technical Co-operation officers, the FIARDC is now to be strengthened to up to fourteen with locally recruited staff also increased.

PUBLIC SECTOR DEVELOPMENT

Banking

With the prospects for development and recommendations made by the 1976 Shackleton Report for a 'fully fledged banking operation', the independent international bank Standard Chartered is establishing a branch in the Falklands. This will be the first of its kind in the Islands, offering the facilities and expertise of any normal banking concern. The bank will become the first independent source of credit and the first advisory body on financial matters. Initially the bank will take over the present operation of the Government Savings Bank.

Brewery

On 25 February 1983, to coincide with the Islands' 150th Anniversary Celebrations, Everards Brewery Falkland Islands Ltd was officially opened with the tasting of their first brew of Burton-upon-Trent style best bitter beer, to be labelled and retailed as Penguin Ale. Conceived by Everards of Burton-upon-Trent, the plan for a brewery in the Islands was prospected in October 1982, construction of the brewery commencing in mid December. The plant, made by Robert Morton DG Ltd of Burton-upon-Trent, is the most modern mini-brewery yet developed, with a nominal $2\frac{1}{2}$ thousand pints per brew, or the equivalent of 10,000 pints per week production. With a capital cost in excess of £100,000 the new brewery hopes to market a quarter of the Islands' total beer consumption.

Service businesses

With the likelihood of increased business possibilities in the Islands and the already increased population, a number of firm proposals have been made by people from the United Kingdom to come to the Islands and set up local businesses in Stanley. Fish-and-chip shops and snack bars are proposed, and laundrette and dry-cleaning services are expected by the end of 1983.

Agriculture

In the 1976 Shackleton Report the team made a strong case for the creation of smaller farm units by the division of the larger farms. Following the purchase and division of Green Patch (*see* page 238), a West Falkland farm, Roy Cove, was subsequently offered for sale; it was purchased by the Falkland Islands Government, sub-divided and re-sold with extended credit facilities to six new owners. In February 1983 further West Falkland farm land, owned by Packe Brothers and including land at Fox Bay East, Dunnose Head and a section of Port Howard, was purchased by government with UK government funds for an agreed £500,000, for division into smaller units. In March 1983 the San Carlos Sheep Farming Company announced that they also sought to sell their holding of 107,000 acres and 27,000 sheep and they offered the farm to government at an asking price of £500,000 with a view to subsequent sub-division.

It would seem that opinion on the merits of sub-division is divided, with increasing pressure by some to see the Shackleton Report implemented and some larger farms bought up and divided. Others show concern about the feasibility, success and economic viability of sub-division. In the House of Commons on 8 December 1982 Mr Pym, the Foreign and Commonwealth Secretary, outlined a development package for the Falklands following much of what Lord Shackleton recommended. The Report's recommendation on the purchase and sub-division of the Islands' large farms, however, was discussed with a great deal of caution. Mr Pym maintained that a gradual approach to land re-distribution would be more in keeping with the Islands' existing rural population and also more consistent with a realistic approach to immigration prospects.

The Shackleton Report considered the merits of sub-division as both economic and social insofar as the creation of the smaller farms would provide opportunities for some more Falkland Islanders to have a stake in the land. The Report also saw some opportunity to integrate the smaller holdings with other diversification, such as horticulture and tourism. However, from studies and experiences of the existing sub-divisions such as Green Patch, the 1982 Report did make the following comments.

> It is too early to draw any firm conclusions as to the success or otherwise of these developments, but the following observations may be made:
>> In the newly created small units, the method of farming has not changed, that is, minimum supervision and the division of each farm into camps for the various classes of sheep.
>> There has been little or no co-operation over sharing of facilities and use of pasture.
>> Stocking rates are up but higher wool clip may not be sustained; fleece weight has decreased.
>> Labour productivity has improved.
>> There would appear to be a strong commitment amongst the new owner-occupiers to the Falklands, and the general appearance of the farms has improved.
>> The cost of providing infrastructure to service a number of small farms is clearly greater than that for a low number of larger farms. Even so, opportunities will be presented for units connected to the new Stanley–Goose Green road.
>> Government tax revenue will fall as a result of the creation of new small farm units.
> Taking account of the observations made above we have not changed our view that the creation of small farm units is desirable, although we would urge a more positive attitude towards co-operation over resources among the new owners.

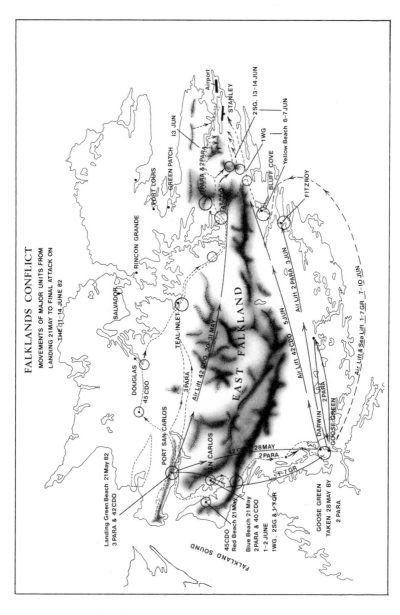

The Falklands conflict, 1982: movements of major British units from landing on 21 May to the final attack, 11–14 June

The question arises as to whether smaller farm units might also be created by tenancy and share farming arrangements as well as by selling off the land.

Concern for the sub-division proposals is perhaps reflected in the above findings by the Shackleton team itself. Many of the adverse points have been raised by those who recommend restraint on any large sub-division programme. It is also pointed out that many shepherds and land workers do not want the worry of owning their own land, but would rather live within the shelter of a larger farm community, which the division of some of the farms will destroy. Over a period of some 150 years the pastures of the Falklands have changed through sheep farming and it may be questionable whether they have improved or in the main deteriorated in quality. What is not clear is if the more intensive stocking that sub-division is to bring will merely aggravate this situation, especially as Shackleton has already indicated that the method of farming does not appear to have changed on the sub-divided farms. As there are merits in both arguments it would seem that more 'homework' needs to be done, perhaps with a view to finding more of a compromise.

Agricultural Enclave

With the establishment of a garrison and the intensified need for fresh produce, the Government's Development Officer has received a number of firm proposals for the setting up of poultry farms, a piggery, and field and protected horticultural units which it is proposed might be set up along with a planned new dairy unit on land near Stanley.

Wool Mill

Plans are under way to establish a small-scale private wool mill at Fox Bay East (West Falkland), processing raw Falkland Island wool through all stages to various items of knitwear. Small industrial sample equipment will be used, producing approximately 50kg per week in the first instance with plans to increase up to about 250kg per week. It is proposed to allow the project to grow and develop gradually, and the possibility of expansion, including capital reinvestment in larger plant, is not ruled out once the foregoing 'pilot plant stages' are covered. It is proposed to sell wool at all stages of production, ie raw double-skirted fleeces, scoured wool and ready-carded slubbings for hand spinners, as well as knitting wool and yarns for weaving, and finished knitwear. The latter is expected to be the main outlet.

Salmon Ranching

Following an initial investigation by a team from Stirling University in January 1983, proposals are already in hand for building to commence on the first hatchery for a pilot salmon-ranching project at Camilla Creek, near Darwin, East Falkland, by late 1983. Initial funds for this project are to be provided by the new Falkland Islands Development Agency. If the return of salmon is satisfactory it is expected to follow by commercial production at Darwin and the establishment of a number of satellite hatcheries and production units on both East and West Falkland. The results of the pilot scheme are expected to be known in three to five years' time.

Radio and Telephone

Since the establishment of a garrison there has been a very substantial increase in the amount of traffic handled by the Cable & Wireless Co installation. To cope with the increase, two telephone channels operating seven days a week for ten hours a day commenced operation in December 1982. The telex channels were also increased, to two. Telegram circuits, originally half speed, have been up-graded to full speed. In keeping with modern communications systems, the Falklands will also be applying the use of satellite communications through a Standard B earth station, one channel bringing a twenty-four hour telephone link to the Islands. In conjunction with such a service it is envisaged that 'card telephones' will also be installed.

POST-WAR AND REHABILITATION

External Air Communications

In the 1982 Shackleton Report it was stated that 'the establishment of regular civil air communications with the Islands is an absolute priority. Without it, little or no development would take place, the economy would decline further, and the sense of isolation would probably be unacceptable to the majority of Falkland Islanders.' Now that the air connection with Argentina has closed for the foreseeable future, alternative routes have to be found. All the alternatives, however, call for the need of a larger runway, to operate the type of aircraft required for such a service. A further critical factor is the military requirement; for this reason alone a much larger airport is required, to take widebodied jets making the flight from Ascension Island. In March 1983 it was announced that a number of British contract firms would be asked to tender for the construction of a new airport, on a new site near Fitzroy some thirty miles to the south-west of Stanley.

THE FUTURE

For a community that has known only peace and isolation to be subjected suddenly to an invasion, a conflict, re-occupation and now a sudden surge of new development, all in the space of some ten months, the impact has unquestionably been severe. In some measure or another every household has been drawn into one or another of these situations and the trauma has been difficult to throw off. Immediately following the conflict the Islands have seen a new form of 'invasion' with the establishment of a garrison : large amounts of equipment, materials and personnel for the military establishments and also for the rehabilitation of the islanders' facilities have poured into the islands. An overwhelming number of investigating committees, media personnel, labour and experts looking at a wide range of matters have visited the Falklands in recent months to evaluate the needs of the community and the future development of the Falklands.

On 8 January 1983 there was a different form of impact on

the Islanders: a momentous occasion when the Prime Minister, Mrs Margaret Thatcher, made an unexpected visit to the Falklands. Her informal and very emotional visit was greeted with great enthusiasm; it became a common factor on which people could leave aside much of the trauma of the war by showing their own emotions. The Prime Minister's visit also did much to allay the fears of many Islanders about the British Government's policy towards the future of the Falklands.

Shortly after, The British Nationality (Falkland Islands) Bill received its final reading and was passed by the House of Commons (March 1983). The Bill provides for Falkland Islanders to become British citizens with the right of abode in the United Kingdom.

On 2 February 1983 a Parliamentary Select Committee on Foreign Affairs arrived in the Islands, to make a report to the House of Commons about British foreign policy in relation to the Falkland Islands and other South American states, in the light of recent events in the South Atlantic. In contrast to the emotional visit by the Prime Minister, the enquiry brought home the hard reality of the existing situation in the Islands, not uncommonly referred to as 'Fortress Falklands'. In the course of the hearings, questions were asked which left many islanders in little doubt that ultimately there had to be a different solution to the present situation. There has to be a peaceful and definitive solution which a geographical fact dictates must have some connection with Argentina in the future. How that connection is made of course is still an embryo yet to be born. It is difficult in the long term to visualise a solution which does not involve the United Nations, perhaps in some form of trusteeship role in the larger framework of a multinational treaty, on similar lines to the Antarctic Treaty.

Antarctica and the Falklands and its Dependencies have much in common; although their environments differ, they are marginal areas of man's existence, and as such have never known any human indigenous populations. They are also areas of dispute. Their greatest similarity is that they are in a global context unique ecological areas holding important collections of wildlife. Is there any reason why the Falkland Islands should not be drawn under a new international umbrella, with Antarctica, to form an even larger reserve—not just for the benefit of man's development, but one where the natural development of such unique ecosystems can have some guarantee from man, so that they too can have a chance of survival?

BIBLIOGRAPHY

ANDERSSON, J. G. *Contributions to the geology of the Falkland Islands* (1901–3)

BAKER, H. A. *Final Report on Geological Investigations in the Falkland Islands 1920–2* (1924)

BOUGAINVILLE, ANTOINE LOUIS DE. *Voyage autour de Monde* (Paris 1771)

BOYSON. *The Falkland Islands* (Oxford 1924)

BRIDGES, E. LUCAS. *Uttermost Part of the Earth* (1948)

CAWKELL, M. B. R., MALING, D. H. AND CAWKELL, E. M. *The Falkland Islands* (1960)

CROWE, PHILIP KINGSLAND. *The Empty Ark* (1967)

DARWIN, CHARLES. *A Naturalist's Voyage round the World in HMS Beagle* (1860)

DAVIES, T. H., DICKSON, I. A., McCREA, C. T., MEAD, H. WILLIAMS, W. W. *The Sheep and Cattle Industries of the Falkland Islands* 1970

DAVIES, WILLIAM. *The Grasslands of the Falkland Islands* (1939)

DISCOVERY COMMITTEE. *Report on the Progress of the Discovery Committee's Investigations* (1937)

ELLIS, J. M., Col Sec. *Falkland Islands Centenary 1833–1933* (1933)

FANNING, E. *Voyages Round the World* (1834)

FALKLAND ISLANDS COMPANY. *The Falkland Islands Company, 1851–1951* (1951)

FALKLAND ISLANDS GOVERNMENT. *Colony of the Falkland Islands, Estimates* 1969–1970

FALKLAND ISLANDS GOVERNMENT. *Shipping Registers. Falkland Islands Government 1842–1871, 1930–1971*

FALKLAND ISLANDS GOVERNMENT. *Biennial Reports. Colony of the Falkland Islands 1940–1969*

312

BIBLIOGRAPHY

FALKLAND ISLANDS GOVERNMENT. *Despatch Books (Inward and Outgoing) 1842–1930; Miscellaneous Letter Books 1832–1842; Miscellaneous Letter Books 1842–1870*

FALKLAND ISLANDS GOVERNMENT. *Annual Summary Reports of Education Department* (Falkland Islands Government Publication)

FALKLAND ISLANDS GOVERNMENT. *Falkland Islands Annual Stock returns to 1970*

FALKLAND ISLANDS GOVERNMENT. *Government Gazettes* (Secretariat, Stanley).

FALKLAND ISLANDS GOVERNMENT *Records of the Colony* (Secretariat, Stanley)

FALKLAND ISLAND PUBLICATIONS. *Falkland Islands Magazines* (1889–1933); *The Penguin Newspaper* (1927–1938); *Falkland Islands News Weekly* (1938–1944); *Falkland Islands Weekly News* (1944–1949); *Falkland Islands Monthly Review* (1958–1971)

FALKLAND ISLAND PUBLICATIONS. *The Falkland Islands Journal* 1968–1969–1970

FALKLAND ISLAND PUBLICATIONS. *Christ Church Cathedral* 1892–1967 (Govt Printing)

GIBBS, J. G. *Report of the Department of Agriculture* (1937–1946)

HALLE, THORE G. *On the geological structure and history of the Falkland Islands* (Upsala 1912)

HELSBY, JOHN. *Notes Relating to the Port Louis Murders.* (Government House Library)

HM STATIONERY OFFICE. *Annual Colonial Reports* (Blue Books 1871–1922)

HM STATIONERY OFFICE. *Discovery Expedition First Annual Report* (1926)

HM STATIONERY OFFICE. *Discovery Investigations Second Annual Report* (1927/1928)

HM STATIONERY OFFICE. *Colonial Development Corporation Reports* (1951)

HM STATIONERY OFFICE. *Falkland Islands Economic Study 1982.* Chairman: The Rt Hon Lord Shackleton KG, PC, OBE (1982)

HM STATIONERY OFFICE. *Falkland Islands Review: Report of a Committee of Privy Counsellors, 1983.* Chairman: The Rt Hon The Lord Franks OM, GCMG, KCB, CBE (1983)

HUNT, THE REV R. J. *The Livingstone of South America*

BIBLIOGRAPHY

HUNTER CHRISTIE W. W. *The Antarctic Problem* (1951)

LAWS, M. A. *The Seals of the Falkland Islands and Dependencies* Vol 2 No 2 (1951)

LEBEDEY, V. *Antarctica* (Foreign Languages Publishing House, Moscow 1959)

MCWHAN, FORREST. *The Falkland Islands Today* (1952)

GOV MIDDLETON. *Memorandum on the Sheep Farming Industry of the Falkland Islands* (1924)

MILLAM, REV P. J. *Bishop Stirling, First Bishop of the Falkland Islands 1869–1900* (1969)

MOORE, D. M. *The Vascular Flora of the Falkland Islands BAS, Scientific Reports No. 60*

MUNRO, HUGH. *Report of an Investigation into the Conditions and Practice of Sheep Farming in the Falkland Islands* (1924)

MURPHY, DR CUSHMAN. *Oceanic Birds of South America* Vols I and II (1936)

NORMAN AND FRASER. *Giant Fishes, Whales and Dolphins*

PEPPER, J. *The Meteorology of the Falkland Islands and Dependencies 1944/50* (1954)

PERNETTY, D. *Histoire d'un Voyage aux Isles Malouines fait en 1763 et 1764* (1770)

SCHULTZ, G. *The Falkland Islands* (1891)

SHACKLETON, THE RT HON LORD. *Economic Survey of the Falkland Islands* Vols 1 and 2 (July 1976)

SKOTTSBERG, CARL. *A Botanical Survey of the Falkland Islands* (1907–9)

STIRLING, BISHOP. *The Falkland Islands and Tierra del Fuego* (1969)

STRANGE, IAN JOHN. *Beauchene Island. Polar Record* Vol 12 No 81 (1965)

STRANGE, IAN JOHN. *The Falkland Islands a South Atlantic Bird Haven. Animals* Vol 6 (July 1965)

STRANGE, IAN JOHN. *Seals of the South. Animals* Vol 8 (December 1965)

STRANGE, IAN JOHN. *Survey of Seal herds in the Falkland Islands. 1965–1966*

SMITH, JOHN. *Condemned at Stanley* (1969)

SNOW WILLIAM, PARKER. *A Two Years' Cruise off Tierra del Fuego, the Falkland Islands etc.* 2 Vols (1857)

BIBLIOGRAPHY

STRANGE, IAN JOHN. *Les Iles Falkland Paradis des Oiseaux. Le Monde Animal* (March 1966)

STRANGE, IAN JOHN. *The Falkland Islands.* (Geographical Magazine, April 1968)

STRANGE, IAN JOHN. *Marine Mammals of the Falkland Islands.* (Pacific Discovery Journal, Californian Academy of Sciences, vol XXII 1969)

STRANGE, IAN JOHN. *Enthauten Mahnérobben Wie Steht Es Um Die Robben Auf Den Falkland Inseln.* (Das Tier June 1969)

STRANGE, IAN JOHN. *The Wise Men of West Point. Animals* Vol II (February 1969)

STRANGE, IAN JOHN. *World Wildlife Yearbooks.* 1968–1969 and 1970

STRANGE, IAN JOHN. *Schafe Gegan Die Vogel Der Falkland Inseln.* (Das Tier October 1970)

STRANGE, IAN JOHN. *Conservation in the Falkland Islands* (Oryx (1972 Vol XI No 4)

STRANGE, IAN JOHN. *De Fauna Van de Falklands* (Artis No 5 January/February 1973)

STRANGE, IAN JOHN. *The Silent Ordeal of a South Atlantic Archipelago* (Natural History Vol LXXXII No 2 February 73)

STRANGE, IAN JOHN. *Ravaged Falkland Islands* (Geographical Magazine February 1976)

STRANGE, IAN JOHN. *The Falkland Islands: Steps Toward Conservation* (Pacific Discovery November—December 1977)

STRANGE, IAN JOHN. *De Robben Van de Falklands.* (Artis September —October 1977)

STRANGE, IAN JOHN. *Sealion Survey in the Falkland Islands* (Oryx November 1979 Vol XV No 2)

STRANGE, IAN JOHN. *The Thin-billed Prion*, Pachyptila belcheri, *at New Island, Falkland Islands* (Le Gerfaut, Institut royal des Sciences naturelles de Belgique Brussels 1980, 70: 411–45)

STRANGE, IAN JOHN. *Breeding Ecology of the Rockhopper Penguin in the Falkland Islands* (Le Gerfaut 72: 137–88, 1982)

STRANGE, IAN JOHN. *Unmentioned Crisis in the Falklands: Wildlife Survival* (Animal Kingdom, Zoological Society Magazine, New York, Aug/Sep 1982)

STRANGE, IAN JOHN. *The Passing of a Lifestyle* (Geographical Magazine December 1982)

BIBLIOGRAPHY

STRANGE, IAN JOHN. *The Bird Man* (Gordon & Cremonesi 1976)

STRANGE, IAN JOHN. *Penguin World* (Dodd, Mead, New York 1981)

WHITINGTON, G. T. *The Falkland Islands* (1840)

YOUNG, C. D. *Report on Pasture Improvement Experiments carried out in the Falkland Islands during 1965–1968* (1968)

YRIGOYEN, HIPOLITO SOLARI. *Asi Son Las Malvinas* (1959)

YRIGOYEN, HIPOLITO SOLARI. *Las Malvinas de Hoy* (1966)

INDEX

Numerals in italics refer to illustration pages

INDEX

Bisley, FI successes at, 175
Black Tarn, 23
Blackburn River, 26
Bleaker Island, 27, 33, 220
Blechnum, 202
Blomfield, Sir Arthur, 89
Blue grass, 230
Bluff Cove, 283
Bodie Creek, 29
    bridge, 143
Bombilla, 25
Bougainville, Antoine Louis de, 47, 48, 51, 52, 53, 104, 167, 184, 192, 223
Boxwood, 203
Boy Scouts, 176
Boys, Capt, 70, 72
Boys Life Brigade, 177
Brandon, Dean Lowther E., 44, 88–9, 165, 180
Bransfield, RRS, 127, 131–2
Brenton Loch, 25
Brewery, 303
Bridges, Thomas, 92, 93
Brisbane, Capt Matthew, 57, 58
Bristol, 152, 155
Bristol, HMS, 99
British Antarctic Survey, 19, 127, 131, 132, 140, 151
British Government, 69, 72, 137
    talks with Argentina, 245
British Meteorological Service, 19
British Nationality (Falkland Islands) Bill, 310
British settlement, 52–3; surrendered to Spain, 54; restored to Britain, 54; abandoned, 54; return of British, 57; colonisation, 58–60, 61; lawless element, 65–6
Broadcasting service, 146–8
Browne, Adm, 75
Brunel, Isambard K., 155
Brunel Society, 155
Buckingham, Duke of, 111
Bull, Rev Charles, 87, 88
Burwood Bank, 181, 182
Button, Jemmy, 92
Buzo Tactico, 248
Buzzard, Red-backed, 211
Bryon, Capt John, 52, 183, 220, 223
Byron Heights, 25, 33

C130 transport aircraft, 271
Callaghan, Governor, 37, 79, 98, 126
Camargo, explorer, 47
Camoena, mutiny on, 178
Camp, the, 14, 15, 237
    camp tracks, 142–3
    education, 163
    life in, 159–61

    vegetation, 202–3
Campbell, Capt, 198, 199
Canberra, the, 277
Canopus, HMS, 99
Cantara Mountain, 23
Cape Carysfort, *49*
Cape Dolphin, 52
Cape Horn, 13, 47, 66, 126, 155, 156, 186, 211
Cape Meredith, 20, 31
Cape Pembroke, 31, 174, 248, 270
    beacon, 19, 134
    lighthouse, 19, 134–5, 144, 145, 157, 174
Cape Tamar, 52
Carancho, 211
Carcass Island, 33, 188
Carcass, sloop, 52
Cardinall, Governor, 117
Carnarvon, Earl of, 29
Carnarvon, HMS, 99
Carrington, Lord, 252
Catherine, schooner, 76
Cattle, 105, 106, 114, 219
    and settlements, 34
    decline of wild, 106–7
    hunted by gauchos, 107–8
    introduced, 104
    poached by sealers, 105
    population today, 113
    wild, 82, 104, 193
Central Office of Information, London, 43
Cerro Monte, 25
Challenger Expedition, 29, 32
Challenger, HMS, 58
Challenger, Mount, 283
Channon, Henry, 19
Chapman, Thomas, 183
Chartres, 230
Chartres River, 26
Chata Flats, 25
Chelsea Pensioners, the, 66, 72, 97
Choiseul Sound, 25, 26, 284
Christmas bush, 202
Cinema, the, 176
Cinnamon grass, 230
City of Philadelphia, loss of, 157–8
Clairac, Ramon, 55, 104, 193
Clarke, George A., 164
Clarke, Mrs, 164
Clayton, Lt S.W., 54
Cleopatra, HMS, 104
Clifford, Governor, 182
Clifford, Sir Miles, 45
Clift, Capt Hiram, 69, 71, 72
Climate, 17–24
Clio, HMS, 57
Coal, 29–30, 169
Coastlines, 25
Cobb, F.E., 19

318

INDEX

INDEX

INDEX

326

INDEX